C000280516

HOW TO BE YOUR OWN
MANAGEMENT
CONSULTANT

Edited by **CALVERT MARKHAM**

HOW TO BE YOUR OWN
MANAGEMENT
CONSULTANT

Consultancy

tools and techniques

to improve your

business

REVISED EDITION

**KOGAN
PAGE**

First published in 1999
Revised edition 2001

Apart from any fair dealing for the purposes of research or private study, or criticism
or review, as permitted under the Copyright, Designs and Patents Act 1988, this publication may only be reproduced, stored or transmitted, in any form or by any means,
with the prior permission in writing of the publishers, or in the case of reprographic
reproduction in accordance with the terms and licences issued by the CLA. Enquiries
concerning reproduction outside these terms should be sent to the publishers at the
undermentioned address:

Kogan Page Limited
120 Pentonville Road
London N1 9JN
UK

Kogan Page US
22 Broad Street
Milford CT 06460
USA

© Calvert Markham, 1999, 2001

The right of Calvert Markham to be identified as the author of this work has been
asserted by him in accordance with the Copyright, Designs and Patents Act 1988.

British Library Cataloguing in Publication Data

A CIP record for this book is available from the British Library.

ISBN 0 7494 3690 5

Typeset by Saxon Graphics Ltd, Derby
Printed and bound in Great Britain by Biddles Ltd, Guildford and King's Lynn
www.biddles.co.uk

CONTENTS

SECTION TWO: BUSINESS DEVELOPMENT AND PERFORMANCE IMPROVEMENT

LIST OF FIGURES

LIST OF TABLES

LIST OF CONTRIBUTORS

THE RICHMOND GROUP

The chapters in this book have been written by practising management consultants, all of whom are members of The Richmond Group. The Richmond Group is the UK's leading consortium of independent, certified management consultants. Its members are:

- experienced specialists in their areas of expertise;
- Fellows or Members of the Institute of Management Consultancy and thereby holders of the internationally recognized qualification CMC – Certified Management Consultant;
- in independent practice or in a small firm of five or fewer consultants.

The Richmond Group has a lively programme of meetings, common interest groups, networking, and joint business and practice development. It is therefore able to facilitate the linkage between a business need and the consultant or team of consultants who can meet it.

The Richmond Group can be contacted on 0870 606 0094. More information is available on the website at *www.richmond-group.co.uk*

Calvert Markham, after early experience with ICI, entered the world of consultancy with PA Management Consultants, where he specialized as a human resources consultant. He moved to Spicer and Pegler Associates, where he developed their human resources consultancy practice and then left to set up his own practice. Shortly thereafter, he formed

Consultancy Skills Training Ltd, of which he is Managing Director, to pursue his interest in consultant education.

He has been involved with the Institute of Management Consultancy for many years, serving on its Executive Council and, in particular, the Professional Development Committee. In 2001, he was awarded the President's commendation for services to the Institute and profession. He is also a long-standing member of the Richmond Group, and has served on its Council for many years, as well as being Chairman 1998–99.

Calvert Markham is a past Master of the Guild of Management Consultants, of which he was one of the founding members.

He is also the author of *The Top Consultant* (also published by Kogan Page) and *Practical Management Consultancy*.

Clive Bonny is a founder of the Salopian Business Association, a fellow of the RSA, and a past Chair of the Richmond Group. He has held board level and management roles for multi-nationals and small businesses, working in Central and North America, Africa and the Far East. He is qualified to advise on the international standards of Investors in People and Business Excellence. His UK business, at www.consult-smp.com, develops individuals and organisations through coaching and interim management.

Bill Boynton is Managing Director of Kingsland James Limited, the consulting and services group whose mission is to inspire and to assist its clients to be outstanding in the eyes of tomorrow's customers. This consulting work is undertaken with well-known clients in service industry sectors including retail and financial services.

He is a Cambridge graduate with marketing and business development experience initially with the Mars Group. Twenty years international consulting experience followed at Inbucon and P-E International, where he was Managing Director of Corporate Consulting before establishing Kingsland James.

Widely experienced in the issues surrounding customer focus, he leads change programmes to assess the quality of relationships with customers and reposition businesses for competitive advantage.

An expert in the measurement of customer satisfaction, he leads the design of customer feedback information systems to monitor performance, reward employee achievement, strengthen customer relationships, and bring the voice of the customer into the boardroom.

Bill Boynton is a past Chairman of the Richmond Group.

John Dempster is a management consultant with more than 25 years' experience as a consultant and 10 as a chief officer in government. He is a Chartered Management Accountant and Fellow of the Institute of Management. For the book he has drawn on his experience in engineering manufacture in the Midlands, printing, horticulture, banking and finance. Currently he specializes in Business Continuity Planning, teaching life management to senior executives and assisting companies with business in Russia. He lives in Guernsey and works internationally.

Chris Edge has a varied experience including, when only 23, the role of Manager of Accounting for General Electric's London offices running an office with over 35 staff. He has also held similar senior finance positions with small, medium and large complex corporations in Canada, the USA, Saudi Arabia and the UK. Many of these have required very complex financial routines, with complicated foreign exchange transactions.

As a management consultant Chris has assisted organizations with their divergent requirements around the world. His clients have included those from the banking, hospitality, IT and technology sectors.

Carol Harris has run her independent consultancy practice Management Magic since 1986, specialising in the development of people and organisations. She has worked in the public, private and voluntary sectors and has several years' experience in general management at Board level in a national organisation. Carol is a Fellow of the Chartered Institute of Personnel and Development and was, for four years, Chair of the Board of Trustees of the Association for Neuro-Linguistic Programming, a small professional body. She is the author of *NLP: New Perspectives, Networking for Success* and *Consult Yourself – the NLP Guide to Being a Management Consultant*, creator of the audiotape series *Success in Mind* and Publisher/Editor of the magazine *Effective Consulting*.

David Jefferson originally qualified as an engineer, began working on advanced business applications of IT and moved into management consultancy shortly thereafter. He has worked on IT issues as manager, director and consultant. His 25 years in the industry have given him an understanding of why the real-life use of IT falls short of its potential. He has worked with clients of all sizes to improve the disciplines of directing IT investment towards key payback areas. He now specializes in the application of IT to the customer-facing parts of the business, and particularly the Internet. He is on the Council of the Computing Services and Software Association and an occasional contributor to management magazines, and is the Chairman of the Richmond Group 2001–2002.

Graham Johnson BSc, MBA, CEng, MIEE, is an independent consultant specializing in BPR, IT and organizational change. Currently Managing Director of JFS Consultancy Services, Graham commenced his career at British Telecom International where he was responsible for facility management of customers' systems. Following this, he joined Deloitte Haskins & Sells as a senior management consultant.

As an independent management consultant for more than 10 years, Graham has provided his expertise to over 14 major blue chip organizations, often working at board level. Graham has undertaken major organizational change in several leading finance organizations, and acted as mentor to senior management. He has also acted as an expert witness in legal disputes.

Peter Jones is a consultant in human resources management and organizational development and change. He helps directors, managers and their teams to think through business and organizational issues and plan and implement change programmes, and identify the values and behaviours that they want to encourage and model for themselves. His clients have included public and private sector organizations across a range of sectors and he held senior HR director and manager's posts before becoming a consultant. He is a Fellow of the Chartered Institute of Personnel and Development.

Dr Mike Kearsley is a Fellow of the Chartered Institute of Personnel and Development and an independent management consultant formerly responsible for all business development training for Coopers and Lybrand. He was a top-performing IBM salesman and manager and the Group Marketing Director for Marsh McLennan, international insurance brokers. He was also the MD of his own direct mail and word-processing business. He has been an associate of several European management development centres and has been a tutor on the MCBS/Surrey University MSc course in consultancy skills. He is the author of many articles in the area of business practice and consultancy development. He has researched extensively in the area of 'sales reluctance' – the difficulty many consultancies and professionals have with sales activity.

Steve Kennett is a Chartered Marketer and Fellow of the Chartered Institute of Marketing and of the Chartered Institute of Personnel and Development. Thus he embraces the disciplines of sales and marketing with training and personal development.

He started his career as a chemist in a research department at ICI before moving to industrial marketing research and product planning.

He joined an engineering group and set up their commercial research department before taking on sales management and marketing roles, finally joining the board with responsibility for group activities throughout Europe.

Steve was seconded to the Civil Service to assist in leading investigations into the efficiency of major UK undertakings such as gas, coal, NHS, and food retailing for the government of the day. Since 1970 Steve has worked as a consultant advising clients on the effectiveness of their sales and marketing activities.

He is the author of many articles on sales and marketing topics. Steve is a liveryman of the Worshipful Company of Marketors and a member of its court.

Bill Peace is an American business executive turned consultant and now lives in the UK. He has held senior positions with Westinghouse Electric (sales/marketing and general management in the electric utility business) and United Technologies (president of the Carrier air-conditioning business in Europe). As a consultant, he specializes in business performance improvement, executive mentoring, and management team effectiveness. Bill has worked extensively in the engineering, manufacturing, healthcare, financial services and retail sectors; he is listed in *Who's Who in the World*.

Dr Peter Tomkins, following a sophisticated senior marketing and general management career with Mars Confectionery, Ernst & Young, and Encyclopaedia Britannica International, set up the specialist strategic management and marketing consultancy firm D.M. Management Consultants Ltd (DMMC) – concentrating on market entry, best practice reviews, acquisitions/joint ventures, e-commerce integration, database specifications, and senior management recruitment/search, particularly within the direct marketing, database and loyalty/relationship marketing arena. DMMC has an extensive list of blue-chip MNC and international clients in this field.

In 1995 Peter was elected President of the UK Institute of Management Consultancy and became International Marketing Trustee of the ICMCI. He is a Fellow of the CIM, a liveryman of the Worshipful Company of Marketors, on the visiting faculties of several business schools and serves on a number of boards.

ACKNOWLEDGEMENTS

My wife threatened to divorce me if I wrote another book, so I took on the task of Editor, thinking it would be less onerous. It wasn't. So my thanks must first be to her for her patience.

Next, I must thank the contributors drawn from the membership of the Richmond Group. Although only a handful of people, they have more than 250 years of consultancy experience between them and it is an honour to be able to tap into that experience.

Finally, I am sure that they, like me, will acknowledge a debt of gratitude to our clients. Not only do they provide us with our livelihood but also with the opportunity to practice our skills and develop our experience. This book represents some of the fruits of that experience.

PREFACE

The market for consultancy has grown rapidly in recent years. In part this has been because organizations, having been re-engineered and downsized, no longer have the capacity or, sometimes, the wish to undertake projects that a few years ago would have been resourced internally.

But a further value of consultants is that they can bring a freshness of thinking to an organization, and it is this that this book addresses. It will be especially valuable to the manager or executive who is not currently using consultants but wonders what perspective a consultant might bring to his or her enterprise. Those contemplating a career in consultancy – or practising consultants – should also profit from this book.

It has been written by a team of practising management consultants, all of whom are deeply experienced in their areas of specialization. All belong to the Richmond Group, a consortium of management consultants, working as sole practitioners or in small practices, who are qualified members of the Institute of Management Consultancy.

So the book is a practitioner's view. It is not comprehensive – it would be unwieldy if it were – and maybe it is not perfect. In these two respects it is much like a management consultant! But – like a good management consultant – it should stimulate thought, help articulate a vision, and support you in developing the performance of your enterprise.

Calvert Markham
August 2001

INTRODUCTION

Gone are the days when the management consultant was a rare esoteric specialist, bringing mystic arts to client organizations. Now consultants abound. So why should anyone want to know how to be his or her own management consultant?

The reasons why organizations employ consultants are usually:

- They do not have sufficient skills in house to carry out a particular task.
- They need the skills only for a temporary period.
- The consultant has access to technology (however defined) that is otherwise inaccessible.
- The organization wants an independent or fresh view.

Consultants bring value, however, in their own right:

- They can see what needs to be done.
- They know how to do it.
- They make it happen.

And it is to help the reader deliver this value that this book has been written. But if you are to be your own management consultant, you are also the client, so you need to take a client's view too. So the three questions above become:

1. What ought to be on my business agenda?
2. What needs to be done to address these agenda items?

3.   Can this be done within current resource constraints, or are additional resources needed?

Much of the value of a consultant lies in knowing what questions to ask. Probing questions result in items being put on the business agenda, and the first of the questions above is crucial.

How can you sort out what should be on the business agenda? If something is clearly going wrong, then it is an obvious candidate – it demands your attention. But beyond this, how can you determine items of a developmental rather than a remedial nature?

This book can help. Under the heading of 'Diagnosing what has to be done', Section 1 of the book gives an overview of the consultancy process, and some general ideas about thinking about your business in totality. These chapters give a general introduction to what may be of interest or value to consider in more detail in the organization.

Section 2 then looks at improving the performance of the main functional areas – how you engage with your marketplace and manage operations. Then in Section 3 we look at infrastructure and resources, which underwrite performance in these areas. Neither of these sections is meant to be comprehensive – nor is this meant to be a textbook – but each is intended to stimulate your thinking and prompt ideas on what you might put on your own organization agenda.

Having decided what needs to be done, you have to decide how to go about doing it, and you will find each of the chapters has suggestions for this too. There are abundant checklists, which will lead to ideas for action. But the observant reader will notice that there are two words that appear frequently throughout the text – they are 'change' and 'culture'. One of the definitions of a consultant is 'an agent of change'. The success of a consultant lies not just in knowing what needs to be done; it consists also of enabling the client to do it. And this requires a skill in managing change. The ease with which any change can be implemented depends in part on corporate culture, so many of the chapters touch upon this theme. And the topic of introducing and implementing change is dealt with explicitly in Section 4.

But there is a third component that influences success, in addition to change and culture, which is the quality of the consultant himself or herself. This is addressed in Section 5: how you look after yourself and how you engage with other people will affect your performance as a consultant.

Consultancy is often thought to involve being able to answer questions, and that is partly true. But even more important is the ability to know what questions to ask, and for consultants these fall under three headings:

- What changes need to be made?
- What are the prevailing circumstances in this organization that will affect how this change might be introduced?
- How can I help?

Use this book to stimulate your thinking under these headings.

DIAGNOSING WHAT HAS TO BE DONE

CHAPTER ONE

CONSULTANCY AS A JOURNEY

Calvert Markham and David Jefferson

Ask any member of the top management team if he or she understands the business and the answer will probably be 'yes'. In many cases this is because 'no' is clearly an unacceptable answer. Asked the same question at the beginning of an assignment, a management consultant would answer in the negative. Obvious perhaps, but the difference is that consultants can now ask the questions which enable them to learn how the business really works. They question assumptions that the organization regards as obvious and often get answers that yield great insight.

In this chapter, we use the metaphor of consultancy as a journey. If you are going to undertake a trip of any kind, it is useful to have a map of the territory. In the world of business, maps will be expressed in terms of the 'theories' or 'models' that you have about business in general, and your business in particular. If you are to get an insight into how the business works, and a detailed understanding of the predicaments that confront it, then you need to use these models explicitly to map your starting point and destination. So we start with a view of some models – ways of looking at organizations and structure. But if you are to be your own consultant, you must start with a clean sheet and an objective mind. So you will have to begin by clearing your mind of the things you think you know about the business. Finding the curiosity to ask all the questions is important. A manager is often a particular type of person whose learning processes work best when talking. So, if you are collecting information by discussions with other people, guard against answering your own questions!

MAPPING THE TERRITORY – USING BUSINESS MODELS

One of the most powerful ways of eliciting information on the nature of the business is building models of various kinds with the assistance of others working in the business. Invariably the models show patterns that are new to everyone. This is primarily because you will be modelling things that managers generally do not study closely when performing their day-to-day work. Let's examine how a consultant might look at a business which is new to him or her. The first objective is just to build a new understanding, as well as collecting the information that can be used later to identify needs for action.

The organization chart – formal and informal

This is the most basic of descriptions of the business. It illustrates the hierarchies of your organization and the main functional areas. As a manager you may know these things instinctively. Nevertheless drawing this structure can be used as the starting point for the discovery of needs. In drawing the chart, pay careful attention to reporting relationships and the management of key corporate assets. Use interviews to secure the information, or at least validate it, rather than your own understanding. When you have completed this exercise you may be surprised by how different the actual diagram is from your personal intuitive view before the exercise was carried out. Now you can begin to see that the process of building a model has enhanced your understanding of the business.

Remember that the formal, published, organization chart (if one exists) rarely reflects the reality of relationships. Who talks to whom, who has high or low influence, how decisions get made, in practice will often be different.

So it is often well worthwhile drawing up an informal organization chart. This will perhaps be in the form of a network, and can yield an invaluable insight into the real communication and political processes in the organization.

While we are on the organization chart, why not make the next step and invite several key people to study the chart to correct it to fit their own understandings. Notice how the perceptions of different individuals may not be in accord with your own observations and intuition. You can also use the building of a model to collect information from people, which involves them in the acceptance of its outcome.

The financial model

We all need to produce budgets for future expenditure. The business has a budgetary structure dictated partially by the set-up of the accounts system and partly by the historical organization and its main functions. The management domain of each budget-holder determines the structure of the budget and how it builds to a corporate financial whole.

The budget is an expenditure model of the business, and is one of many possible financial models. It is useful to explore the accepted fiscal pictures of the business and become familiar with the building of financial models of the business. Imagine how you might need to build alternative models if success in the future meant shutting down some historically important part of the business.

There are software packages that can handle the modelling process on a personal computer. These packages allow the trading picture and capital structure to be modelled. With such modelling tools you can escape from the structure laid down by the chart of accounts in the accounting system and ask probing 'what if?' type questions. This gives new insights and raises new questions. Where are the key assets of the business? Where are the major cost or revenue areas? Some caution is needed when making conclusions because it is easy to model financial structures that in the real business world are impossible. Expert assistance from a management accountant can help with these.

The value model

Most businesses pride themselves in doing some things extremely well. Their output is therefore useful and has value to their customers. The business acquires resources like money, time, knowledge, people, etc in ways designed to create value and 'mould them' into a form suitable for sale (a product). A well-managed business will find that the products it sells have considerably greater value than the sum of their components and the cost of the effort to assemble them. A value-added model gives insights into operational areas of key importance to the product or service.

So in the value model, a car company produces cars of value; an oil company breaks up crude oil into components, like petrol, which have increased value as a result; a hotel operator manages space and services to provide value to guests; an accounting firm or legal practice acquires knowledge and skill and sells them in the form of services which are of value to clients.

Whatever your business, there is a value model which can be created. Showing how your organization acquires the key resources, manages its value-adding processes, and delivers value to customers/clients will give you new insight into key elements of your business, which are the source of your competitive advantage.

The business process model

The day-to-day operation of the business depends on thousands of administrative tasks. They are interrelated and they interlink with one another. Some are simple, like perhaps ordering stationery, others are more complex, like perhaps managing the construction of a new warehouse; some relate to day-to day trading matters and some are part of the management of the infrastructure of the business.

Building business process models at a detailed level is a substantial task, but like other modelling tasks it gives insight into the business.

This area has been one that has given rise to some legendary strategic advantage applications. One example is the question, 'What processes link us to our customers and can they be changed to lock customers to our supply?' Answering that question enabled one company to take a market-leading position.

Contingent or empirical models

'Contingent' or 'empirical' models are a posh way of saying they are models you have made up! But they are valuable as they will help you to make your current assumptions about the business explicit. You can test the models so produced, and use them to direct your enquiries into what is really going on. So use models as learning tools. But remember that a model is an incomplete abstraction from the real world and cannot be used to predict the future behaviour of your business with any certainty at all. Don't confuse the map with the territory!

What can we learn from business models?

We've described some basic model types, and there are many others. They can form the basis of your search for areas where performance improvement could lead to strategic advantage.

Perhaps an organizational model starts an investigation into human resource management looking at careers, competencies, skill sets and training needs. A computer system to manage human resources is the need identified, and an IT project can then be set up with terms of reference. An example from real life was a company that had to process huge numbers of redundancies rapidly at the shutting down of a plant. With the proper information to hand, they were able to minimize disruption to staff and to other parts of the organization.

Perhaps a budgetary model shows a particular sensitivity of product profitability to materials management, purchasing, lead times and supply chain planning. Systems of this type are often credited with profitability increases.

Perhaps a value model shows that value to the customer is generated in a part of the business that receives insufficient attention. It may show that resources are being misdirected, or it may show scope for developing a product still further, so as to create a proposition more attractive to your customers.

DESTINATIONS: PLANNING FOR COMPETITIVE ADVANTAGE

As a means to understanding the business and its key areas, these models will help you to explore and to share ideas. When you have built some exploratory models of the business, you can use them to plan a way ahead. For example, if you are looking at IT, superimpose on them the location points of your known IT assets (ie applications, hardware, networks). Note where you have historically placed your IT investments. Then note locations where no investments have yet been made. These areas can then be studied further.

A similar approach can be used in respect of other elements of the business. For example, what about the detail, accuracy and timeliness of management information? What are the key operational decisions that are made in the business? Does the quality of management information match these? The same question might be asked about investment decisions.

Similarly, you could look at sales and marketing activity. For example, do rewards for sales people (both tangible and intangible – this latter being about what is praised and publicized) match the value of business? (A common mistake here is that customer acquisition is given more recognition than customer retention, when the latter might be of more value.)

But we also need to consider the business as it might be in the future. This is about planning – or strategy.

The changing environment

It would be comforting to think that your business might continue next year very much as it is this year. This security of tenure is increasingly rare. In the past you could depend on a national economy which was relatively well understood. Nowadays, global trade is making it difficult for national governments to protect businesses, industries and their economies from the changes that are taking place on a global basis. Competition is less easy to understand when it comes from abroad. The economics faced by a competitor in another economy may not be the same as your own.

Moreover, there is now a huge amount of research being carried out in all areas in the developed world and this is leading to new technologies and new products, as well as new businesses, new economics and new competitive forces. This activity leads to greater confusion for planners and managers who must prepare for the years ahead. Will any of these new products result in the obsolescence of your products? Will new manufacturing and value-adding processes render your business uneconomic?

You can assess the environmental forces at work by conducting a PEST review. This is an acronym covering the main headings under which you look at the environment:

- political;
- economic;
- social or sociological;
- technical

This is described in a little more detail in Appendix 1.

Changing competitive forces

There will be organizations whose activities may threaten your secure trading position. They might not be competitors in the traditional sense of an organization providing a similar service or product; they could be putting up local labour rates or stealing your staff.

Here you could conduct a SWOT review. Again, this is an acronym, with the initial letters standing for Strengths and Weaknesses of your own organization, and Opportunities and Threats in the marketplace. This analysis method is described in Appendix 1.

Conducting PEST and SWOT analyses can surface areas meriting further attention; indeed, they can be used to identify important issues that need addressing urgently.

ARE YOU ABLE TO MAKE THE JOURNEY?

The high rate of change in the business world means that a 'once and for all' solution to any problem is not going to work, or at least not for long. What is needed is a process for identifying and meeting business needs on a continuous basis and for the longer term.

You need to maintain the business and its systems in an acceptable and effective state, and in tune with the changing environment. A management consultant should therefore seek to build evolving solutions, changing continuously under your management, and at a pace the business can reasonably afford.

Some businesses operate in markets and territories where there is little change from one year to the next. In this situation management may reasonably believe that the resources and processes it uses do not need frequent review. There will, however, be pressure to upgrade the organizational infrastructure from time to time. There will also be important new opportunities that require IT and other investment.

There is a danger that planning and budgeting for these investments will be a source of annoyance if management are not regularly dealing with investment issues. But it is likely that within a few years the environmental changes will bring them to the end of the era of comfortable static operation. The way management then handle change will be important to their longer-term success. The manager of such an organization should therefore ensure that the management team is equipped for the situation when it arises. So infrastructure review should always be on the agenda, even if the outcome most of the time in the static organization is 'do nothing'.

Is the organization fit for change?

An organization that needs to be successful in a changing environment in order to succeed in its business must beware inflexible attitudes. New rules, new ways of working, and new management attitudes to change all have a bearing on success. So the problem facing management is the one of keeping the organization in tune with the various elements of the environment which are key to business survival.

Here are some important factors needing attention.

Learning

Organizations have always evolved with the changes in their environments. When the pace of environmental change was slow, they were probably unaware that they were experiencing a slow process of learning and managed adaptation. Organizations today need to create more deliberate learning programmes because the rate of change is rapidly approaching the rate at which they can comfortably adapt.

This is illustrated by the formula:

$$L > C$$

which says that for survival, the rate of learning (L) in an organization must exceed the rate of change (C) that it is subject to.

Managing the mechanisms for learning is now a strategic task, and management need to be selective in the way they deploy their learning resources, what they study, and how much they can afford to learn by experimentation, failure and further experimentation.

Using external consultants might give you rapid access to information. On the other hand, conducting research for yourself, you can focus more narrowly on discovering what is appropriate for your particular business. This may be a better use of resources than using a consultant.

The process of learning cannot be restricted entirely to theory, and may involve live running or prototyping trials with the full involvement of operational staff. Their cooperation and enthusiastic involvement in the learning process are vital. This demands a great deal of flexibility, so that learning projects can be carried out on a timely basis. When such learning projects become a feature of day-to-day work, there will be a need to provide greater resource at least initially so that operational work is not disrupted.

Implementing change

In the future there will be more change to the working environment than heretofore. For organizations pursuing a policy of always keeping up to date this will mean moving rapidly and seeking to capitalize on the benefits of the latest technologies in all areas of the organization.

Staff and management who use new systems will need to move more into the driving position, having greater control over what is done and when. There will be significant demands on their time to be involved in the management of change as well as learning and operating changed work practices.

Organizations in which staff accept and implement change with skill will have a competitive advantage over those that do not. Moreover, the evidence is that change in which those influenced have a say in design and implementation has greater acceptance and success.

Management and staff attitudes

Flexibility and the implementation of change on the basis we are faced with today are unlikely to be possible with staff and management attitudes that prevailed only 10 years ago. Organizations that were designed to be static will not change overnight to a format of adequate flexibility. This is a matter of changing people's expectations and attitudes so that the necessary learning and development work can be carried out effectively and with the courage and commitment of all levels of the organization.

Organizations wishing to move with agility in implementing change will find that the staff re-education process takes time. It is also not as easily controlled as teaching skills on courses. Many aspects of staff expectations, attitudes and behaviours are deeply embedded and confirmed over time by the company business culture. Releasing the flexibility required for rapid organizational change will require a change in the company culture.

What about people's reactions to the idea of change?

The culture of an organization has many dimensions. It is the sum total of the attitudes and behaviours which are accepted or encouraged in your company. It is embedded in the people of your organization; it has variants by seniority and by function; and it is very difficult to study. It is one of the most powerful human forces in your organization, and it is important to understand its impact.

If you are to be your own management consultant, what you really need to know is that culture emanates from the chief executive and the top team. When their behaviours start to change, only then will the culture of the organization start to change.

Cultural extremes

In an organization that has operated in a static format for some time, staff will not be accustomed to change. Since it is not a frequent occurrence, staff may have anxieties about the impact of change. Indeed it may be accepted that there is a tacit management agreement not to inflict change on staff. Staff and management may find considerable comfort in their predictable and static work regime, and any threat to this might be strongly resisted.

Evidence of the existence of this type of culture in your organization may be present in people's statements about the company, or the departments in which they work. Some examples might be:

- 'We are right, and this is proved by the fact that we haven't changed for many years.'
- 'Some companies don't do things our way and they get into trouble.'
- 'I remember Mr Smith who tried that. It didn't work. He didn't get on and eventually left.'
- 'Mr Jones has been with us for six months now. He's not like us so I expect he will move on.'

When you begin to tune in to the culture statements you'll appreciate where your organization is locating itself between the 'static position' and the 'flexible position'.

There are no goods or bads or rights or wrongs in culture. There are only relative levels of the usefulness for some business purpose. A strongly change-averse culture will inhibit progress. As a contrast, a culture that embraces change for its own sake is at the opposite end of the spectrum. Both extremes are dangerous, one having disasters of omission and the other having different disasters of commission.

Some change inhibitors are healthy. So also is a strong desire for change. Together they create the debate that is the driving force for the learning process.

Understanding your culture

Operating as your own management consultant, you will need to begin the process of cultural realignment by discovering where you are.

Begin by making up a list of statements which might evoke a cultural response. Can you anticipate how people in various parts of your organization might respond? Here are a few words you might use as starting points: learning, sharing, rules, power, insecurity, fear, anxiety, improvement, punishment, failure, future, waste, success, achievement, discipline, reward, change, competition, argument, self-respect, integrity, humiliation, honesty.

Cultural statements might be items like the following:

- We do not fail.
- We could always do better.
- We like to be involved in decisions.

See if you can build a list of statements that typify attitudes amongst your staff.

This is of course a thinking exercise and is not to be taken as the basis of a questionnaire or a culture change programme, but it will help to form an impression of the culture of your organization.

Evolving your company's culture

When you understand where you are culturally, it is probable that you will want to encourage the culture to move gradually towards a position that is more supportive of change.

The way forward is to undertake many projects having a higher than usual profile and manage them, giving evidence of some of the new elements of culture you need people to absorb. Training courses and more staff access to your corporate visioning and strategy thinking will also reinforce the acceptance of new ways.

Another word of caution . . . It would be indiscreet to describe this as an exercise in culture change. It most assuredly is not. In truth it is just management leading staff to handle change in a new way, and to espouse some new behaviours which are supportive of the sorts of project that will become common in your organization. You manage the projects and the culture will adjust. The stimulus to adjust is the project portfolio itself.

You may of course select projects for your personal involvement on a judicious basis. If you wish to delegate responsibility lower in the organization, you may safely do it on a project.

If you wish to change the traditional response to 'failure', you may undertake some risky learning exercises and reward the project leader on the value of the learning in spite of the failure to implement a system. If you wish to show that going on training courses is not an admission of failure, you might send some of your best people on courses.

The key activity in being your own management consultant is in the diagnosis of cultural position, and in selecting the particular actions to take. Using this approach, your power to make gradual, useful and sustained change is greater than that of any consultant. It will, however, require your longer-term commitment and that of senior management.

To that end it is probably necessary to include the planning and budgeting of this work as part of corporate planning and strategy setting.

New definitions of success and failure

There are important controlling features of static cultures and one of the most common is the failure/blame/punishment dimension. As attitudes towards the importance of learning improve, there is a point where the use of blame and punishment becomes counter-productive. Senior management then need to acquire leadership skills to replace power-based control. They must encourage exploration, experimentation and training as ways of acquiring knowledge to keep ahead. If failure in a learning project is seen as dangerous to career advancement, the learning process will be severely constrained.

New types of objective setting and performance monitoring are needed to maintain a balance between relevant learning with planned payback and the uncontrolled spending on training for its own sake. A new vocabulary of objectives, deliverables, accountabilities and leadership will help to indicate that an organization is changing.

Learning projects must have learning deliverables and objectives, leadership and a way of capturing the new knowledge for the good of the organization. Formal documentation of all activities is a key way of ensuring that knowledge acquired is captured and can be made available to others.

GETTING STARTED

Providing appropriate technology to all of the areas of your business will certainly happen more readily with a 'learning' culture and 'inclusive' management approaches. Involving many levels of staff in change decisions is part of finding and installing good workable solutions. This is not cosmetic nor is it a staff communication exercise; it is real. Delegation to lower levels in the organization brings better commitment and better solutions and reinforces the flexible learning and knowledge-sharing ways of working. To go this far is to embark on a journey of continuous change and learning which will not allow a return to the old static ways.

Senior management support is vital

The commitment of the whole senior team is vital to the long-term success of any project. Senior management need to maintain their leadership position in these processes and the pace needs to be maintained. This management style is a journey made up of many projects. Individual projects have their ends and their deliverables, but the corporate journey has no end.

Is everyone present?

In the early stages of a series of learning projects, the organization will begin to change its nature. With proper support, training and involvement, most staff will stay part of the team; regrettably a small number may not.

As the changes take hold, some people will find that they are unable to function in the new business as they did in the old. If they are unable to make the adaptation themselves, you may find that they will work to bring the organization back to its former static ways so that their behaviours will again be successful. In some cases there will be a parting of the ways with these few and management must provide for this to happen in a way that is not damaging to the new organization not too traumatic to the individuals affected.

Since some of those who cannot make the journey may be senior, the preparation must be carried out with some care and discretion.

Is the journey optional?

There is a well-known (and false) syllogism that goes:

- 'Something must be done.'
- 'This is something.'
- 'Therefore we must do it.'

This leads to the management phenomenon of 'refuge in action' – 'so long as we are doing something, everything is all right'. But the art is doing the right thing.

Careful analysis is required to take stock of where you are and where you should be; and then you have to make the journey!

CHAPTER TWO

DIAGNOSING THE HEALTH OF YOUR BUSINESS

Bill Peace

A business – even a one-person business – is a complicated organism, not unlike the human body. Many things can go wrong, but fortunately most of us are healthy, and in many cases where some function is out of order, steps can be taken to put it right. Similarly, many kinds of problem can arise in a business: most businesses are reasonably healthy, though with a bit of exercise or change in diet they could become stronger, more energetic. When a business does become ill – even seriously ill – steps can be taken, in most cases, to put it right.

The role of a management consultant has sometimes been compared with that of a company doctor. And in the same way that a doctor – whatever his or her specialization – needs to know about anatomy, physiology and the major human systems (such as nervous, blood circulation etc), so too does a consultant have to understand the complexity of an organization.

This notion of complexity is important. At first glance, a small business may seem rather simple, with simple problems requiring uncomplicated solutions. A casual glance may suggest that the human body is pretty simple: pairs of arms, legs, eyes, ears and a mouth – all we need to get around, move things, see, hear and communicate. But as we all know, below the surface, it's not quite so simple.

Consider, for example, Peter Richards' accountancy practice. He works from an office at home, providing accounting services to 84 clients, all of whom are locally situated individuals or small businesses. It seems simple enough. Peter responds to questions from his clients. He gathers data from them, and prepares accounts and filings for the Inland Revenue.

But let's look at what lies beneath the surface. Peter must develop the ability to obtain new clients, both to grow the business and to replace clients who move elsewhere. Should this be done with advertising, or by word of mouth? Where should he advertise? Which clients will offer referrals?

Peter must keep up to date with current accounting practice and changing tax regulations. Which journals should he read? Which seminars and courses should he attend? Peter's office at home will include a phone, PC and fax. Will a photocopier be cost effective? When the PC crashes, what effect will this have on the business? What complexity of software can be justified in terms of improved productivity and customer service? How will he learn to operate the software? Should the typist who comes in twice a week come in three times?

Then there is Peter himself. A quiet, self-effacing individual, he has always disliked people with big egos. But eight of his current clients and two very interesting prospects are anything but humble. How well will he deal with these clients?

Even this one-person business presents a complicated mix of:

- Peter Richards' skills, experience, attitudes and needs;
- the support systems (physical, financial, emotional, etc) that keep the business going;
- client relationships across a broad spectrum from warm and secure to rather shaky;
- relationships with others who influence the business: Inland Revenue, professional bodies, competitors, allied practices, etc.

To tell the whole story of Peter Richards' accounting practice would take a good-sized book. And the same could be said of any small business.

If we hold the view that a small business is a rather simple activity, we risk treating only symptoms. We return to medieval medicine, when the apothecary was consulted about which herbs would allay which symptoms, without any understanding of the *cause* of the illness. We need to get to grips with the complexity of business if we are to diagnose its health accurately.

TEN VITAL SYSTEMS

In order that we may be, in effect, physicians for our own businesses, it is important to have a view of what can cause a business to be ill (or healthy). There are 10 life support systems in a business, all of which must function well for the business to thrive. Five of these are front-line systems that connect the business directly to customers and the market-place. These five are strategy, sales/marketing, product/service development, product/service delivery, and after sales service.

Then there are five support systems, which contribute to the front-line systems, making sure they are both effective (meeting customer/market needs) and efficient (competitive). These support systems are human resources, technology, finance, information systems, and management.

Figure 2.1 shows how the vital systems relate to one another and the marketplace.

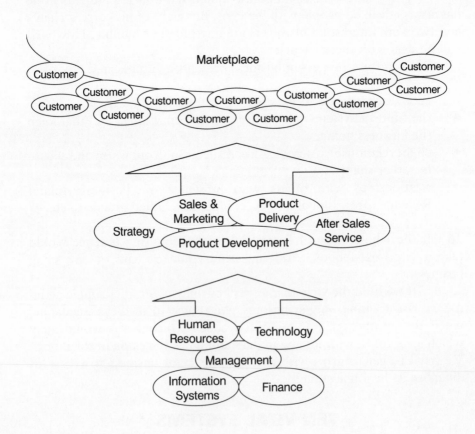

Figure 2.1 Ten vital systems

Front-line systems

Let's look at some examples to better understand this complicated thing we call 'our business'.

John and Mary Wells' business is called 'ServiceLab'. It has been operating for six years and has a client list of 57 laboratories, mostly at hospitals, but some in healthcare products and service companies. ServiceLab retains a resource pool of qualified laboratory technicians; nearly all are graduate chemists and biologists. Many have particular specialities: blood analysis, tissue pathology, etc.

The business turned over £524,000 last year, with a pre-tax profit (not counting the owners' salaries) of £58,000.

Strategy

When they started the business, John and Mary didn't think about 'strategy'. Instead, they saw a need to provide 'agency' lab technicians on short notice to clear overloads, and provide sickness/holiday cover. Having worked (and met) in a district general hospital laboratory, they knew their idea could work only if they could become aware of customers' needs and respond quickly with qualified personnel.

They approached several hospitals and obtained agreement from the laboratory team leaders that the leaders would fax each month's lab rota (showing any openings or needs for backup) to ServiceLab before the month started. Meanwhile, John and Mary pay a small 'retainer' to lab technicians who will make at least 48 hours per month available for assignments from ServiceLab. On a PC in the office, Mary matches client needs with technician availabilities. In most cases where a client calls in at 9.00 am for sickness cover, ServiceLab can have a covering technician on site in the afternoon, from a pool of 'technician mothers' who wish to work only part-time.

In addition to this rapid response, ServiceLab faxes an evaluation sheet to each client after every assignment. The returns are not only monitored; they are shared with the assignee. The message to both clients and technicians is: 'We provide a quality service!'

Perhaps they didn't write down their strategy, but John and Mary certainly have one. By connecting themselves very closely to their customers and responding quickly with qualified technicians, they effectively lock out their competitors.

The strategy for your company is that which responds to your customers' needs in ways that make you different from your competition. The best strategies are not only responsive to particular customer needs; they are difficult for competitors to copy. These best strategies tend to involve capabilities or processes. The capability might be the ability to provide a special skill or to make use of unique technology. In ServiceLab's case, their differentiation involves process: the way the company does business or puts its key tasks together. ServiceLab uses a direct fax link with its customers to gather data quickly. Some of its clients have converted to e-mails to which the rotas are attached as Excel spreadsheets.

Compare the Wells' strategy with the more typical strategy for an agency business. Someone in the agency office waits for 'need help' calls to come in. (Usually, these calls go out to several agencies.) The agency starts making calls to its roster of potential staff. If a 'hit' is made, the agency calls the client back, and if no one has got there first, the agency will get the business. All too often, though, the agency can't find someone quickly enough to beat the competition, and sales suffer. So do profits. Being different in the way you serve your customers is essential to success.

Sales/marketing

Let's stay with John and Mary Wells as we examine the sales/marketing system. While definitions vary, marketing tends to involve the positioning of the business and its products or services in the marketplace: it's about customer perceptions. Sales is more about securing individual pieces of business – day-to-day orders.

Advertising (and public relations) are usually part of marketing. ServiceLab doesn't do any advertising. Its competitors do: Hospital Staff spends £1,850 every month on adverts in *Health Services Journal*. John Wells' view is that lab team leaders don't pay much attention to these adverts, but they do like to attend the bi-monthly seminars that ServiceLab arranges. Starting at 5.00 pm with tea and biscuits in a pleasant venue, there is a presentation by an outside expert or laboratory scientist (ServiceLab pays his/her out-of-pocket expenses), followed by a discussion. Then, there is wine and a light buffet. John introduces the speaker (and the invitations go out in ServiceLab's name), but it's pretty low key: just a few brochures in the reception area. During the wine and buffet, John and Mary circulate amongst the attendees, paying particular attention to potential new clients.

John also spends a good deal of his time visiting potential new clients. This is more marketing than selling. Most of the day-to-day selling (securing orders) is done by Mary working at the PC in the office, sending out confirming faxes and e-mails, and making phone calls where necessary. John takes with him a laptop PC so that he can show potential new clients how the ServiceLab system works: typical rotas, staff credentials, client evaluations, response times. It's real and pretty impressive. ServiceLab's business is growing. A dilemma for the Wells is whether they should expand geographically in the same business, or expand into other agency sectors within their current geographic area.

For your company, the sales/marketing system must convey to your customers and potential customers a clear image of what your company is. What adjectives or adverbs will come to your customers' minds when they hear the name of your company? Are those the adjectives and adverbs you want them to think? Equally important, the sales/marketing system must bring in customer business, regularly, steadily, at sensible prices and with the right expectations about the products or services you will provide.

Hospital Staff spends quite a lot of money on marketing. In addition to their advertising, they spend about £75 on each client 'decision-maker' for a Christmas hamper, with a thank you note from the managing director. Amongst those decision-makers, though, they are thought of as a 'bit of a sweat shop'. Effective marketing?

There are five Hospital Staff salesmen calling on medical laboratories in the UK. They don't really 'sell' anything. This is done, hit or miss, by the 'coordinators' in each office. The sales people identify new contacts, invite old contacts out for a 'pint and a pie' (generally without much success), and try to extract a promise that the client will call the local coordinator each time there's a vacancy. These five salesmen have a total cost of £236,000, or about 6 per cent of sales. To put it in another way, Hospital Staff would be more profitable by about £200,000 per year if it had no sales staff.

Product/service development

Julie DeAngelo and her boyfriend, Philip Cowan, started a bakery three years ago. Philip had worked as a pastry chef in a small, upscale restaurant, and Julie, an enthusiastic amateur cook, had studied marketing and logistics at a local college. Their business, 'With the Grain', serves restaurants, specialized food shops and a few, small supermarket chains. The products are relatively unique breads and sweet pastries, all delivered daily (except Sundays and bank holidays) to customers within 50 miles of the bakery. Last year, With the Grain turned over £215,000, and broke even, after paying Julie and Philip £35,000 in salaries.

With the Grain has a 'tried and true' portfolio which includes about two dozen varieties of breads, rolls and pastries, available consistently on a year-round basis. These products, unique in appearance and flavour, and often of ethnic origin, are all on the delivery vans as they go out each morning. But in addition, With the Grain offers a further half dozen varieties which are 'new treats', or seasonal breads and pastries.

Because the large supermarkets are continually following the product trends which small, independent bakers prove out, Julie and Philip vowed at the outset to stay continually 'at least one jump ahead'. Their 'new treats' are both sales enhancers and potential replacements for tried and true products whose sales have declined.

Philip and Julie have evolved a method for developing new treats. On Sundays, they pore over ethnic cookbooks from the library. At least once a week Philip will experiment with one or two recipes, often altering them to suit his own ideas. Some of these experiments are very promising; others are much less so. Once a month, Julie will go to London and tour the bakeries, carrying with her a basket of samples, with recipes, from With the Grain. If she sees something in a bakery that interests her, she'll offer to trade recipes and samples with the proprietor. The consequence of this activity is that With the Grain constantly has a dozen new breads, rolls or pastries under development. About every two months, Julie and Philip will take a selection of their potential 'new treats' to a charity meeting or event. These are meetings typically attended by the kind of customers who trade at the restaurants and shops served by With the Grain. In return for tasting their products, Julie and Philip get comments and reaction on their potential new treats. They also leave behind small listings of where With the Grain products can be purchased locally.

For With the Grain, product development is the key to survival and profitability. Last year, two independent bakeries serving the same county as With the Grain have ceased trading. Both offered staple products that are produced by the mass production bakeries or baked by the supermarkets on their own premises. These bakeries could not sell enough of their products, at prices above cost, in order to survive.

Product/service delivery

But With the Grain also uses its product delivery system to charge premium prices and avoid the powerful reach of the supermarkets.

With the Grain has two significant investments: in Philip's

kitchen, with its kneading machines, trays, ovens and packaging stations, which starts work at 3.30 am, most mornings. Assisting Philip are
an apprentice baker and 3–4 local students earning a bit of extra money.
The other important investment is four delivery vans, of various sizes
and ages, all leased or on hire purchase. Each van is fitted with a bin for
each of the varieties of breads and pastries. The vans are driven by
retirees chosen for their sales experience. They're paid a commission
for 'tried and true' sales and a higher commission for 'new treats' sales.
The driver/salesmen are briefed on successes at charity tasting events
and a restaurant proprietor is likely to hear, 'Your customers will love
this Georgian bran bread – the Children's Aid Council thought it's won-
derful!' The vans start loading at 7.30 am and most are on their way by
8.30 am. Each van has a route assigned, and while most customers
(those who purchase at least £10 daily) are visited each day, others are
seen on alternate days, again based on the £10 minimum purchase.

Delivery runs are usually completed by early afternoon, and the
driver/salesmen are then free to visit prospective new customers. These
must not be within one mile of an existing customer (quarter of a mile
in towns), must not add more than 10 minutes to the route, must be
willing to buy £10/visit for a one-month trial. The driver/salesmen get
a 'bounty' for each new customer obtained.

There is a goods received form for each customer, which is completed on the premises, signed and returned to the office where Julie
scans it into the system. 'Day-old bread' (of which there is 10–25 per
cent) is given to local charities. The cost of ingredients in the bread is
less than 10 per cent of sales, so while Julie and Philip don't want to
waste money on ingredients, they are more concerned about not having
the product a customer wants.

Product production and delivery is a tightly integrated system at
With the Grain, starting with Julie's forecast of volumes by product,
based on data off the office PC (and her intuition), which she prepares
at the end of each day for the next day. Most customers get daily personal attention, and the opportunity to try something new to please
their customers. Most information flows are linked to the PC, and even
the left-over bread is put to good use.

The two bakeries that went out of business had a much less formalized approach, particularly to distribution: no forecasting, no
scannable forms, no driver/salesmen (just deliverymen), and no careful
route planning. Frequently they were making stops to deliver less than
£5 of bread. With the price pressure from the supermarkets, this was a
recipe for disaster.

After sales service

The after sales service system is perhaps well illustrated by the case of Wainwright Compressors Ltd. Wainwright is a dealer/installer of small to medium-sized air compressors for industry. The company, now owned by Karen Wainwright, was started by her husband Joseph 22 years ago and is franchised to sell three lines of air compressors of various capacities up to 1,000 cfm and output pressures up to 100 bar. Karen, widowed for the last two years, runs the company with the help of a son, John, who is sales director. There are 23 employees, a turnover of £2.1 million, and pre-tax income of £305,000 last year.

When Joseph started Wainwright Compressors, there was essentially no site work (installation or service), unless a customer called in with a problem. The business was selling air compressors. Now, about 50 per cent of turnover and 70 per cent of profits are coming from work on customers' premises, or in the small rebuild shop. Wainwright began installing compressors (foundations, electrics and piping) just over 10 years ago. And, five years ago Karen persuaded Joseph to move aggressively into after sales service. At first it was mostly site maintenance labour and more of a push to sell parts. Gradually, however, Wainwright introduced its customers to three tiers of service contracts. The least expensive contract provides all parts at a discount, and site labour within one working day (also at a discount) for a fixed annual fee. The most expensive 'hi rely plan' guarantees a compressor availability of at least 98.5 per cent, with all parts and labour included in the higher annual fee. Wainwright service technicians inspect and maintain these machines quarterly, and Wainwright refunds a portion of the annual fee if the target is not met. Next, Karen moved into 'rebuilds': taking used compressors in trade, reconditioning them in the shop, and selling them with a comprehensive guarantee at discounted prices. Last year Karen decided to offer on-site service for five makes of competitive air compressors. Her service business is growing at better than 15 per cent per year. The additional involvement after the sale has been well received by customers, many of whom can remember the company's slogan: 'We keep the pressure on!' Karen's view is that more interaction with her customers also gives her the inside track when a customer is thinking of purchasing a new compressor.

Contrast the approach taken by Wainwright with Mercury Compressors, who are dealers of the largest selling brand. If a customer requires installation, Mercury refers him to one of its 'installation partners' (local mechanical and electrical contractors). Mercury also has a list of 'preferred maintainers' to whom it sells parts and whom it recommends for any site repair work. While Mercury is more than three times the size of Wainwright, its return on sales is 8 per cent (vs. 14.5 per cent for Wainwright), and its sales growth is about 3 per cent (less than half of Wainwright's growth).

But after sales service is not applicable only to capital goods. At ServiceLab, every client is asked to provide feedback on every assignment. If there is anything negative reported, Mary will call the client or John will visit. At With the Grain, Philip or Julie speaks on the phone personally to every customer at least once a quarter. And Julie watches the purchase trends of every customer. If a popular product is dropped or sales trend downward, that customer will get an immediate call, followed, in some cases, by a visit. The cost of keeping existing customers is a small fraction of the cost of finding new ones.

Support systems

Human resources

Let's consider the five support systems that complete the anatomy of the business. Human resources are a vital part of any business: the right people can make a very healthy business; the wrong ones will make it very ill.

ServiceLab is a people-intensive business, and John and Mary Wells experienced more people problems than they anticipated: employees who lied about qualifications, who made unwanted advances to client staff, who falsified attendance records, who refused to accept assignments they had volunteered for, etc, etc! ServiceLab now has a cadre of about 90 technicians, who are well liked by clients, are reliable and enjoy their work. The problem is that there is a constant turnover of these 'stars'. Without effective recruitment and screening, the number of stars would decline. Over time, ServiceLab developed a unique process for finding, hiring, evaluating and promoting new staff to stars (who get the best assignments). ServiceLab's primary source of new employees is a polytechnic college. As soon as new students enrol in relevant study programmes, ServiceLab contacts them with an offer of lab assistant's jobs (a necessary source of income to the students). The Wells also sponsor a pre-graduation 'taste the wine' event every year as part of a process of knowing the graduates, where they will be working, and staying in touch with them. Mary speaks personally with every new technician before and after the first few assignments, and each potential star receives written feedback. Stars and potential stars also receive a monthly 'newsletter' of client activities and assignments. John says: 'If we didn't get the people side of our business about as right as it can be, we'd be dead!'

So good human resource management is essential in even a small business: finding, and recruiting the right people. And bear in mind that, in the same way that a business has to provide products to its customers, it has also to provide an attractive 'prospectus' to its people, that will encourage the best staff to stay.

Technology

Technology may often be part of the strategy: the ability to offer a unique or unusual capability to customers. If this is the case, marketing will feature the technology in its image-building efforts, and urge customers to remember the company for the technology it employs. Technology may be in the centre of the product/service development system: we want to use this technology in our product or service. Technology is likely to be present in the product/service delivery or the after sales service system.

When Wainwright Compressors first went into the rebuild business, for example, it was necessary to bore out scored cylinder liners. (The cylinder liner provides a smooth inner surface to the cylinder against which the piston rings slide to assure a tight seal. Scored cylinder liners – caused by grit in the lubricating oil – lead to poor compression and inefficiency.) Because of the tight 'interference' fit between the liner and the cast cylinder, Wainwright had to send compressors out to a machine shop, which removed the liners on a boring mill. This represented the highest single element of cost in the rebuild work: typically £15–25 per cylinder.

But now, a piece of homemade technology has made a real difference. Wainwright technicians use resistance heaters, shielded with mineral wool insulation, to heat the cylinder casting to about 400°F. A special tool made by the shop foreman and consisting of steel fingers which extend from a central hub is inserted into the cylinder and adjusted to engage the cylinder liner. A made-to-measure plastic disc is used to close off the bottom of the cylinder, above the fingers. Shielded thermocouples are attached inside and outside the cylinder, then dry ice is packed inside the cylinder. When the thermocouples show a temperature difference of about 500°F between the liner and the casting, the liner can be withdrawn with ease. The procedure is also used to install replacement liners. Scored liners can now be removed in batches at a cost of less than £5 per cylinder. This one application of technology has taken rebuilds from a marginal business to a profitable one.

Finance

The finance system is not just about invoicing and the control of receivables and payables, it is also about providing management with a clear, nearly real-time, view of what is going on in the business.

When Julie and Philip started With the Grain, the accounts were kept by Julie in a ledger, and on a quarterly basis their accountant would come in, pore over the ledger with Julie and put together a profit and loss statement for the quarter, as well as a balance sheet. Usually, there were surprises: the book value of ingredient stocks didn't match the actual, or the book value of cash flow didn't seem to match the bank statement, etc. Julie and Philip argued about what had happened and why. After six months, they agreed that they couldn't continue with the manual ledgers. They bought a 'shrink wrapped' package of financial software, which not only generates monthly P&L statements and balance sheets, but also keeps track of the level of ingredient stocks, prints cheques to creditors, reconciles the bank statement, keeps track of VAT, and shows which debtors are overdue.

For many small businesses, capitalization is an important issue. If there is not enough capital (cash to pay the bills) the business will be unable to grow. If too much money has been borrowed, the business is at risk of failing, particularly if there is a decline in sales and there is not enough income to meet the interest and principal payments, as well as other expenses. Defining the right capitalization of the business is a key function of the finance system.

Information systems

Information systems have two fundamental purposes: automation and providing information. Automation is about efficiency: using a computer to do something which it will take a human being a lot longer to do. A good example is the scannable goods receipt form used by With the Grain. Julie DeAngelo can scan all of a day's sales into the office PC in less than half an hour. Seconds later, the day's sales can be seen in figures and graphically. Just to get a total for the day used to take her two hours before the software was installed, and then all the invoices had to be prepared manually.

As to the information providing role of information systems, you'll recall that Mary Wells is able to take data from faxes coming in from her 'stars', and prepare a master schedule so that she can see at a glance who's available to meet a client's needs. The faxes come onto the office PC. Mary copies data from individual stars and pastes it into a master Access database. No need to flip through over 100 pages of faxes to see who can go to Reading tomorrow morning.

Management system

The last, but certainly most important system in this living thing, your business, is the management system: you! The management system assures success in many ways:

- by defining and implementing the right strategy;
- by designing and putting in place effective processes for sales/marketing, for designing and delivering products/services and for serving the customer after the sale;
- by continually measuring how well the systems are working and improving them continually, as well;
- by using appropriate technology and information systems;
- by hiring, developing and motivating the right people (and sometimes by dismissing the wrong ones);
- by putting in place a sound financial system, including the right level of capital.

By the same token, if management doesn't get this list of tasks right, the business will certainly struggle, and it may fail.

And management has one essential role which is not included in the above list: maintaining the culture and morale of the organization.

Culture is not something 'which happens'. Culture is the result of the behaviour of management and the values that management demonstrate. Managers control the culture. Similarly morale is in the hands of management. Certainly, external forces can have positive (or negative) influences on morale, but we have seen companies facing extremely difficult external challenges where morale was high. That excitement, that 'by gosh, we can do it!' buzz in these companies reflects a confidence of the people in their managers, of the managers in the people, and of everyone in the strategy and action plan.

At this point, you will perhaps agree that your business, any small to medium business, is a complex organism, where much can go wrong (and right).

TWO TREATMENT PLANS

What to do if things aren't going well? There are two basic treatment plans. The first is the macro approach, which takes the broad view and will help us to distinguish whether we are running a ServiceLab or a Hospital Staff. The second approach, while not exactly micro, is more detailed. It should be used when we're pretty well convinced we've got the basics right, but we want to get another step forward in performance. It's possible that the detailed method – if pursued with an open mind – will throw up a great new improvement, like cutting costs in half in a major area, or taking a new approach to customers, which opens a far larger market. The danger in starting with this more detailed method – business process analysis – is that unless it is approached with plenty of lateral thinking, we could relieve some symptoms without addressing the illness.

Macro diagnosis

The macro approach to evaluating the health of your business relies on plenty of 'second opinions' and a list of tough diagnostic questions.

From whom should you seek second opinions? Any thoughtful person who knows your business and who wants to see you succeed. Employees are a good place to start. Two comments about getting second opinions from employees. First, try to get a balance of views from people working 'at the coal face' as well as from the managers to whom they report. The people who are actually doing the work may have quite a different perspective than the bosses. It is not unusual for the bosses to lose touch with the mundane problems in the business. Second, it needs to be very clear that you really want to hear what your employees have to say. At Mercury Compressors, for example, management has been using 'Team Brief' to communicate with employees for the past five years. A set of 'briefing notes' is put together monthly by the MD, and these are then cascaded down through the organizational hierarchy at workplace meetings. The problem is that this is all 'tell' and no 'listen'. Moreover, the MD is very seldom seen talking to people in their work locations, outside his office. If the MD of Mercury started asking his employees for their views, he would almost certainly be treated with some scepticism, and end up hearing what people thought he wanted to hear.

Try to get the views of the 'heroes in the culture'. These are the people to whom other employees listen because they are intelligent, persuasive and have character. They also tend to influence the behaviour of others. They may not be managers – in fact, you may sometimes consider them to be nuisances. But if they have some time to think constructively about your questions, it is unlikely they will try to mislead you. Rather, they may give you some startling insights!

Customers are an excellent source of second opinions. Try to focus on the ones who don't buy as much from your company as you might wish. Ask the large, sophisticated, demanding customers for their opinions. Be aware of one serious shortcoming with 'customer surveys': customers don't always know what they'll want tomorrow. *You* may think of something that will absolutely knock their socks off, but if you had asked them beforehand, they might have told you they wouldn't be interested. This unpredictability is particularly evident when the innovation is about style (the bikini swimsuit wasn't a design that women requested), or about technology (Apple, not its customers, promoted the concept of the software 'window').

Your suppliers certainly have their own views about trends in the marketplace. They may also be a very good source of information about what your competitors are doing. As you listen to your suppliers, you'll need to try to distinguish between genuine industry insights and supplier propaganda. Perhaps the best test is to evaluate the extent to which your supplier will benefit from your accepting the opinions or advice they give you. If the supplier includes a dose of disagreeable medicine for himself, better listen carefully!

Competitors – particularly at trade shows – can be very interesting sources of information. Much of it will certainly be self-serving. But you may also get some surprisingly candid answers to tough questions like: 'How do you find your new clients?' Salesmen on the company stand like to talk, and even if your name badge identifies you as a competitor, you may find it possible to exchange views on trends in the marketplace. To avoid any possible impropriety, it is better to avoid any discussion of prices or specific sales opportunities. But if they are handing out price lists or customer reference lists to the public, there's no reason for you not to ask for one!

The published financial reports of your competitors may also provide some interesting 'benchmarks' for your business. (For some competitors, you may need to go to Companies House in London to get reports of registered companies whose shares are not traded on an exchange. For those that are traded, it's a simple matter, as a private investor, to ring up the company and ask for a copy of their annual report and accounts.)

Once you have received reports from your competitor(s), there are lots of questions you can ask, and many of the answers will be there for you:

- What do they say about strategy?
- What particular market sectors do they serve?
- How are they doing in each sector?
- As a percentage of sales, how do their expenses compare to yours?
- What growth have they achieved?
- How does their turnover per employee compare to yours?
- How does their value added per employee compare to yours? (Value added is sales less purchases; a higher value added per employee is a measure of efficiency.)
- How do their key balance sheet indicators compare to yours: inventory turns, debtor days, creditor days, gearing, etc?
- What do they pay their top people?
- How does the average salary per employee compare to yours?
- Etc.

At the end of this chapter there is a list of diagnostic questions which may be helpful to you in thinking about the health of your business and in talking to employees, customers, suppliers and competitors. The purpose of the macro diagnosis is to give you a view as to how well each of the ten vital systems that make up your business is functioning.

Business process analysis

The second treatment plan is business process analysis. A few years ago we probably would have called it 'business process re-engineering'. You may remember that the term generated a lot of hype and was 'on every manager's agenda!' A bit like a bull market, excessive expectations were created, too many people bought in without understanding, and the stock dropped as people realized that the fountain of youth had not been discovered. The reality is that BPR (or BPA) is a good utility and it will deliver dividends – but it's not a panacea that will reform your business overnight.

BPA is the evaluation and alteration of the tasks that make up six or seven of the vital systems in a business. BPA will help us:

- take out unnecessary cost;
- improve quality provided to the customer;
- increase the value of our products/services;
- reduce the time it takes for important events to happen (like delivering products).

The reason that BPA can be so effective is that almost all of the cost, quality, value and time in a business is embodied in the tasks that make up the six or seven vital systems. The seven are the front-line systems plus the finance and human resources systems. (We said 'six' because in a small company there may be no formal process for the strategy system.) By 'process' we mean the series of tasks performed, and the way they are performed, measured and managed.

In all companies, there's a 'way we do things here'. It may not be written down in a procedure, but experienced employees know the way (process) and they can show new employees how to do it. There's the way we do our sales and marketing. There's the way we develop new products/services, and deliver them, and service them. There are specific ways we handle our people and our financial matters. In large companies there is typically a 'strategic planning process' by means of which the strategy for the next several years is developed, communicated and (hopefully) implemented.

Generally, there are no processes for technology or information systems. Rather, these become embedded in other systems, where they are more visible and tangible. If we analyse these other systems thoughtfully, we may find that much could be gained from better use of technology and information.

Also, there isn't a management system that is explicit enough that we can analyse it in the objective way we'll be describing below. There is usually a 'management style' that manifests itself in somewhat different ways under varying circumstances. The consequence of this is that culture and teamwork problems (or problems with management style) can't be addressed by BPA.

Nor will BPA address problems with the strategic definition of the business. We can analyse the strategic process, and we may alter it until we think we've got a great process. But we may still have a poor strategy. Strategy is not entirely scientific (although good strategy contains scientific elements); it is also an art, containing elements of intuition and faith. BPA can't deal in intuition and faith.

Finally, BPA is not the right tool to analyse whether the financial structure of the business is right: whether we have sufficient capital of the right type. This issue we address in Chapter 10.

Even with these disclaimers, BPA, used sensibly, can be very effective in improving the health of your business significantly – even dramatically!

There are many good books on business process re-engineering. If your company is going to undertake a major effort in BPR/BPA, you may find it helpful to read through one or two. Similarly, there are quite a few software packages that promise to make your flow charting much easier. All these methods and sales pitches tend to be confusing. Which is the best way? Actually, once you've analysed two or three business processes, you'll probably have your own way. The best way is what works for you. There are, however, a few principles to bear in mind:

- First, you need to establish the purpose or goal of the business process (why are we doing all this?).
- Map out the tasks in logical order, so that you and your colleagues can look at the big picture together.
- Solicit input from people who actually do the work to make sure the 'as-is map' is correct.
- Use operating data to help quantify the performance of the process: how much it costs, how long it takes, how frequently errors occur, etc.
- Now, critique the 'as-is map':

  - Are all these tasks necessary?
  - Does management have visibility of what's going on?
  - Are people given the information they need?
  - Do managers (and employees) have sufficient control?
  - Can any steps be automated?
  - What can be done to reduce errors and cut costs?

- Starting with the goal of the process and a clean sheet of paper, draw a 'to-be map' of the process. Creativity and lateral thinking are essential here. Think the unthinkable! But finish with a reality check to be sure that your new process will work in your company with your employees.
- Use people who aren't involved in the process, but who are perceptive and innovative, to help with the critique and with the design of the 'to-be process'.

Rebuild Compressor BPA

Let's look at an example from Wainwright Compressors. Six months after she started the compressor rebuild business, Karen Wainwright was frustrated. That new segment of the business was losing money and was growing slowly. Her intuition told her it should be doing much better. With her son John (Sales Director), Bob Kenny (Shop Foreman) and David Weiss (Company Accountant), she set about BPA for compressor rebuilds.

They identified the goal of the process to be: 'To obtain suitable "bodies", rebuild them to run reliably, and sell them at at least 40 per cent gross margin, such that a compound growth rate of at least 25 per cent per year can be obtained.' (The gross margin on new compressors, excluding any installation work, is typically 25 per cent.)

Karen, John, Bob and David identified the major tasks and put them on yellow Post-it notes on a large sheet of brown paper on the wall in Karen's office. The 'as-is map' looked like Figure 2.2.

Some of the tasks actually consist of a number of sub-tasks, and these could be mapped, as well, if the additional detail were useful and informative.

Karen, Bob and David were able to identify the following additional facts:

- For the last three months, compressors were coming in for rebuilds at a rate of about five per month.
- Of the first 10 compressors that had been rebuilt and sold, three had failed within the 90 days. Two had bearing failures and one had an insulation failure in the motor. In all three cases it was necessary to provide labour as well as parts, because of customer dissatisfaction. The average cost of this warranty work was 22 per cent of the price of a new compressor.
- Sixty-four per cent of rebuilt compressors required new cylinder liners. Sending the body out to a machine shop added about two weeks to rebuild time and typically represented a cost of 24 per cent of the price of a new compressor.
- Other parts and labour provided by Wainwright averaged 12 per cent of the price of a new compressor.
- Thirty per cent of compressors rebuilt to date required extensive work because they were not serviceable to begin with. This work included motor rewinds and replacement of major parts such as piston rods and crankshafts. These rebuilds raised Wainwright's costs from 12 per cent to 44 per cent of a new compressor price.

Karen then drew up the following financial summary:

Item	Percentage of new compressor price
Cost of body	20.0
Wainwright's parts and labour	12.0
Warranty costs	6.6
New cylinder liners	15.4
Unserviceable rebuilds	9.6
Total	63.6

With a selling price of 60 per cent of a new compressor, the reasons for the losses had been made clear.

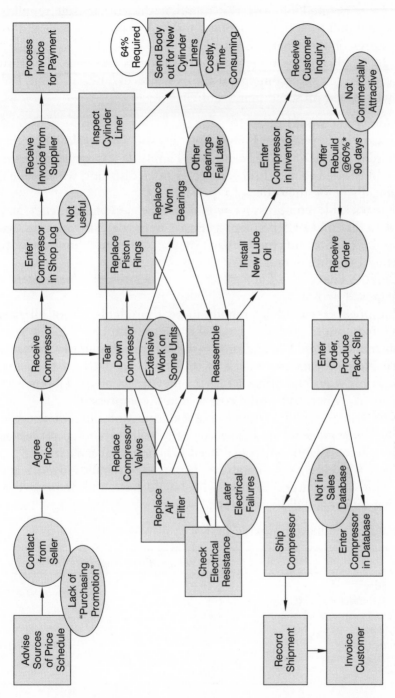

Figure 2.2 Rebuild compressor – 'as is'

* 60% of new compressor price, 90 day warranty

John pointed out that he found it difficult to sell rebuilds, because he didn't trust their reliability, and he had no data (as he did for new compressors) of what was in stock.

In looking at the objectives of the process and what they now understood of the shortcomings of the as-is process, Karen, John, Bob and David agreed on some significant changes:

- Wainwright would offer 20 per cent of the price of a new compressor for serviceable bodies only against a new sale. For other sources a price of 15 per cent would apply. It was agreed that this could be used to avoid pressure for a price discount, which would typically be on the order of 5 per cent.
- Unserviceable compressors would not be accepted, except at a token discount of 5 per cent against a new sale. Any of these that would require any more than 30 per cent price equivalent to rebuild would be scrapped.
- Cylinder liners would be replaced in house, using the new method proposed by Bob.
- Compressors would be rebuilt more thoroughly, using all new bearings, and a wash and bake of the motor stator.
- All rebuilds would be run on a test stand for 30 minutes to assure reliable performance.
- Rebuilds would be offered with a one-year parts and labour warranty at 70 per cent of the cost of a new compressor.
- Wainwright would promote the exchange of old compressors when new units are sold. The sale of rebuilds would be promoted to customers with a marginal need for additional capacity.
- There would be a sales database of completed rebuilds in stock and rebuilds in progress, so that John would have a clear picture of what units are/will be available.

The financial summary prepared by Karen now looked as follows:

Item	Percentage of new compressor price
Cost of body	20.0
Less sales promotion effect	(5.0)
Wainwright's parts and labour	18.0
Warranty costs	2.2
New cylinder liners	5.1
Unserviceable rebuilds	Nil
Total	50.3

Against a selling price of 70 per cent, this yielded a gross margin of 42 per cent.

The 'To-be Map' of the compressor rebuild process is shown in Figure 2.3.

While the process maps say nothing about sales volume, John Wainwright felt sure that with better quality rebuilds he could grow the business rapidly, with monthly promotional mailings to selected customers. One year after the changes were implemented, rebuild volume was up to nine per month, and two years later it was up to 14 per month. Margins have stayed at about 40 per cent.

Karen Wainwright has since used BPA to evaluate Wainwright's human resources and finance systems. While in those two cases the results were less dramatic than for compressor rebuilds, she feels that she was able to reduce employee turnover via a better recruitment and induction process. She also avoided an additional hire in accounting.

DIAGNOSTIC QUESTIONS

In this chapter we have considered how to assess the health of your business. Here are some diagnostic questions that will help in the macro diagnosis mentioned above.

- What is the definition of my business? (What customers do we serve, how and why?)
- What makes my company different?
- How do we sustain the difference?
- How do we stay ahead of competitors?
- How well do I make my business known to customers?
- How well do I convince them to buy at the right price and the right terms?
- What services do I provide to customers after I have sold to them?
- Are my costs competitive?
- What actions could I take to increase margins/reduce overheads?
- Is my quality at least very good or excellent?
- Is my product/service easily available to customers?
- Can I really see what's happening in the business, day to day?
- Am I using up-to-date technology?
- Are my information systems effective and efficient?
- Relative to competitors, is debt a large portion of my capitalization?
- Do I have enough cash to grow the business profitably?
- Does the management team respond smoothly to change?
- Are employee (and management) behaviours consistent with the needs of the business?

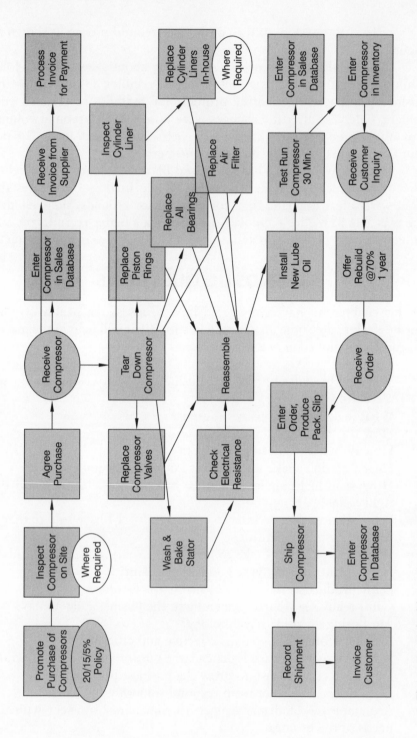

Figure 2.3 Rebuild compressor – 'to be'

BUSINESS DEVELOPMENT AND PERFORMANCE IMPROVEMENT

CHAPTER THREE

MARKETING

Steve Kennett and Peter Tomkins

The reality for most businesses today is anchored in the marketplace. If no one wants your product or service, then your business will fail. So we start this consideration of performance with the marketplace – the environment in which the organization trades.

Two questions that a consultant needs to ask on behalf of the client organization are: 1) How do we understand the marketplace? and 2) How should we best engage with it?

These questions apply to the internal consultant, the not-for-profit sector and public service organizations as much as they do to commerce at large. Every group of stakeholders can be thought of as constituting a market, and the principles of marketing can be applied to each of them.

WHY MARKETING?

Marketing started in the 19th century with the development of advertising posters and hoardings, yet it is less than 50 years old in the form we have it today. Marketing has developed as a consequence of the convergence of time and space in which improvements in transport and technology have the effect of figuratively moving places towards one another over time as the travel-time required between places decreases and distance declines in significance. Less than 50 years ago, possibly less than 20 even, who would have thought it possible to surf the net or to have perishable goods such as snap peas available at supermarkets all year round as though there were no season? Who would have thought it possible that even the smaller business would operate powerful computers, or that mail order would be used to sell business products in addition to consumer items? And what for tomorrow?

Markets are becoming more complex

There is no doubt that markets are becoming more complex. The futures market is just one example. It developed through the need of manufacturers to establish the future cost of raw materials such as cocoa, wheat, tin and copper. Now this activity includes money, where companies with long-term contracts seek to reduce the risk that their income will change in value over time or between currencies.

But complexity is evident around us. The effect of time–space convergence means that geographical boundaries are less important today than they used to be. Events take less time to happen than before. In the computer industry competitive advantage gained through introducing new products is measured in days rather than weeks or years.

Nowadays companies seek sources of low-cost labour wherever it can be found around the world. This action has undermined labour stability in those developed countries that have lost whole industries, such as shoes, clothing and shipbuilding, to the Third World. Even so, the majority of those products made in Third World countries continue to be consumed in their traditional geographical markets.

Competition is becoming increasingly more aggressive as suppliers seek to win a greater share of their market for the products or services they offer. In a free market economy, so the theory goes, the price of a commodity would move in inverse proportion to its availability. Thus, the more available a commodity, the lower its price, and vice versa. But such views, often espoused by economists, externalize non-cost items such as service, credit and reliability, which can dominate purchasing decisions, changing the relationship between supply and demand.

In past years, management called for generalists, not specialists; and marketing was the province of large companies with considerable resources. But nowadays large companies can be as nimble as small ones, so marketing is one of a number of specialisms needed to run businesses of all sizes. It is an increasingly important and critical component of business activity.

Marketing attempts to understand the forces that drive market behaviour. It is a way of thinking that puts market focus at the forefront of business activity.

Given all this, there are still only three main strategies an enterprise can follow. These are to:

- win new customers;
- sell more to existing customers in a given time;
- keep customers for longer.

Most organizations will plan to use a mix of these according to their circumstances. For example, a newly formed company will seek to win new customers (after all, every customer will be a new customer). Others, who are successful in gaining customers yet have difficulty in keeping them, will seek a combination of the first and third strategies, while those who are in a static market may expect to follow a combination of the second and third. The way you choose your strategy is fundamental to the future success of your business. Many of these aspects are dealt with in other chapters; here we deal with marketing as a subject.

UNDERSTANDING MARKETING – OR MORE IMPORTANTLY, WHAT DOES IT MEAN FOR YOUR BUSINESS?

Marketing is the process by which you identify and then engage with the market for your products. Most successful companies now seek to maximize the lifetime value of their customers – that is, how much a customer, or a group of similar customers, contributes to your profits during the time they do business with you.

There is nothing new in this. In the same way a company will expect its production people to know its manufacturing activities in detail (such as output, productivity, scrap rate, cost, and so on), so it should expect its marketing team to produce equivalent information about its customers and the markets in which it operates. There are differences, of course, and you wouldn't be surprised to hear that marketing has more unknowns and greater uncertainties than other management specialisms.

Even so, successful marketing has a number of key ingredients. Success is more likely if the five points listed below are present and maximized in an enterprise:

- the **right product(s)**;
- the **right target audience(s)** (ie marketplace);
- the **right promotional channel(s)**;

- the **right price(s) and proposition(s),** which you will be able to get only through appropriate research;
- the **right timing(s).**

Success is highly likely if these five 'Rights' are maximized within a dynamic and sustainable balance. There is a need constantly to refocus and re-assess your company's products or services and the market segments into which they are sold. In the past this has not always been the case and this perhaps is one of the major causes for failure. So let us take a closer look at each of these points.

Products and brands

It is almost impossible to discuss products without mentioning brands. They are so tied up with one another that sometimes it can be difficult to tell them apart. Yet the difference is important. Many of the successful brands are what we know as 'house brands' or 'major brands'. Examples include well-known names such as McDonald's, Heinz, Ford, Tesco, Nike and Kellogg. All sell a range of products associated with their name, which may be brands in their own right (for example, The Big Mac, Heinz Baked Beans or Kellogg's Cornflakes). House brands tell us about the overall values attached to the range such as value for money, quality and exclusivity. Brands that are one of a range associated with a major brand have to support the overall concept of the range as well as the 'house' image. Not easy!

It takes many years to develop a brand that has meaning for customers. Possibly it is the biggest investment a company will ever make. And as a result it is the constant preoccupation of marketing managers and of the company.

In some cases a company will be too successful and lose control over its brand identity. In such cases their brand becomes a general name for a commodity. Examples of this include Hoover, Biro, Formica and Cheddar cheese. Champagne houses are fighting a huge battle to prevent the word 'Champagne' from being used by makers of sparkling wine in other areas. Yet to the consumers any sparkling wine is loosely called champagne, even though they know it is not 'real champagne'. So while Champagne houses may have won the legal battle, they may be losing it with the public.

For smaller enterprises, it is as well not to proliferate brand names. It is far more manageable and effective to use one name, possibly that of the company, and to make sure it is used in a way that enhances the value of the company and its range of products to its customers.

The more unique and exclusive your products are, the more likely you are to achieve sustainable commercial advantages for your business. Typically beneficial USPs (unique selling points) include:

- branding, ie widely recognizable within your marketplace;
- quality/integrity/excellence;
- customer satisfaction;
- distinctive image/packaging;
- perceived value for money (VFM);
- niche exclusivity;
- innovation, 'leading edge'.

Products with these features can typically extract a premium price within their marketplace. If your products are less so, or essentially undifferentiated within your sector, it is most likely that you will be competing within your chosen marketplace as a commodity and vulnerable to larger competitors' discount pricing practices. A way to combat this weakness is to consider redesigning/repositioning your product(s), creating additional features/benefits that could provide an added-value edge.

Here is an example to illustrate what we mean. Twist drills, the things one puts into an electric drill to fix things about the house, are a commodity item. High proportions are imported from abroad; industry uses them by the score. Some while ago a British manufacturer of such drills realized that their locally made products were unable to compete with imports, and gradually their share of the market ebbed away. It got to the stage that they sold more from abroad than they made in their factory. The consultants who were called in soon realized that this company's problem stemmed from what Theodore Levitt called 'marketing myopia' – short-sightedness. Their perspective was based on the view of 'this is what we've always made'. When the problem was looked at from the customer's point of view it became evident that twist drills are only bought for what they will do for the customer, rather than for what they are. In reality drills are bought because customers want holes. By redefining the business as 'hole provision', numerous avenues of opportunity were opened up, many of which were in growing markets and using technology not readily available elsewhere. People will always need holes; they may not always need drills to make them.

Know your marketplace – or, who are your existing and potential customers and those of your competitors?

Any established business should have a list (whether on paper, or more often nowadays on computer) containing a variety of information, on its current and recent customers, their purchases of existing and past products and so on. The characteristics of these customers, be it by size, geography, SIC codes, uses, sector(s), order patterns and volumes etc will provide vital information key to identifying prospective customers with similar characteristics. What is not easily predictable (without specific market research or test campaigning – see later sections) is the ability to convert these prospects into buyers of your products – the more benefits/features, commensurate with VFM pricing, the more likely your business is to succeed!

For example, take a small restaurant chain selling vegetarian foods that was founded in the 1960s. It has had a chequered history, going into receivership in 1992, and changing hands several times. The new owner has refocused on what customers want, and now it is a rapidly growing and profitable business. The results of the research that underpinned the change showed that only 20 per cent of customers are vegetarian and most were women. By refurbishing its outlets, and changing the emphasis from vegetarian foods to providing menus that are 95 per cent fat free, nutritionally balanced, and with a strong emphasis on flavourings, demand has grown significantly and the company is considering opening further branches in the UK and abroad. All this stems from establishing what their customers want.

While the cost of formal market research studies may well be beyond the means of small and medium-sized enterprises, a low-cost pragmatic approach may suffice to start with. Let's say, for example, that your company sells stationery to other businesses and that you have decided to increase your sales volume without reducing your margins. What should you do? Well, let's first examine the records to find out what type of customer produces the most business for your company, those who produce the highest margins (taking into account the cost of making deliveries), and the mix and proportion of products each takes, on average. As it is people and the machines they use that consume stationery, comparisons of existing customers' purchases against the number of office staff they employ will enable you to gain more useful data.

By now you may well be asking questions about the emerging picture. Why is it, for example, that some customers seem to buy more per employee than others do? Is it reasonable to assume that those with the highest consumption are the most loyal to your company? If so, then we have a fair idea of how much our other customers are giving to our competitors. So what can be done about this? It is from such information that the need for marketing plans emerges. (This sort of exercise makes an ideal vacation job for a university student, especially one studying marketing or business studies.)

A critical unknown is the 'locked-in' competitor with long-term contracts (often across a range of products) providing significant discount, and sometimes service benefits, for volume purchases. But even companies with long-term contracts to supply often keep a second supplier in the background, as insurance. Indeed the converse of this is well worth considering, by becoming a preferred supplier ('partner') for your own existing valued customers, to reduce desertion by future 'promiscuity' to your competitors. The better the relationship that you establish, in a genuine meaningful way, with your customers, through understanding their needs (carefully through tracking on databases), the more likely you are to succeed. The marketplace is now much more of a 'global pond' and every customer is a fair target, often from the most unexpected supplier sources.

As competitiveness increases, even for your most successful products, are your pricing and the way you provide attractive offers sufficient to entice new customers and retain your longer-term loyalists? Large branded goods companies rarely discount. They sustain consistent pricing through creating high perceived brand-values consistent with prevailing sound quality and service. Whilst smaller businesses may not achieve such a high level of perceived brand-value, it must be a key aspiration within its proposition and pricing platform.

Understand your competitors

How well do you know, and importantly understand, those who are competing against you? What is your share of the potentially available 'pot(s)' by volume or sterling penetration within your chosen territory(ies)? By this we mean the proportion of your sales as a percentage of the volume sold into your geographical market (by weight or units) and a similar calculation of the percentage by value. The output of this analysis will give you a good indication of the strength of your presence with customers, and may point to some weaknesses, too. For example, a company with 10 per cent volume and 20 per cent sterling penetration is likely to be selling at the high end of the price range of your market segment. Conversely 30 per cent volume and 10 per cent sterling penetration may indicate that you are selling on price alone, and possibly missing profitable sales gained through upgrading your product range.

It is always a good idea to get the annual reports of your major competitors. Trade press and newspapers are a good source, too. Industrial sector statistics (government, trade bodies etc) exist and without commissioning expensive market research it is possible to assess your position in the marketplace and your potential to gain a share for your products. To establish a view on what the marketplace thinks about your competitors (and indeed your business!) a variety of sources are available. For a start you may talk to current, past and prospective customers. Also, you may commission specific market research (telephone research or mailed questionnaires) and indeed listen to your sales team for feedback.

As most businesses sell to other businesses, it is possible to talk to end users to get a better picture of the market. For example, some time ago a company that makes crucibles (for use by foundries to melt metal) tried without success to forecast demand. This company had contacted their crucible users to ask their view of the future demand but the answer they got was so confused that it was not possible to form a credible forecast. The marketing person who later became involved, asked the crucible customers the proportion of various metals they used in the crucibles and the markets each served. From this it was possible to construct reasonable estimates of the industries the foundries were dependent upon, ie the end users. As a next stage, each of the industries was assessed for the prospects of their future growth or decline. When this was correlated with the data provided by the foundries, it became possible not only to forecast the likely demand for crucibles, but to take a reasonable view of which foundries were vulnerable to the changes that were to take place as well as those that were more likely to grow. Not only did the forecasts prove to be reliable, but also the additional information enabled the company's sales force to focus on those foundries that were most likely to grow. This enabled them to steal a march on their competitors.

Timing

Timing is another key variable worthy of greater attention by management. Most marketplaces have key time-scales; these include seasonality, budgetary controls (such as year-end), financial year-end, end-user demand (ie your customers' customers), education new year, car registration date, tender dates and contract-end dates. These are very different across the differing sectors, yet they need to be recognized and inter-preted carefully to ensure optimized handling within your market plan-ning initiatives. By making your sales and marketing efforts coincide with the time your customers make their purchasing decision, there is a greater likelihood of your getting the best value for your marketing investment.

As examples, we have found that by writing to managing direc-tors on a Thursday or Friday, the response is double that gained from letters posted at the beginning of the week. Also, we have found that managers of local firms are more likely to attend a free breakfast meeting (so that it doesn't interfere with their normal day), than attend meetings at other times of the day, including late afternoon and early evening. The greetings card business is possibly the most seasonal busi-ness; at one time most of such firms' turnover was concentrated into a few hectic weeks. No wonder, therefore, that they have tried to spread the buying season by promoting new events for cards (Easter, Father's Day and Mother's Day, for example).

Methods and channels of sale

It is important to understand how you and your competitors access the potential marketplace(s). Whilst you may currently be using only one channel such as direct mail; there may be others equally viable for your products. Typical routings include:

- wholesaler/intermediary/agent/franchisee;
- sales force (regional, national, etc);
- direct sales person/key account management;
- direct marketing;
- direct mail (including direct catalogues);
- telephone marketing (inbound, outbound);
- direct response advertising (trade press/radio/TV);
- inserts (trade/business journals);
- e-mail/Internet/Web site.

Different segments of your potential market need to be accessed via dif-ferent channels; for example, a detergent manufacturer may divide the market into trade customers for industrial-scale detergents (sales force/key account) and consumer customers for home-use detergents (via wholesalers, to retailers). Also, it is necessary to avoid pricing and branding conflicts. You may need to adopt different branding for each distinct segment.

Know your environment

The environment within which businesses now operate is increasingly controlled by legislation from Europe. Relevant laws and regulations proliferate and management needs to be aware of, and assess, their impact on their products, channels and customers. A list of these is given in References and Bibliography.

There are a number of industry bodies that businesses can turn to for advice in these areas, plus knowledge of prevailing self-regulatory codes of practice, which are also listed in References and Bibliography.

GETTING THE FACTS FOR YOUR BUSINESS

Before you can initiate and build a marketing plan there is a key need to gather information pertinent to your business and the marketplace within which it operates. The following are sources and ways to developing such information.

SWOT Analysis

This technique is described in Appendix 1.

A well-executed SWOT critique with a marketing focus undertaken by management, or by independent consultants on its behalf, will provide an invaluable understanding of likely forward needs.

A basic SWOT analysis need not be lengthy or too detailed, provided the information is correct. It may contain statements such as:

Strengths	We have been in this business for 50+ years and know the main customers well. Our design competence is far in advance of our competitors. We have a superb reputation for responding to enquiries quickly and of providing a design and build service.
Weaknesses	The market for our traditional business is declining. Our production is inefficient; it has high costs, high scrap, with long and unreliable lead times. We are not well known outside our traditional business.
Opportunities	We could become a design consultancy. We could subcontract our manufacturing requirements. New (identified) markets for our design and manufacturing technology are emerging.
Threats	Our main competitor is gaining competitive advantage and market share through buying up smaller companies and concentrating manufacture on fewer sites. We will be bought out, or close, if we do not get on top of our production problems.

There is enough in this example, which was taken from a real-life situation, for most managers to make up their mind as to what actions they would take to improve matters. The debate for the board is what priorities and time-scales to set.

Market research

External independent market research studies covering your sector or marketplace can provide invaluable insight into what potential customers say they like or will do, in relation to your products or the marketing of them. The nature of these studies can be either qualitative (focus groups, feature questionnaires) or quantitative (volume telephone research, direct mail questionnaires, representative large panels etc). Focus groups provide attitudes or views held by individuals in that group about the product, service or activity under review. Quantitative research will determine the extent to which the population in question holds these views.

It follows then that for major studies it may well be necessary to commission both types of research if an overall picture is to be gained.

Such research – if carefully constructed – can provide vital 'expectation' information on your product(s) and their features, as well as volume information as to market size, price elasticity, etc. Such commissioned studies can be quite expensive, usually from £10,000 to £50,000 upwards, and require careful briefing in line with your business aspirations. The Market Research Society (see References and bibliography) is a useful source of reliable qualified practitioners; always obtain two or three quotations.

A related area is for a business to carry out its own customer survey(s). This may be undertaken in conjunction with externally commissioned research or alone. Some external help may be needed to format the questionnaires (for telephone or mailing completion) to ensure maximum uptake and valid outputs. Do remember that these findings will be purely based on existing (or recent) customers rather than the wider prospect universe.

However, even the best market research may not give you reliable information. Ford's Edsel model of the 1950s was designed on concepts fully tested by market research, yet sales of the car flopped – it was Ford's largest failure at that time. The only true test is to sell your product. You should also know that the majority of new product launches, even those that have been extensively researched, fail in the marketplace.

CREATING YOUR MARKETING PLAN

So now, with an understanding of the key components required for effective marketing together with a deepened knowledge of your product(s) and the prevailing marketplace, you are able to pull these elements together within a marketing action plan.

Firstly, most people would agree that the experience of military strategists that 'no plan survives contact with the enemy' applies equally to marketing as well as to business planning. The planning process has so many uncertainties that detailed long-term planning is for most organizations a waste of time. What one needs to be able to achieve is a credible plan in outline that will last for the length of the capital investment involved, and in detail for the ensuing 12 to 18 months.

The time horizon of the capital investment makes good sense. A nuclear reactor for electricity generation may take up to 30 years to plan and build and have a life of, say, 50 years beyond this. For such a plant, any plan will have to be certain of its understanding of the long-term growth in demand for electricity. Contrast this with that of a market stallholder. Such a person has little money tied up for the long term; in fact he or she may turn their capital over each week. Their detailed plan (if it can be called that) will be to make the best purchasing and selling decisions each day. A longer-term plan could be to put some money aside for retirement or a rainy day. Most of us, however, have to consider a time-scale somewhere between these two extremes, such as the economic life of plant and equipment. In either case no realistic marketing plan can be made unless it is in support of clear corporate objectives.

As we have said earlier, all plans have an element of uncertainty, which implies risk. Not all companies have the same view of risk and this must temper your marketing plan. The art is to create a balance between opportunity and risk within the constraints of the business. It follows therefore that competing companies can adopt quite different marketing plans. Copying one's competitor's actions is not to be commended!

No two marketing plans will be identical in structure, form or content. You should build on your strengths (known or perceived) and recognize wider opportunities and competitor vulnerability within your intended marketplace. In addition you should aim to minimize your weaknesses. Your plan will have marketing objectives and delivery targets set within the context of your overall business plan. It is likely that it will be looking forward, in at least overview, some 2–4 years. The initial year's intended marketing initiatives will be provided in depth usually within or alongside your business's annual budget or planning package. This will need to spread the key intentions and tasks by campaign, project entity, and people over the 12 monthly operating cycles.

Within the framework of your marketing plan, as well as the existing ongoing marketing elements, there are likely to be experimental areas, such as product trials, market and campaign testing etc. We will explore these in more depth shortly. It must always be remembered that market research can only indicate what people *say* they will do or like, whereas the acid test must always be actual purchase behaviour (ie doing) and only testing can ascertain reality.

Product testing

From the fact-finding work it may well have become clear that there is a need for new products, modification or range extensions. Dependent upon the product areas your business is in, this could be an expensive commitment. Hence such testing requires separate budgets to isolate the costs associated with such diversification – this allows either 'wet' (prototype product available) or 'dry' (product not available, only campaign response measurable) testing with 'roll-out' (ie scaled up) promotional/development cost extrapolations undertaken. Payback, ie return on investment, ratios need to be agreed with financial management as to long-term viability.

Campaign testing

Traditionally a business may have relied upon a particular marketing channel such as a sales force, but now may have found other potentially profitable ways of selling. These may need testing to find out whether they live up to expectation. It is important to isolate the associated costs and revenues so that their relative effectiveness can be measured, as the following example shows.

A few years ago, a small seller of specialist software used by human resources (HR) departments sought to find ways of reducing its sales costs. Up to that time the software had been sold by advertising in trade magazines and this was expensive. Discussions with a few key customers showed that while the software is used by HR people, they were comparatively unfamiliar with using computers and relied on advice from their IT department. So the questions arose of whether it was better to sell to IT or to HR departments, and would they respond better to direct mail. This was tested by switching advertising to IT journals, and by writing directly to a sample each of IT and HR managers. Mailing just paid off. But the real benefit came through getting the letter right. Trials showed that sales took off by writing to the HR Director and referring him or her to the IT department for approval, and in other cases to the IT manager and mentioning how the HR department would appreciate their recommendation.

As well as alternative channels, other key elements are often test marketed, eg the promotional offer(s), the creative/copy approaches, etc. Major changes need to be isolated from the main campaign approach, so that the impact can be assessed once results are available; always measure change against existing controls.

Marketing resources

Clearly resources must be allocated towards the marketing tasks set out in the marketing plan.

For most small businesses a key issue is how far to have marketing resources in house or to buy them in – ie contract. There is no magic solution to this. It is primarily a factor of scale commensurate with the degree of 'hands-on' control needed. In most smaller businesses the senior manager responsible for marketing is also likely to have other responsibilities, eg sales, commercial, purchasing, and may have only one executive responsible for this function. In some circumstances careful selection and contracting of external suppliers is crucial. This would usefully include advertising, media selection, creative work and copywriting, specialist printers, telemarketing shops, database handling bureaux, list managers, brokers, mailing and fulfilment houses etc. And should you put work out (as you invariably will to a greater or lesser extent), then ensure you meet the key personnel who will handle your work. Often it is a good idea to point to the possibility of making a longer-term commitment, but do not do so until viable working relationships have developed.

Performance measurements etc

By now you may feel that all the detail required necessitates a huge document. Detail does lead to volume, but this need not be so in every case. In those assignments where we have been asked to help turn a company round, the plans were done figuratively on the back of an envelope – at least to start with. The detail came later. The most important part is to be able to measure progress. Many businesses fail to know, on a timely basis, what is happening (or often not happening!) until significant problems or shortfalls occur.

For many businesses the pressure of time on business managers can mean that activities to measure progress get put on the back burner. It is always possible to find more important and urgent things to do. Besides, it can be boring. For smaller companies the three-monthly VAT reporting periods are ideal opportunities to check progress. Don't just leave this to a bookkeeper; make use of the valuable information that is generated.

For larger companies we strongly recommend establishing appropriate performance measures on a monthly (or more frequent) basis within key variables clearly measured against plan and budget. In particular, you should identify variance from plan by line, channel of sale, campaign and so on, of volume, costs (of all types), margins produced, discount levels, and competitor activity. In direct marketing campaigns key control criteria include response percentage, average order value, cost/response and cost per sale – by each type of media/campaign codes. Some businesses use ROS (return on sales – the net profit before tax as a percentage of sales) and SOCE (sales on capital employed – net sales divided by total assets minus current liabilities).

Not only should these key ratios, trends and statistics – relevant to your business – feature in your marketing plan; they need to be incorporated within the overall business or financial plans of the operation and its reporting packages (with clear identification of key variances), so that performance achievements against key targeted intentions are readily identified, allowing timely corrective actions to be initiated.

SUMMARY AND KEY ACTION POINTS

In this chapter we have tried to give you a brief overview of the marketing function and of marketing planning. Marketing is an activity that attempts to understand the forces that drive market behaviour. It is a way of thinking that puts customer focus at the forefront of business activity. Over the past 50 years marketing has grown from being the province of large companies to one of a number of specialisms needed to run all businesses.

As a consequence of time–space convergence, markets and marketing are becoming more complex. Thanks to developments in other fields such as transport and communications, companies can source goods and services wherever a good deal can be made. This has led to manufacturers outsourcing to low-cost areas in the Third World, and to the loss of whole industries in developed countries. Even so, consumption of these goods remains in the West.

Brands are an integral part of marketing. They convey the overall values attached to a range of products that have meaning to customers. While larger companies may use a range of brands, we think that smaller companies will benefit more through keeping to one brand and using it in a way that enhances the value of the company to its customers.

A thorough knowledge of one's customers, potential customers and competitors is fundamental to success in marketing. Research to gain information can be conducted at different levels. Starting with internal data on who orders what and when, and the use of published statistics, research by major brand holders will include projects to establish customers' attitudes, market testing and advertising awareness.

A SWOT analysis provides a focus for market planning. It allows you to identify the strengths and weaknesses, opportunities and threats to a company and/or its brands. Marketing plans must support the objectives of the business and work within the constraints of the business and of the marketplace.

There is no best way of planning. All plans carry an element of uncertainty, which implies risk; therefore it is important to ensure that progress towards the achievement of objectives and targets is measurable and that the results are fed back into the business as a part of the management process.

CHAPTER FOUR

WINNING AND MANAGING SALES

Clive Bonny

Marketing metaphorically sets out your stall; sales are about specific transactions. Selling is the lifeblood of any business. It is also a high-cost and high-risk activity. This chapter will help you to improve the planning and management of sales, both direct business to business, and through distributors.

It examines key processes, from identifying an appropriate channel or buyer through to the point of contracting, for sales of low and high value products and services in a wide range of markets.

DIFFERENCES BETWEEN SALES AND MARKETING

There is an acronym beloved of salesmen: AIDA. It suggests that there are four steps involved in decision making: Attention; Interest; Desire; Action.

The activities of both marketing and selling guide the prospect through a similar decision-making route. However, whilst marketing helps develop and match the product or service to the broad audience, the sales process is more focused on showing exactly how the offering will satisfy the need of a particular customer.

There are three fundamental differences between selling and marketing: in time-scales (marketing tends to be longer term); in measures (market share versus sales volume); and in management (market brands rather than sales relationships). Selling therefore tends to be focused more on people than process, but both activities must complement each other. Imbalance towards marketing creates high awareness but few decisions, and imbalance towards selling creates low awareness and consequently fewer decisions again. Selling will play a more important role when the buyer's decision-making process is more complex, and requires person-to-person advice or support, whereas marketing becomes prominent when coverage is key.

The starting point in sales is to look at ourselves from the perspective of our potential customer. Their view of suppliers who canvass them is often significantly different to the suppliers' perspective. They may be suspicious as previous victims of sharp practice or, more commonly, exaggerated claims. They are likely to have been canvassed many times by suppliers who have not researched possible needs before making contact and subsequently waste the prospect's time. They could be busy people who are reluctant to change. These factors demand an approach that is carefully researched and sensitively implemented. Sales strategy should therefore be driven by customer needs and executed in a way that demonstrates an explicit understanding of those needs.

WHY PEOPLE BUY

Customer expectations focus on a few supplier qualities that tend to remain unchanged. These are:

- perceived value (ie costs balanced by benefits);
- the supplier's ability to deliver what is offered;
- the supplier's willingness to extend themselves to meet special needs;
- a relationship of trust.

People like to buy, and not be sold to, and they will buy for different reasons. Some are goal-oriented, some wish to fulfil dreams, others want to minimize fears. Observing how people buy will help us identify their motivations, and this in turn can help us choose the most appropriate way of selling to them. The process of buying usually involves three steps:

1. Why do I need this?
2. How will I decide?
3. Where and when shall I buy?

The process of selling should therefore help answer these questions, and

in doing so build trust, show competence and make it a positive purchasing experience. The sales process at its simplest level is:

1. Understand needs and wants.
2. Present options and a solution.
3. Identify concerns and ask for a decision.

Sales planning and control

A strategy of customer orientation requires skills in planning, probing,
listening, empathizing and persuading. It requires detailed knowledge
of business aims and resources, offerings and marketplace. Above all it
demands an attitude reflecting honesty, hard work, enthusiasm and
resilience. Anyone involved in managing salespersons must ensure that
these competencies are developed, maintained and regularly checked.
The fast pace of product development results in an increasing perception of sameness between competitors. A key differentiator is the
quality of the salesperson's skills and, where offerings are similar, the
buyer invariably chooses the salesperson who is the most skilled.

It is often said that 'To fail to plan is to plan to fail'. There
should be a written sales plan focusing on business goals. Constituent
parts can include:

1. background profiles on customers, prospects and competitors;
2. contact schedules of who will be contacted, how and when; these
   should be prioritized to address the highest value opportunities;
3. forecasts of monthly results and key activities;
4. reporting processes to keep management informed of activities,
   results and resource needs;
5. contingencies to overcome possible obstacles.

The plan should be drafted by whoever is responsible for its implementation, and submitted to management for approval. This will ensure
ownership and agreement by relevant stakeholders, and facilitate a clear
link to the supplier's overall business plan. Objectives described in the
sales plan should include not only financial targets but also activity-
related goals as illustrated in Figure 4.1.

The monitoring of activity ratios can provide an effective
diagnosis of potential problems long before a shortfall in results
becomes visible. Activity-based performance standards can highlight
skills deficiencies in specific areas such as letter writing, appointment

- Achieve quarterly forecast accuracy of at least 75 per cent
- Respond to all written sales enquiries within two days
- Average X miles per visit
- Report on unsuccessful tenders within one week
- Achieve a ratio of one in five appointments from cold calls
- Obtain Y orders per 100 quotations
- Maximum Z percentage discount per order

Figure 4.1 Activity-related goals

making by telephone, qualifying client needs, face-to-face presenting, and proposal-writing. Such standards can help salespersons manage themselves to make the best use of their time and direct training given into the area most needed. If there is a sales team, it also provides the opportunity for team members to compare activity ratios with one another and identify best practice from those with the best performance ratios. These measures can be charted graphically on a weekly or monthly basis so that the under-performance can be quickly addressed. For long sales cycle times (three months or more from initial contact to final contract) activity ratios are an essential management tool.

A sales strategy based on identifying and matching customer needs requires time to be invested in fully researching those needs. Whilst the marketing function can analyse the broad needs of a targeted industry or group of prospects, there is no substitute for direct contact by salespersons to identify specific needs of individual prospects. This is particularly important in higher value product sales and in selling less tangible services.

Qualifying needs

Common sources of information to help identify the prospect's need will fall into two categories – those outside the prospect's organization and those inside it. Outsiders who can be approached include trade associations, customers, suppliers, and anyone who has knowledge of the prospect's business. Inside the prospect we can elicit the support of a number of people who can help us qualify if an approach is worth making, and to whom. Such requests for help and information should always be accompanied by an open statement of purpose, explaining the desire to find out if the prospect could benefit from our offering. People will react positively to candour and object strongly to subterfuge.

Direct approaches to the prospect can often be made to their marketing department who can mail back product literature, newsletters, press packs and annual reports. The latter can highlight company challenges, policy makers and future aims.

Telephoning the personal assistants of executives can also identify the decision-making chain for your offer, and sometimes identify competitor activity.

Different approaches

Research will enable the qualifying and prioritizing of 'suspects' into 'prospects' who are potential buyers; the next step is to plan the initial approach. This will be largely determined by the type and size of unit sale. High quantity and low cost products may demand direct mail and telephone selling. Low quantity, high cost products will usually involve a longer cycle of personal meetings to educate, inform and persuade. The most complex sales usually involve high value intangible services such as technical consultancy advice. Consulting services introduce many more variables than tangible products, and can carry high perceived risk for the buyer. Consultancy advice is less easy to specify, cannot be readily returned if faulty, and is less easily costed and evaluated. Such differences magnify risk and uncertainty to buyers whose decision criteria will then become weighted towards personal relations rather than product specification. The greater the perception of risk to the buyer, the greater the need for direct contact, longer decision-making time and increased skills in relationship building. At this end of the spectrum the main differentiator is the person and not the product, and consequently a key focus for a services supplier will be generating quality face-to-face time to build trust and overcome the 'FUD factor: Fear, Uncertainty and Doubt' in the mind of the buyer.

The challenge for a lower cost product provider is still significant, in so far as the buying activity involves the same processes but the journey must be navigated in a fraction of the time. A telesales process must therefore generate attention, interest, desire and action within only five minutes, including an analysis of client needs and decision processes.

Both fast and slow sales cycles usually require analysis of decision-maker types. These range from purchasing agent and budget-holder to influencer and end-user, and doing this early is critical to next steps. Buyer types can also be stereotyped, which is particularly useful when selling time is short and we have to move quickly onto their wavelength. The *systematic* buyer will want product details whereas the *decisive* buyer prefers bullet points. The *amiable* buyer will enjoy sharing personal pleasantries, whereas the *impulse* buyer prefers information on applications.

The ability of the salesperson to identify the buyer's personal style, and adapt his or her approach accordingly, will result in the buyer absorbing the messages effectively and being more inclined to accept the proposition.

The same principles can be applied to planning sales entry into a new organization. If the client culture is *systematic*, ie belt and braces, then we can anticipate protracted hierarchical decision making. If *decisive*, then we should be brief and fast moving. If *impulsive* we should be wary of changes of mind; if *amiable* we should emphasize a consultative approach. Understanding buyer chemistry is critical and our sales process must be significantly adapted between those who want a commodity and those who look for an experience.

MANAGING THE SALES TEAM

Communications

An effective sales manager will be close enough to the salesperson's prospects to ensure that the right mix of personal chemistry is occurring. The role of a sales manager is to create results through others, and an effective manager can only do this by being close enough to observe not only what is being done but also *how*. The manager must balance time between the office and the field and balance time analysing past events and planning the future.

Communications should create focus within the sales team and a key task of the sales manager is to facilitate them. There should be clear objectives so people know what success looks like, and how it contributes to the organization. Standards and values should reflect how the team is expected to work (ie reporting procedures or demonstrating sensitivity to client concerns). Paperwork should be minimized with the application of technology, and reports should focus on usable qualitative information such as call plan, activity summary, market intelligence, business forecasts. Above all, there should be regular news going to the team regarding company updates, sales successes, competitors and team results. Salespeople often feel isolated in the field and need a two-way flow of information to keep them in touch with colleagues and the company.

Recruitment

The sales manager should be able to recruit, develop and appraise salespersons. The starting points for this are the job description and person specification. Job descriptions can specify what outputs are required and person specifications describe the attributes of the ideal jobholder, ie inputs. It is vital to specify these accurately. If the person specification is too vague, then you could recruit a low calibre salesperson; if it is too demanding, the role may not be filled. The manager should encourage existing staff to recommend candidates with a finder's fee from contacts with friends and associates, and make the vacancy known through the local Business Link and colleges. Although these may not supply ready-trained salespersons, they can provide people suitable for sales support roles who can eventually be promoted. Without succession planning of this kind, a sudden loss of a salesperson can result in a gap of several months before a replacement is found and trained to the same standard.

When recruiting salespersons it is vital to process applications quickly as good candidates are rarely available for more than a few weeks. Advertisements should always include a telephone number. If the job requires telephone skills, the quality of initial telephoned responses can be appraised as part of the sifting process. A particular difficulty in recruiting salespersons is their ability to mask their own potential weaknesses. It is therefore vital to check claims regarding core competences. This can be done by creating short simulations of activities, eg a role-play to make an appointment by phone or a presentation of a sales plan for the territory. Candidates should be asked to bring evidence of claimed successes (eg copy of a sales award or client testimonial), and can be introduced informally to others in the team to get feedback on personal chemistry. Reference checking should always occur by telephone direct to previous managers, verifying factual claims and ascertaining their view of potential weaknesses.

Finally the recruiting manager should always remember to sell the job and the company to each candidate. A tailored information pack should be given to short-listed candidates, they should feel welcomed by all staff, and a press pack of company achievements should be available in reception for their review (not removal). Such support can make the difference between a candidate choosing you or your competitor.

Training and performance management

Once recruited, there should be a structured induction covering the business, the marketplace, all internal contacts and the job requirements. A person should be appointed to coordinate induction (ideally a member of the team) and verify that information is both absorbed and understood. The process should include job accompaniment with performance being formally appraised at the end of a probationary period. This will create a clear sense of purpose, and ensure that untrained people do not damage customer or prospect relations. It also prevents the salesforce inheriting a lame duck who interviewed well but could not apply his or her knowledge. Under-performers in a sales team often affect the rest of the team.

Ongoing training and development is the responsibility of the sales manager. The most effective development method is on-the-job coaching, allowing the trainer to observe what happens and how, and to give feedback on performance immediately afterwards. Feedback should be packaged in a 'praise sandwich' – ie positive accomplishments, what could improve, and again what went well. Constructive criticism is more likely to be absorbed in this way and acted upon. Coaching should employ open questions rather than statements so the learner considers possible courses of action for himself or herself. Records should be kept of individual salesperson strengths and weaknesses so that trends are identified and people can team up with the most appropriate partners to exchange good practice. Whilst the best diagnosis of training needs occurs through observation at work, activity statistics will also identify issues. Activity ratios (referred to earlier) should be regularly analysed, published and compared between team members to enable them to benchmark themselves with the best performers.

In some instances the use of an external specialist trainer or coach can improve team performance in the field as the feedback is likely to be more objective, and new ideas from outside the team can be introduced and applied quickly.

There are many different training methods appropriate for salespersons and a training plan should not rely on just traditional classroom-based study. Role-plays and simulations at sales meetings, summarizing key points on cue cards, supplying audio tapes for travel time, and appointing internal experts on key topics (eg competitors) will all help the sales manager break up the training tasks into manageable proportions. When training has been provided it should be followed up afterwards to establish what was learnt, how it was applied, and the benefits accrued so that the investment in time and money can be evaluated to improve subsequent delivery. With no assessment of training outputs, it is not possible to establish its value.

Forecasting

A key output of effective salesmanship is the ability to forecast accurately. Forecasting is important for cash flow and inventory management. Inaccurate forecasts result in too much or too little inventory, and insufficient cash flow to pay for fixed costs. The consequent effects can impact many areas and ultimately can critically damage the business. There are a number of factors affecting forecasts which are outside the control of the salesperson, eg the market economy, exchange rates, competitive activity, etc. However, the main factor affecting forecasts lies within the control of the salesperson – prospect qualification.

Qualification begins as soon as information about the prospect is collected. At its basic level this includes names and job titles of decision-makers, their buying history, and expressed wants, budgets and timeframes. At this level of qualification it may not be possible to predict anything more than a 50 per cent possibility of winning their business. As the sales cycle progresses it becomes more possible to predict the timing and likelihood of contract. The number of successful meetings, qualifying additional needs, a request for proposal, a presentation and a feasibility survey will all contribute to escalating probabilities from 50 per cent to 90 per cent. Additional factors may reduce chances – for example a change in decision-maker or policy or involvement by competitors.

Such issues should be factored into the overall equation so that a realistic weighting is given to forecast business. Thus for four prospects of orders valued each at £10,000, if the probability forecasts are 50 per cent, 60 per cent, 70 per cent and 80 per cent the overall forecast value should be £26,000 rather than £40,000.

Additional correlation factors can be based upon a salesperson's abilities to forecast accurately, as this can also vary. This is calculated by comparing forecasts with actual business closed. An optimistic salesperson who has been forecasting 25 per cent more than actual in the previous periods may require a reduced weighting to compensate until the skill issue is addressed. Prospect lists of sales in progress are therefore an essential control system. They should detail client name, potential value, percentage current probability based on agreed criteria, order date expected, and next action by the salesperson. If there is no follow-up appointment date to progress a decision to the next stage, the salesperson may lack the control to develop the sale.

These lists should be updated at least monthly, even weekly, to ensure forecasts are based on accurate information, and as this is company-critical information, forecast accuracy should be included as part of the regular appraisal process. Competitor involvement will have a significant effect on forecasting, often reducing margins and deferring decision timing. Although marketers will collect broad information about competition, the salesforce is in a better position to gather up-to-date tactical information due to their exposure in the field. There should therefore be a system in place to collect and aggregate such data so that appropriate counter-tactics can be applied. This could include special offers, price incentives, product improvements and new services. Loyal customers are a useful source of information, and the poaching of competitor staff can also help. An increasing phenomenon is the *secret shopper* where a competitor will masquerade as a prospect. Sales and support staff should be alerted to such activity and be shown how to qualify new prospects before releasing sensitive information. Blanket tenders through third parties (eg consultants) are sometimes used to obtain a detailed picture of an organization's financial, operating, product and support infrastructure. Market research questionnaires should also be treated carefully.

Sales force structure

Turning to sales force organization, there are four ways to organize a business-to-business structure: by region, vertical market, product type or major account. The pros and cons of each option are as follows. By region promotes local relationships and is simple to administer, although service quality may vary between regions, and major national accounts may experience coordination difficulties. Regional structures tend to suit high levels of simple repeat business for small to medium-sized clients. A vertical market approach (ie specialists for local government, professional services, manufacturers) enables customers to have suppliers with a higher understanding of their business sector, and lets the supplier focus resources on profitable sectors. Clear distinctions between sectors are necessary and sales staff require a good knowledge of business needs and applications. This is suitable for more complex transactions requiring longer-term advice and guidance on specialist applications.

Product specialization allows high levels of technical support through a knowledgeable sales force, but this can result in an over-emphasis on product knowledge at the expense of market requirements or customer needs. A major account structure allows the supplier to focus on clients with the biggest payback and can generate high quality key term relationships. However, this can result in longer sales cycles to win new business, and result in different service levels at the expense of smaller clients.

Overall, for business-to-business sales, the major account structure is commonly integrated into the other structures because of the greater long-term benefits. Those include a deeper understanding of client needs, improved product development and service delivery and more opportunities for cross-selling additional offers over a period of time.

An example of how this occurs is shown in the following case study.

DEVELOPING A MAJOR ACCOUNT

The aim of this case study is to show how a consultant worked with a successful business to improve its position as a market leader.

The organization

Mark Wilkinson Furniture Limited designs, manufactures and sells handcrafted kitchens and bedroom furniture. Its products, originating in the leafy village of Bromham in Wiltshire, are widely regarded as the embodiment of quality English craftsmanship.

Owner-managed by Mark Wilkinson and his wife Cynthia, they employ over 100 people in Bromham, and sell direct to the public in showrooms across the UK, and through retailers and agents worldwide.

Mark Wilkinson says: 'From the very beginnings of our business in the early 1980s we have taken the view that a forward-thinking, responsible attitude to the environment is central to our business. This means being responsible to everyone who works for us in terms of ensuring their health and well-being at work.'

The challenges

The business is labour-intensive in a retail industry, which is notoriously affected by economic peaks and troughs. These are difficult to predict or control, and the directors are acutely concerned to protect their employees' livelihoods under all economic conditions. 'The gradual building of a loyal, skilled and happy workforce is the cornerstone of our business,' says the Chairman, and he approved a skills audit of all showroom personnel and key managers up to director level. The purpose of the skills audit was to identify skills development needs for those involved in business development activities to ensure that the company could maintain its market leadership.

The company decided that impartiality was important for the skills audit, so they retained an experienced external consultant.

The implementation

The first steps were one-to-one reviews with the consultant, in order to identify the strengths and areas for improvement of each jobholder. This simulated assessment centre processes under informal circumstances, at the end of which jobholders' priorities were aligned with company goals, and a skills development plan was produced.

This review identified the main priorities for development as relationship management internally between managers and staff, and externally between salespersons and clients.

As the additional development needs had not been budgeted for, the consultant submitted a proposal to the local Business Link, seeking a financial subsidy for a number of complementary projects to address the requirements. These included:

- developing plans for sales, marketing and customer service;
- tailored workshops for showroom staff;
- improvement to the appraisal system;
- coaching and mentoring programmes for managers;
- workflow analysis for factory personnel;
- reviewing and improving the dealer training programme.

The Business Link agreed to sponsor part of the costs with a subsidy of several thousand pounds supporting the use of the same consultant so that continuity was maintained. Managing Director Cynthia Wilkinson committed the company to an investment of 24 consulting days spread over a 12-month period to enable change to take place without disruption to busy schedules, and with sufficient time to reinforce progress.

The outcomes

A new sales and marketing plan was produced, providing a common focus for the many differently located teams and a more effective tool for the directors to assess progress. Function heads were appointed for customer service and distributor sales, and the consultant also facilitated the production of their own business plans.

All showroom staff participated in workshops building their relationship management skills. These engendered team working and motivation, being highly interactive, and involved the sharing of *success stories*. The dealer training programmes were improved in both design and delivery, to the extent that participants stated them to be the best in the industry.

Factory managers launched a workflow analysis programme, which resolved bottlenecks in the manufacturing, storage and order processing areas.

The line managers were involved in developing a more effective appraisal system so that staff could appraise themselves and manage their own performance more effectively.

The consultant took on the role of coach and mentor for a few key senior individuals, resulting in behavioural change perceived positively by managing director and staff alike.

Managing Director Cynthia Wilkinson comments, 'The stakeholders in our business include not only directors, but also our staff, suppliers, customers and our community. For every new customer order we plant a tree. Actions like this and our people development programmes represent our philosophies and motivations for managing our business.'

Last year the business grew by 20 per cent – just like the trees planted!

BUSINESS PARTNERING

In the case study above, the customer took advantage of a single source to deliver a number of different tailored services for a wide range of employees. The customer obtained a reduced cost through a 'bulk' purchase of consultancy via the local Business Link. The quality of services was consistent as it came from the same source. There was no time wasted on repeated briefings of requirements to different deliverers. The knock-on effects of servicing different but related areas was measured more widely and consequently led to more effectiveness.

Where major account servicing is provided on a larger scale by a sales and support team, it can build team spirit and reduce costs with more synergy within the supply team. This can lead to sales staff influencing purchasing patterns, customers contributing to product development and creating a cycle of improved service. The long-standing nature of the relationship can help the supplier build customer need satisfaction into the business plan and strategy. Over a period of time it may be possible to integrate supplier and customer systems and procedures (eg online order processing) and harmonize quality controls. Eventually this can lead to strategic supplier alliances or partnerships allowing substantial information sharing, mutual problem-solving and cost reduction.

A typical example of this is in the increasing number of alliances between product manufacturers and service suppliers. A small computer manufacturer or reseller may find themselves competing with larger organizations who offer a full 'turnkey' solution, wrapping their own brand of consulting services around the hardware sales. In this instance the smaller business sometimes fails to win because the client perceives them as merely selling boxes, and not understanding the strategic issues linked to the introduction of new technology. The smaller hardware supplier could establish an alliance with a non-competing IT consultancy whose specializations in IT strategy, project management or training could be jointly packaged as a single offer to the client.

This would reposition the hardware supplier as a 'one-stop shop' and enable their involvement in decision making both within strategy and across other areas of implementation. Eventually such a partnership can help the hardware provider to learn how to set up and deliver their own consultancy services. Customers are increasingly demanding more choice in their purchases and more flexibility from suppliers. Partnership arrangements can be a fast and cost-effective process to meet such demands or offer differentiation without the costs and risks of building in-house resources.

The stages in developing a partnership will include:

1.   identifying a product or service, which will enhance the value of your own core offer;
2.   researching the perceptions of its value amongst customers and prospects;
3.   defining and costing the new offer with a non-competing organization who are willing to transfer knowledge and who are not intent on building their own brand to compete;

4. agreeing terms of reference, mutual responsibilities and contact management details to manage relationships;
5. piloting and responding to feedback;
6. sharing information and team working at all levels are prerequisites for success and both parties need the skills and systems to support this.

THIRD-PARTY DISTRIBUTION

Whilst the focus of this chapter has been on direct business-to-business selling, distribution networking and selling through third parties should not be overlooked. A local distribution network can replace or work alongside direct salespersons. This can involve distributors, agents, wholesales and retailers. The benefits of low-cost coverage and faster local response can attract customers, and standards of service must be consistent throughout the network. The distributors themselves should be treated as a customer by the original supplier, who should be aware of the distributors' needs and motivations. A distributor may look for a number of benefits from the supplier: offerings which attract, product information, technical support, marketing support, training, loyalty or incentive schemes, ease of contact. This requires a comprehensive support plan.

The support plan can specify the quality standards expected of the distributor, for example inventory maintenance, staff training, customer satisfaction measures, and delivery timeframes.

For displayed products there should be consistent visual standards, sometimes covering not only merchandising material but also literature, building layout and dress codes. These will reinforce a brand image and give customers the security of consistency. To minimize 'performance scatter', benchmarks should be specified and successful performers should be encouraged to share how they achieved the standards. The star performers may need an incentive to share their experience with others.

An example of this is as follows: the distributors of an electronics supplier were performing with significantly different results and it would have been too costly and taken too long for the supplier to have visited all outlets to identify the problems and implement solutions. Instead the supplier hired an independent consultant to facilitate a series of business development workshops at head office at which the distributors shared and developed ideas between themselves to improve performance.

The process included new product launches, competitor briefings, meetings with supplier support staff and teamwork exercises between distributors. As a result all attendees felt they benefited in different ways, and under-performers were able to learn not only what to do differently but how to implement successful practices from those who had performed better.

The amount of control a supplier can exercise over distributors depends upon their status as either independent or franchised. Franchisees must not supply competitor products, whereas independents can, and use this to play off suppliers against each other. The supplier must decide the degree of control they want or are able to exercise, and can offer varying degrees of support in tune with the degree of commitment by the distributor. Suppliers can take financial stakes in networks and simply increase representation levels to exercise control. These varied options should be regularly analysed so that events alone do not dictate distributor development strategy.

Distributors themselves can influence the resources available to them by drawing up a business plan for the suppliers' approval. The format of a plan could include sales and marketing objectives, customer care and loyalty incentives, training, direct marketing activities and performance review processes. Distributors should be encouraged to develop their own ideas rather than be directed centrally as they will feel greater ownership and commitment. Their ideas may well be transportable to others in the network too. Sales conferences are useful vehicles to help this, creating teamwork and the opportunity for good performance to be recognized in front of the peer group.

Praise and recognition through public presentations will motivate distributors, and can be linked to the performance standards important to the supplier. These can go beyond achieving revenue or unit sales, targeting areas like staff training or customer satisfaction.

An impartial third party eliciting customer views can judge these. Such exercises will focus distributors on customer needs more so than conventional turnover targets. More general communications should be coordinated through a distributor specialist who can develop other communication channels to keep the network informed of relevant news. Management bulletins, newsletters and briefings can ensure the network receives regular and clear information. Staff within the supplier's company also need to be kept informed so they can see the results of their support and focus efforts where they are most needed. It is essential that customers perceive visible team working in the supply chain, and a crucial element is the building of a customer database centrally. Local outlets may need guidelines on what information to collect, such as sales records, advertisement responses and customer complaints. These data can help the supplier identify buying patterns, marketing needs and product development issues. This collection of valuable facts will protect the supplier business should there be any changes of distributor, as well as helping the two parties support each other.

FINAL TIPS

This chapter has outlined a number of ways of winning and managing sales. We will end with two final tips: responding to lost business, and how to get more sales with no extra cost.

Business losses will occur both when prospecting and when maintaining customers. Whilst it is tempting for suppliers to shrug shoulders, 'c'est la vie', and move on quickly without dwelling on negatives, if this happens the opportunity disappears for learning from the event and putting into place loss prevention measures to stop a trickle becoming a stream. All significant losses should be analysed, because many losses are preventable. The supplier should start by examining the processes involved in the sale, whether poor qualification, insufficient cost-benefits or simply not keeping in touch. For an important loss, bringing in an independent analyst will overcome the problems of customers being unwilling to tell the supplier directly what they feel, and salespersons being unwilling to accept responsibility for their own shortcomings. A brief call or visit by a third party can be a very valuable investment.

Finally the simplest and most cost-effective method of winning new business with no cost implications is to ask for referrals. A request can be made not only of satisfied customers, but even during the initial sales cycle, provided a relationship of trust has been established. The process is straightforward: check clients' feelings about your relationship; if they are happy, ask who else they know who could also take advantage of your offering and ask why they may be interested; check if you can mention the referer's name or if they would wish to contact the prospect themselves; then thank them and keep them informed of progress. In doing the latter you will create yet more opportunities to request further referrals leading to more business. If they decline to give a referral this may well be a symptom of an unhappy client, giving you the opportunity of checking and improving their satisfaction levels: a win-win situation. Employ these ideas and the lifeblood of your business will be a stream of clients who keep coming back for more.

CHAPTER FIVE

USING CUSTOMER FOCUS TO GENERATE REPEAT BUSINESS

Bill Boynton

Everyone knows the importance of customers. Without them, a business does not exist. This chapter shows you how to look objectively at just how well your organization is meeting the changing expectations of its customers and the steps you can take to maintain a profitable long-term relationship with them.

THE EMERGENCE OF CUSTOMER FOCUS

A great deal has been written in the past 20 years about dealing with customers. The emphasis on production efficiency and marketing in the 1960s and 1970s gave way in the early 1980s to 'customer care', the first time management thinking specifically addressed the details of 'customers' rather than 'markets'.

Apathy, disregard for customers, and outright discourtesy were not unusual at that time. If customers were accepting of this environment it was only because standards were universally low and because customers' rights had yet to become significant issues for pressure groups and legislators.

Initially, programmes concentrated on training staff to heighten sensitivity to the needs of the customer. Customer care initiatives involving every employee such as that launched by BA at the time of its privatization showed what could be done. However, many organizations imitating the approach were guilty of simply arranging mass 'sheep-dip' training courses which failed to capture the hearts and minds of staff, and which lacked follow-through.

Later in the 1980s, Total Quality Management (TQM) sought to address the issue of serving the customer well in a more comprehensive way, this time with an emphasis on examining business processes, measuring their effectiveness, and engaging staff in efforts to improve. The biggest breakthroughs came in manufacturing, where statistical process control and other techniques demonstrated that attention to detail could transform performance in terms of product defects, repeatability and conformity, lead times and availability. Approaches such as JIT (Just-In-Time) and the growing importance of quality standards, such as BS 5750 (later identified as ISO 9000), also supported these changes.

Though it was claimed that TQM and ISO 9000 approaches are equally applicable to service functions and to service businesses, they frequently fell short for at least three reasons. Firstly, they rarely used a better understanding of the relationship with the customer as the driver for change. Secondly, they were not championed by top management through boom and recession. Thirdly, statistical techniques that could be used to drive out inefficiencies in the closed environment of the company system proved too time-consuming to apply to the diversity of tasks involved in meeting the needs of individual customers.

Big ideas in more recent years such as BPR (Business Process Re-engineering) have done little more to encourage employees to 'think customer'. On the plus side, they have led companies to streamline the way in which service is delivered through simpler organizations and by the effective use of computers and communications technology. The downside has been that employees, certainly those who have worked in large companies, have seen BPR more in terms of downsizing and job losses. Given the stresses of coping with the more rapid pace of change in all businesses, 'continuous improvement' is no longer a management slogan which is guaranteed to enthuse the majority of employees.

Throughout the period, however, increased competition has led more companies in all markets to listen more to their customers, to monitor customer satisfaction, and to invest in better ways of serving them. Often it has been small businesses that have identified what customers want and have set the culture and captured the right values in their organizations to provide it.

Although you will find that the most widely publicized management techniques contain much that is useful, beware. This brief history suggests that none of them alone will provide a template for change based on understanding customers better. The rest of the chapter seeks to provide more relevant solutions.

FUNDAMENTALS OF CUSTOMER FOCUS –
A CHECKLIST

Although detailed solutions depend on the customers and markets being served, past experience of customer satisfaction provides a number of key lessons on which you can base your thinking. Questions are provided in this section to encourage you to take stock of your business.

For every customer who complains, studies suggest that between five and 10 who experience what they regard as unsatisfactory service will not bother to do so. Yet each of these customers is likely to tell five to 10 others of his or her experience. Thus for every complaint known to the provider, between 25 and 100 people will hear of unsatisfactory performance. Whatever the specifics of your business, the message is clear – known complaints are but the tip of the iceberg; other customers will be more influenced by word of mouth than by your organization's communications about its service capabilities.

Q: *First, think about your own experience as a customer (as a consumer and in business), and how often you complain or feel like complaining. What is the evidence of complaints by customers of your business? Are there any indicators of those who feel the service could be better but do not complain?*

It is always important to manage expectations. Customers feel dissatisfaction when services or products do not live up to what they have been led to expect. For example, customers often plan their lives according to delivery promises. If there is going to be a delay, as inevitably happens from time to time, they can be remarkably tolerant but only if they feel they have been given reasonable notice of a change. Many companies fail to communicate with customers about changes, regarding it as too minor or too time-consuming a task. Excellent companies live up to clear principles in this respect. Smart businesses even allow a safety margin in making their promises so that customers are more likely to be agreeably surprised with the outcome.

Q: *Have you ever experienced irritation as a customer when a promise was not fulfilled? How well does your company keep customers informed when promises can't be met?*

Good 'customer recovery' leads to advocates. Even the best organizations slip up from time to time. There is ample proof that companies that apologize and put things right generously and promptly turn potential critics into supporters who then communicate positive rather than negative views to other customers. This finding has led many organizations to seek ways of making the corrective action memorable, either through troubleshooting units or by empowering front-line staff to make amends.

Q: How does your organization behave when these situations arise?

Today's innovation equals tomorrow's expectations. Technology and new competition are leading to faster change. News of improvements travels more rapidly to customers than ever before. More to the point, when customers experience better quality of service in one area of life, it shapes their expectations in others – 'If these people can do it, why can't everyone else?' It is therefore unwise to judge customer expectations by the quality of service you and your competitors currently provide. Newcomers to your market may capitalize on any gap that exists.

Q: Just how good is the service customers get from you and your rivals when compared with the best service you have personally experienced?

It costs four times more to acquire a new customer than to retain an existing customer. This repeated finding is frequently overlooked by companies that have a sales-driven culture which places more value on a 'hunter' who prefers to chase new business than on a 'farmer' who nurtures and builds existing accounts. Studies have demonstrated in a variety of markets that it pays to calculate the lifetime value of an account rather than the profit on the most recent transaction.

When profitability is examined in this way, it usually becomes evident that resources applied to developing existing relationships will produce better returns than investment in new business.

Q: Have you evaluated the relative costs of winning new business and keeping existing customers in your market?

Only excellence will do. For years, companies have thought that their objective should be to achieve a high percentage of 'satisfied customers' as measured by satisfaction surveys. Subsequent analysis of motivations shows that customers seek variety, change and value in some of the goods and services they buy. Research into loyalty has revealed that retention rates can be low even amongst customers who have experienced satisfactory or adequate service. When customers encounter what they regard as excellent service, the proportion of customers who will remain loyal rises substantially. This same group is also likely to make recommendations to others. For these reasons, Quality

Award winners like Xerox set their goals and standards in relation to excellence, and their corporate goals in terms of customer loyalty.

Q: If your customers were asked to rate their satisfaction with your organization's service on a scale from 1 to 5, what proportion of them do you judge would give your company the highest possible rating?

Customers vary widely. Success depends on staff taking responsibility, not working to strict rules from the centre. Many businesses, especially the larger ones, try to treat all customers in exactly the same way. What were originally introduced as guidelines may become rigid rules either because staff refuse to use their judgement, or because the centre equates freedom to act with lack of control over costs. The indications are that companies do best by recognizing that customers wish to be treated as individual human beings and by giving their staff the ability and motivation to make appropriate decisions. A great deal of effort in many organizations is currently being addressed to create cultures that work in this way.

Q: Do all the staff in your organization have real freedom to use their common sense and to do what is fair and necessary to resolve customers' problems and meet their real needs?

The organization's approach to customer satisfaction must be part of its values. Experience shows that good customer service cannot be skin-deep, the result of a special action programme. It appears to be more important to achieve long-term consistency in three dimensions – the image the organization projects, the way management sets objectives and treats its staff, and the experience it gives its customers. As Richard Branson put it in a 1998 lecture, 'We embarked on consciously building [Virgin] into a brand which stood for quality, value, innovation, fun and a sense of challenge. We also developed these ideas in the belief that our first priority should be the people who work for the companies, then the customers, then the shareholders.'

Q: Do you think your customers and staff see your organization in the terms used by Branson? How would they describe your business and what it has to offer them? Does this match the image you communicate in the messages you communicate to the marketplace?

Answering the eight questions in this section will provide a useful preliminary analysis of how customer-focused you and your organization are. Consideration of the points raised will make you aware of the issues involved and ready to start the process of serious review.

A PROCESS TOOL FOR IMPROVING CUSTOMER FOCUS

Figure 5.1 shows the steps that will enable you to develop and implement changes in your approach to your current and potential customers.

1. As a first step, always undertake an analysis of the information you have about your current and recent customers (see below under 'Analysing your customer database').
2. Arrange an in-depth assessment of what customers and front-line staff think about your products and services.
3. Use this information over a period to determine the 'product and service offer' which you believe will achieve high levels of satisfaction amongst your customers over a period of, say, 12 months. Identify the gaps that exist between this 'ideal' and the service currently provided. Assess the extent to which the gaps can be closed by:

- changing the attitudes of everyone in the business to customer service;
- improving people's skills;
- introducing better procedures;
- changing the way you organize (eg hours of service, roles);
- investing in new facilities and systems.

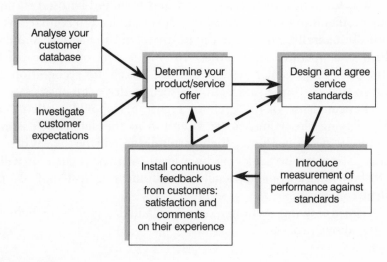

Figure 5.1 Review process

Prepare some outline plans for each of these aspects, discuss them with your staff, and get their views.

4. Involve your staff, particularly those dealing with customers day to day, in the process of agreeing measurable standards for customer service. Everyone should feel that the standards are achievable with current resources and are consistent with the decisions being made in 3 above.

5. Establish procedures that will lead to the regular assessment of performance against the agreed customer service standards. These are likely to be internal measures that concentrate on objective facts about service level provided.

6. Introduce additional methods which will provide regular feedback direct from customers on their satisfaction with the service they have experienced, preferably asking them to compare it with their expectations and experience elsewhere. Ideally this research will quantify satisfaction levels and occur at regular intervals so that trends can be monitored.

7. Ensure that feedback from the customer gets to the people responsible for delivering service and that they have the opportunity to discuss ways of improving it. (Be careful to avoid pursuing errors in a manner that creates a 'blame culture'.) Encourage staff to find ways of eliminating weaknesses in performance, focusing on those that affect customers most and which recur for reasons that can be identified.

The new information obtained from 5 and 6 should be used to maintain the momentum to improve service. It should lead to regular reviews of both the overall strategy for the business and the service standards to which you operate. Staff should be able to feel ownership of this process. Where possible, results can be linked to recognition and reward so that customer satisfaction is seen to drive the business.

Repeated use of the cycle in Figure 5.1 should result in your business paying closer and closer attention to the details of customer expectations and, over time, higher standards will be set. When the business appears to be achieving high levels of performance, it will be time to benchmark your approach to customers against that of other excellent companies.

The following sections contain detailed methods to help you apply the above process.

ANALYSING YOUR CUSTOMER DATABASE

Any efforts to improve customer focus should start with an analysis of your customers – to understand who they are, how they change, and how well their needs are met. The following checklist of questions provides the basis for a quick audit that will also enable you to review your existing practices.

In a small business with few customers, it may be felt that a full understanding exists, but even in such cases, more insights can often be gained from the audit.

Q.   To how many customers has your business provided revenue-earning products and services in the past three months, one year, two years, and three years? Can you segment these customers into markets with different needs?

What is the split of revenue in percentage amongst these customers (highest to lowest) measured by:

- volume/frequency?
- revenue?
- profit, contribution or margin?

Does Pareto's rule apply? (See Appendix 1 for Pareto's rule.) Is the service or product you generally provide influenced by the needs of any dominant customers? Is this a benefit or a constraint to the business?

Q. What has been the percentage change during the past three years in:

- total number of customers?
- number and proportion of new customers acquired?
- proportion of customers who can be categorized as regular, occasional, or lapsed/lost?

Q. What reasons do your established current customers have for buying from you:

- location or geographical convenience?
- your specific understanding of their organization or the industry in which they operate?
- their dependence on your technology or on a product you provide?

- competitiveness of your prices/charges in relation to the quality of service you provide?
- they do not have time or the motivation to look for another provider?
- other reasons?

What evidence is there and how confident are you in these judgements? Are you sure that reasons that once applied still apply?

Q. *What evidence do you have to explain the reasons why new customers have been obtained in the past 12 months?* In addition to analysing the sources of new business (eg sales leads, marketing initiative, referral or recommendation, advertising etc.), try to assess reasons in the terms given for established customers.

Has there been any noticeable change in the type of customers you are acquiring and the amount of actual and potential business they offer?

Q. *What information can you get from an analysis of lapsed customers? (If it is a large population, take a sample over the past year.) What are the respective proportions leaving you for involuntary reasons (no longer require your product, closed down, relocated, died etc) and voluntary reasons (dissatisfaction over price/quality/service, wanted a change etc)?* Do you have any arrangements in place to monitor both the rate of lapsing of customers and the reasons for it, from which plans to reduce the loss rate can be developed? Research amongst customers in a wide range of markets shows that many drift away because they feel their suppliers are remote, do not care enough about them, and make little effort to communicate with them except in respect of new orders. The same suppliers believe that they have been providing good service and are unaware of these customer perceptions.

Q. *Does your business routinely measure the level of service actually delivered to customers who have placed orders or requests for service?* This may be measured in simple quantitative terms, eg:

- percentage delivered at due time/date;
- speed of delivery/response;
- percentage of availability of product or service;
- percentage rescheduled or cancelled by your business.

Have you in the past two years conducted any formal survey amongst customers to find out what they want, and how satisfied they are with what you offer (your products or service)?

Q. *Are there any agreed standards for quality of service to customers? Are they written down and do they feature clearly in training given to staff?* Standards may cover any aspect of contact with customers and prospects when responding to them or approaching them. They may apply to any department which has reason to be in contact with customers by letter, telephone, or face to face.

Q. *Do you have in place a procedure for dealing with customer complaints and suggestions?* In the first place, there need to be agreed guidelines as to what constitutes a complaint (ie expression of dissatisfaction by the customer) and they should be recorded. Are there agreed and documented policies for addressing customer concerns? Is there a procedure to monitor whether customers' grievances are addressed rapidly and effectively, and whether this appears to be appreciated by these customers?

Do people believe they have the authority to resolve complaints and do they appear to exercise it? Does the climate in your business discourage or encourage staff to deal with such complaints?

Q. *What is the quality of customer information in your business?* Do you have their names, addresses and contact details? How up to date are they? Is it a single system or are records scattered across different departments? Do you have records of their contact history? Does this show details of:

- all transactions?
- all contacts, queries etc they have made with your organization?

Is the information accessible by your staff during their contact with customers (so they can convey a good understanding of the customer's business relationship with you)?

Do you have the quality of information that will enable you to plan appropriate marketing, eg offering a new service only to those customers most likely to welcome it?

The answers to the self-audit will enable you to review your business procedures and to plan changes.

UNDERSTANDING CUSTOMERS AND THEIR REQUIREMENTS BETTER

It is important to acquire a clear understanding of what your customers want, the steps they go through when doing business with your organization, and how they view your efforts in meeting their needs.

One of your most important objectives should be to make it as easy as possible for your customers to do business with you. Many senior managers assume this to be the case. However, customers do not have your detailed knowledge of your operation and may find it far more difficult to do business with you than you realize.

Depending on the nature of your business, it is possible to learn more about customers through:

- visits to customers (by managers and staff in all roles);
- observing and videoing/recording what customers say and do when they are in contact with your organization;
- getting your people to use the product or service provided by you or your competitor and to report back on whether it was an easy and pleasant experience;
- reading what customers write to you.

Of the research methods available, *focus groups* have the potential for the greatest impact.

Focus groups

The sole agenda of a focus group is to open up discussion about customers' needs and their experience with your business. Focus groups can be composed in two principal ways. They may typically be made up of representative groups of junior staff who deal with customers day to day. They usually have a good sense of what customers feel and where the organization might be failing to deliver excellent service. Alternatively, groups of customers may be used, perhaps arranging separate groups according to customer profiles or the product/service they have experienced.

Customer focus groups are more expensive due to time required to recruit them, hospitality, and rewards. It is normal to pay consumers £30–50 for their effort in attending and more to business customers who might put a higher value on their time. If your market is fairly small, however, a focus group can be a good way of developing relationships with current and prospective customers.

Focus groups are normally tape-recorded and transcripts prepared which provide a great deal of insight into the details of the relationship from the customer's viewpoint. Good standards of organization are required to set them up and they need to be chaired/moderated with considerable skill to get the best out of the participants. The key ingredients for leading the groups are:

- a warm welcome, hospitable atmosphere, and clear and friendly explanation of how they can help;
- a structure that guides the group through a discussion of the customer experience, while allowing the conversation to flow and inviting contributions from all;
- an ability to get people to distinguish between their feelings, impressions, expectations and actual experience.

You should probably hire a professional to run at least one such group to see how they do so before undertaking to lead one yourself.

Using the information from focus groups

It is possible to arrange customer focus groups so that vision and sound are relayed to another room where staff can observe at first hand. This often has great impact and brings home the reality of customers' concerns to managers and others. Meetings can be held immediately after each focus group to discuss the customers' views and to agree actions to make improvements. The approach can be particularly successful with businesses which operate through several locations and branches, since the staff at each location are likely to respond better to the views of their own customers.

There are also numerous ways to analyse customers' views. One fruitful way is the development of a 'customer journey', which describes, step by step and entirely from the customer's standpoint, what would be an ideal experience or relationship. This will of course be quite specific to the service you offer and the type of customer you serve.

An example is given in Figure 5.2 for a customer of a DIY (do-it-yourself) retail outlet. This example does not represent a particularly futuristic view of what customers want, yet some of the requirements are probably not met currently by any outlet in the UK.

The analysis of the focus group could be presented to show the most relevant comments made under each of the elements of the ideal

As a customer of a DIY store, I would like to:

- find a clean swept car park in which spaces are clearly marked out with directional indicators;

- find immediately I enter either:

  - a staff member who welcomes and guides me to the aisles which contain the items I wish to see; or
  - a large and clear plan of product group/aisle locations and their position in relation to the entrance;

- find aisles which are clearly numbered at floor and aisle level;

- encounter easy-to-see confirmatory signage which is not obscured by displays and which guides me to the product I am seeking;

- find throughout the store a system that allows me to make product queries without having to wait for an assistant to attend;

- see store staff, who are smartly dressed and instantly recognizable in the approved uniforms, evenly distributed about the store;

- encounter staff who can help me find solutions to my needs, but who also have a clear understanding of the limits of their own technical knowledge and how to supplement this quickly;

- find that every item that is boxed contains the product, ie without the need to call up from the warehouse;

- be able to rely on professional advice for more complex items of purchase or those with a technical content;

- find that the checkout area is staffed in relation to the level of customer flow, not in relation to company needs or staff convenience;

- find that a competent backup staff member is available at all times to help resolve matters beyond the competence of the checkout operator;

- receive a receipt, which is fully itemized and easily readable;

- be assisted with heavy or awkward items when I leave;

- be certain that any item may be returned and/or exchanged without fuss if accompanied by the appropriate receipt.

Figure 5.2 Ideal 'customer journey' for the customers of a DIY retail outlet 'customer journey'. This helps to clarify what customers really want and highlights gaps in their present experience.

Once you have prepared an appropriate 'customer journey' for your own business, it can be used as a template with which to assess how well your business is currently performing against each of the requirements of the journey. It is then a short step to discussing the specification with your staff and agreeing with them standards of performance that will meet customers' expectations.

ASSESSING SERVICE QUALITY AND CUSTOMER SATISFACTION

Measures should seek to address both the 'hard' and 'soft' aspects of service quality, and it is helpful to make a distinction between internal measures (information indicative of service quality that you can arrange to capture within your business, often by redesigning systems to produce extra reports) and external measures (feedback from customers which helps you assess performance).

A visit to most outstanding organizations will reveal that their success is partly determined by their attention to detail. They progressively examine different aspects of service and create new measures to check each element. By contrast, poorer organizations are characterized by a belief on the part of management that the effort required to obtain such detailed information is not justified by the benefits it will bring. The point often overlooked is that, in the long term, a policy of encouraging people to monitor service performance in detail leads to higher standards becoming part of the culture of the enterprise.

Internal 'hard' measures

Hard measures are objective measures based on events such as the following:

- speed of response to customers' enquiries;
- average waiting time for customers;
- percentage of enquiries lost because customer would not wait;
- percentage of customer requirements we were able to meet;
- percentage fulfilment of our delivery promises on or before promised date;
- percentage of orders delayed by more than X hours/days;

- average lead time between customer request and provision of service;
- frequency with which we cancelled the customer's order/booking or requested customers to accept a rescheduling of the service delivery;
- percentage of returns by the customer due to inadequate or inappropriate product or service, analysed by reasons;
- percentage of complaints by customers;
- level of refunds to compensate customers for inconvenience.

Measures chosen will depend on the nature of the transaction with the customer:

- Is it conducted face-to-face, by telephone, or by letter, e-mail or other means?
- Is it the rapid provision of a standard product or does it involve a high degree of personalized service?
- They will also depend on the phase of the 'customer journey' – sales enquiry, sales transaction, user query/request for advice, maintenance, etc.

You will need a set of between five and 15 measures, which are indicators of short-term performance as experienced by your customers. They indicate the *outcomes* of your way of running the business and should be monitored weekly and monthly. Major customers may require you to meet their own specifications and need separate reporting.

Your business will need additional longer-term outcome measures. These should indicate:

- customer acquisition (eg percentage of enquiries converted to sales);
- customer retention (percentage of customers in a given period who purchase from you in the next period, or are known not to buy elsewhere);
- customer growth (percentage of new business);
- customer development (change in sales value per customer in a period).

When your main measures are in place, you should encourage staff in different areas of the business to establish their own standards, to arrange the collection of information, and to undertake their own regular assessment of how well they are performing. At this level, measures may be about service to internal customers (ie other departments) and to intermediaries as well as to the ultimate customers of the business.

Internal 'soft' measures

It is also important to monitor the quality of the customer's experience (ie how it feels to be a customer) in addition to the metrics of efficiency described above. This requires the assessment of such factors as:

- the empathy towards and interest shown in the customer;
- whether the customer is allowed and helped to explain his or her real need in full and whether this is understood by staff;
- how frequently customers' needs are met at the first point of contact (being referred on to others or having to call back are particular irritants);
- when there is more than one solution to the customer's request, how well these are communicated, and the quality of advice to help the customer to make a decision;
- whether the customer is offered additional services not requested, in a manner that is seen to be helpful rather than 'pushy'.

Such measures can be introduced through methods of self-assessment and team assessment, which are part of a programme to help staff develop their skills and product knowledge. In the case of one well-known telephone bank, a sample of incoming calls taken by a staff member during the period is replayed by the staff member and supervisor and reviewed against criteria agreed within the bank. It is important to establish a climate in which there is no blame attached to mistakes and opportunities are given for personal development.

External measures – customer surveys

In contrast to internal measures, external customer surveys of various kinds tell you more about customers' *perceptions* of your business.

For some customers, what you provide is of considerable importance and value, for others it may be of marginal interest. Some customers will have clear recall of the transaction or relationship; others may be left with an overall impression. In some cases, the customer will have an established view of your organization based on previous experiences. This view may be slow to keep pace with the changes you make in service.

Despite customers' lack of perfect recall, well-designed surveys will accurately reflect how your customers feel about their experience of your organization. As someone once said, 'Perception is reality', and we ignore the findings of a survey at our peril.

The key principles for planning customer surveys are as follows.

1. Decide what to measure

Examples are: overall customer satisfaction with the total experience and key steps in the 'customer journey', and customer satisfaction with particular services, eg the quality of telephone support or after-sales visits and how these vary amongst particular customer groups.

At this stage, you should consider whether you will invest in frequent surveys so that results from one period to the next can be compared. Normally results at least once per quarter are required to maintain momentum.

2. Decide or take advice on the techniques to use

The main methods that can be considered are set out in Table 5.1.

3. Design questionnaires

This requires considerable experience. The main challenge is to produce questions that will be meaningful, unambiguous and comprehensible to *all* customers who are invited to take part. The questions must be seen to be worthwhile and non-trivial, otherwise a negative impression may be created.

Surveys normally use multiple choice questions to obtain:

- ratings of satisfaction with service;
- what factors the customer regards as important;
- other information to classify the customer and transaction (to permit more detailed analysis).

Researchers have tested many numeric and semantic rating scales over the years to measure customer satisfaction. The primary aim is to obtain objective and consistent responses. Perhaps the best method is to use a scale that seeks to determine whether the customer feels he or she experienced service that can be described as excellent, good, moderate, or poor.

Table 5.1 Survey methods

Method	*Comments*
Postal: Questionnaire is mailed to customer for completion and returned by free-post mail	• Handout of questionnaires by local staff rarely works well [due to staff bias/inconsistency]. • Method requires good customer name and address database for central mailing. • Multiple choice questions normally used to speed completion. Comments can also be invited. Questionnaires can cover considerable detail. • Response of over 30 per cent is possible if the subject really matters to customers. • With a personally addressed letter from the top manager, a postal survey can convey that customers' views are important to your organization. A communications opportunity. • Drawback is that one is never certain about reasons for non-response and whether results are wholly representative. • Low cost per customer.
Telephone: Customer is telephoned by trained interviewer who asks a series of (simple) questions. Multiple choice questions normally used	• Structured (quota) samples of customers can be drawn. • Intrusive, so questionnaires have to be short and simple. • Agencies offer CATI (Computer Aided Telephone Interviewing), which allows questions to vary depending on customer responses. • Costs mount if longer interviews are required.
Face to face: (by appointment)	• Infrequently used to quantify customer satisfaction. • Expensive so usually reserved for in-depth qualitative enquiries into customers' attitudes.
Mystery customer visits/calls: Trained agency personnel contact your organization as if they were customers and rate its performance against a set of criteria	• Method is the best way to determine in detail whether service standards are being maintained. Scope may be limited if costs prevent the mystery customer from making a purchase. • Expensive logistics if visits to many locations are required. • Since the 'mystery customer' is repeatedly undertaking a paid task, lacks the emotional content and 'reality' of responses from real customers.
Exit interviews: Customers are asked to rate and comment on the experience as soon as they complete their purchase/transaction (eg outside a store)	• Intrusive, so has to be short. • Multiple choice questions normally used. • Customer quotas can apply.

In addition to customer satisfaction ratings, a more ambitious line of questioning can also be considered. Figure 5.3 illustrates that exploratory surveys can be designed to find out more about the customer experience.

4. Choose yardsticks to measure customer satisfaction

It helps to interpret a mass of data through a single measure of performance. There are two main options:

- percentage of customers giving top rating of satisfaction, eg 'Excellent'; 4 in a rating scale 1 to 4;
- a customer satisfaction index which combines all results through a weighting system; eg if the customer is asked to rate each service element from 1 to 4 where 4 is the highest, then simply average all the customer scores for each element or express it against a base of 100. An average score of 3.00 using the 1–4 scale would then give an index of 75.

Results from a survey can be presented to highlight customer satisfaction with each element of service. Figure 5.4 gives an example from a mystery customer survey in retailing. It clearly pinpoints the parts of the relationship where the organization can improve.

Choose which of the following words best describe your relationship with your main contact at your bank:					
Warm		Distant		Effective	
Cool		Supportive		Efficient	
Friendly		Inadequate		Unrewarding	

Which of the following words best describe your visit to your travel agent?					
Fun		Interesting		Easy	
Boring		Straightforward		Complicated	
Quick		Slow		Confusing	

Figure 5.3 Customer satisfaction monitors

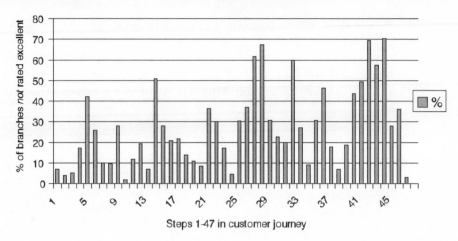

Figure 5.4 Customer journey – retail

5. Decide who should undertake the research and analysis

Some organizations think it will make their staff more aware of customers' needs if they undertake the survey themselves. As a secondary consideration, it saves the cost of using an agency. Before choosing this route, however, bear in mind that it has the following disadvantages:

- customers are unlikely to be candid if approached by individuals who provided the service;
- some staff will be unwilling participants and avoid calling customers expected to be hostile;
- training is essential;
- if you require frequent survey data to track performance, it is often difficult to find dedicated resources at the right time.

6. Determine sample size

If you do not intend to survey *all* your customers, you will need to construct a valid sample.

If only a small proportion of customers are asked their opinions, the change in customer satisfaction measured in successive surveys may be due to variations in the sample rather than to an underlying change in satisfaction.

The sampling rules required to achieve statistical validity are quite complicated. However, a useful rule of thumb often employed by researchers is to examine the reports that will be produced from the analysis of data, identifying the categories and sub-categories (of customer or service attribute, region, branch etc) that are to be monitored. The smallest cell of data should have a minimum of 20 results in each successive survey to establish trends without excessive sampling volatility.

For example, if we require to monitor satisfaction in five customer groups, then each group will need 20 results, ie 100 results will be required. If a postal survey is used, and a response of 20 per cent is expected, it will be necessary to pick a sample of 500 customers to get the 100 results required.

7. Use surveys to get closer to the customer

If your customers are other businesses rather than consumers and you have a relatively small number of customers, the above research methods may be difficult to apply. Other methods can be developed with the cooperation of your customers to examine long-term relationships requiring considerable support and contact. An example is the process of *Joint Assessment* illustrated by Figure 5.5.

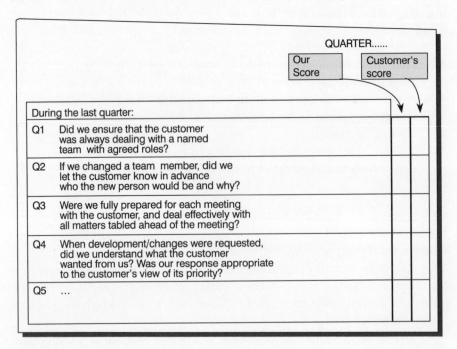

Figure 5.5 Quality of service monitor

Figure 5.5 shows an extract from a questionnaire designed to be completed by staff and by the customers they serve. The process works as follows:

- Design a series of questions that can be put onto an assessment form. Agree a rating scale, say 0–10 where 10 = 'We do this to an extremely high standard', 0 = 'We don't do this but should'. The form could be extended to allow room for comments to each question.
- Ask staff to make an objective assessment of the relationship with each customer during the previous period (eg quarter or year).
- Contact the appropriate person at each of your customers and ask them to cooperate in an assessment of your service quality. Send them a copy of the assessment form to complete and return.[1]
- Analyse results, especially significant differences between what customers and your people say, and study their comments. Ask your team to prepare plans for improving the working relationship with each customer organization.
- Communicate to your customers a summary of the lessons you have learned and the actions you are taking to improve service to them.

Behind the principle of this survey is the idea of tuning your service to your customers so they have less incentive to go elsewhere. It can be extended to find out how you are regarded in comparison with other suppliers and what you need to do to reach 'preferred supplier' status – and achieve an assured flow of repeat business.

---

[1]As a variant to this, send each customer a copy of your team's assessment and invite them to put their own ratings alongside. This will encourage your own staff to be more objective.

CHAPTER SIX

IMPROVING OPERATING PERFORMANCE

John Dempster

The operations function is the arrangement in a business of resources that are devoted to the production of goods and services. Operating performance is improved by using these resources more effectively to produce goods and services that satisfy customers of the business. The operations function applies equally to manufacturing companies and to service companies and organizations.

All companies that wish to have a continuing business will be looking to improve their operating performance for existing products and to ensuring that new products are competitive. Many companies go out of business or are taken over because they are no longer competitive. This may be the result of one or more of the following problems:

- costs of production or services rise with inflation;
- warehouses bulge with stock;
- production areas are filled with work in progress;
- products no longer suit the customer's requirements;
- staff hurry around firefighting and cannot get on with productive work;
- stock is produced that sales do not require;
- there are shortages of stock for urgent sales;
- deadlines are not met;
- customers are kept waiting;
- raw materials received are rejected;
- there is a large 'non-productive' labour force: labourers, inspectors, foremen etc;
- raw materials incur high transport costs to the factory;

- raw materials are purchased through a distribution chain rather than direct;
- finished goods travel long distances to customers;
- sales are made through a distribution chain with many links;
- it takes months to implement design changes for the finished product;
- much stock has to be written off each year as obsolete;
- there is a stack of letters awaiting reply;
- performance targets are not set.

These are some examples of the problems that are met by consultants looking to improve operating performance.

Consultants are asked to help improve operating performance generally in order to enable the business or organization to gain competitive advantage or eliminate such weaknesses. It will therefore be concerned with:

Doing things right – to obtain a quality advantage

Doing things fast – to obtain a speed advantage

Doing things on time – to obtain a dependability advantage

Changing what you do – to obtain a flexibility advantage

Doing things cheaply – to obtain a cost advantage.

Managers are concerned to make continuous improvements to operations but will often call on consultants to achieve a step change in operations performance. Consultants can achieve such a step change because they have the time to study the business, the experience to see what changes could be made and the expertise to know how the changes could be implemented. Managers might achieve the same were they able to make the time available, to gain experience by looking at how competitors and other businesses work and gain expertise through training and study.

But ideas for inclusion on the performance development agenda can come from elsewhere. Increasingly there are publicly funded bodies that facilitate the exchange of information between businesses and how they manage their affairs. It is often useful to find out what arrangements exist in the locality of your own business.

In this chapter, stepwise changes are considered as well as continuous improvement and examples are given of award-winning companies which have achieved such changes in the past both with and without the help of consultants.

SELECTING A PERFORMANCE IMPROVEMENT STRATEGY

There are many examples of businesses that have become more successful by concentrating on the things they are good at and divesting themselves of, or ceasing business in, products that perform poorly. There are also many examples of businesses that have improved their profitability by vertical integration so that they control the whole operations process from raw materials up to the end customer. Equally there are good examples of companies that have improved their profitability by limiting vertical integration and outsourcing those things that can be better done by other companies.

Figure 6.1 gives the results of a survey of 900 executives in 35 countries, showing that the three most popular techniques for improving company performance were: culture change, business process re-engineering and outsourcing.

Two approaches used by consultants in formulating a strategy for operations are shown in Figure 6.2.

It is a matter of selecting the methodology or procedure that suits the organization best. Both require the company to look at its objectives and mission statement and understand those first, and then look at customers to ensure they are being satisfied.

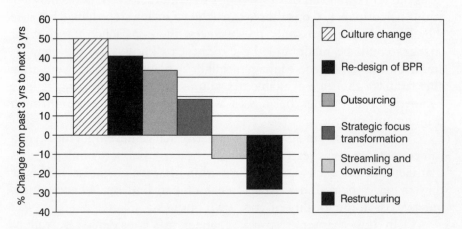

Figure 6.1 Strategic focus on changing corporate culture

The Hill methodology	The Platts–Gregory procedure
• Understand long-term corporate objectives	• Determine the opportunities and threats in the market, noting particularly what the market wants
• Understand marketing strategy	
• Determine competitive factors for winning business or satisfying customers*	• Define the existing operation and how the operation currently performs
• Select the process to be used in carrying out the objectives	• Decide what needs to be done in order to improve.
• Select the infrastructure or non-process structure which will be required	• Produce a revised operations strategy including action plans

Figure 6.2 Formulating an operations strategy

*The Hill methodology is based on the belief that customers have a set of priorities. Some product features are taken for granted (e.g. brakes on a car), some set one product apart from another (e.g. anti-lock braking), and some are delight factors (e.g. cruise control). The strategy should be directed at getting the basics right and delivering the known 'order winning' factors.

CUSTOMERS

Right at the start, it is essential to understand the chain of events or processes in operations that affect customer satisfaction. The process needed for feeding back customers' views to operations will vary depending on the level of customer interaction. There may be:

- no customer interaction, as happens with a long distribution chain where the manufacturer has no direct contact with the end customer;
- passive interaction with customers, where the manufacturer or service provider only responds to customer requests or complaints;
- active interaction with customers, where the customer actually helps to design the product and plays a real part in the operations process, apart from gaining satisfaction as a customer.

Clearly the most effective procedure for ensuring customer satisfaction is where there is active interaction, and it may be valuable to set in place processes whereby both the customer and those in operations become more interactive.

The study quoted in Figure 6.1 showed that global manufacturing industry was indeed now focusing on customer satisfaction, particularly:

- on-time delivery;
- customer perceived quality;
- prompt handing of customer complaints;
- fast response deliveries;
- product reliability.

PRODUCT DESIGN

Design is a transformation process. The resources of technical information, market information, time information, test and design equipment, and design and technical staff are used to achieve finished designs that will satisfy customers' needs in the defined marketplace. During that process, the options are being evaluated for feasibility, acceptability and vulnerability. Designers should consider the four 'Cs' of design:

- creativity;
- complexity;
- compromise;
- choice.

Motor Coach Industries and the Computer Sciences Corporation (one-time winners of the Management Consultants Association's Business Improvement Award for the Best Overall Transformation Project) did so with a project in which the largest coach builder in North America looked at the design process for motor coaches and transformed the whole system to produce models that satisfied customers better, were easier to build and were more readily designed. They introduced concepts of computer-aided design. A single design team was formed working in one large open area. Targets for the design process were derived from market research. This showed that the new design priorities should be:

- passenger excitement;
- problem-free miles;
- whole-life cost of ownership;
- schedule adherence.

Before, the design team had 'cost' as the first priority; now, it has 'passenger excitement'. By using concurrent engineering, with design teams from suppliers as well as their own factory workers, and tooling and process engineers working together with their design team, the design time was cut from the usual five years to three. Ford, Motorola and Hewlett-Packard have adopted similar concurrent engineering design management.

Critical elements of their design success included:

- encouraging concept generation through focus groups within the company where groups from within and outside the company of different disciplines met to consider design options;
- customer research, which was vital;
- looking at competitors and carrying out reverse engineering to check how they produced vehicles.

At Motor Coach Industries, quality function deployment, an analytical, customer-oriented approach to value engineering, was used for product requirement definition to translate a large 'wish list' using tangible and measurable parameters. This helped determine which of the many ideas put forward should be implemented in the new design. One result was that a spiral staircase was designed to enable older passengers to board and alight from the coach quickly.

SUPPLY CHAIN

The supply chain concerns the whole operation from raw material to end customer with the objective of organizing the chain to satisfy the end customer. For some manufacturing companies the supply chain can be extremely long, with two or three stages from raw materials to the factory operation, and a further three stages within the factory followed by three stages in the distribution system to reach the end customer. Any long chain of communication is prone to 'Chinese whispers' (also known as the Forrester effect), in which messages are distorted in the flow along the chain. Communications about changes in demand must be given directly to all members of the chain, as shown in Figure 6.3.

Figure 6.3 Supply chain

Relationships in the supply chain

The relationships between different parts of the supply chain will make a big difference as to how the chain can be managed. There are a number of alternatives:

- integrated hierarchy – this is a fully vertically integrated supply chain within one firm;
- a semi hierarchy – this is a vertically integrated chain under a holding company;
- co-contracting – this is the long-term alliance or partnership between suppliers and customers where the sharing of risks and rewards of technology and innovation can lead to reduction in costs, improvement of delivery and quality and the creation of sustainable competitive advantage.

Co-contracting has become popular especially in the motor industry. Bertrand Faure Seating supply seats to Honda and Rover on a just-in-time basis and cooperate closely with both companies to ensure a smooth flow of excellent products. The company, based in Stanford in the Vale, was once joint winner of the Engineering Industry Sector of the Award for Best Factory given in association with the Cranfield School of Management and published by *Management Today*. Another example, from the retail industry, is Marks and Spencer, which for many years has worked closely with suppliers of fresh vegetables and clothing in partnership arrangements and generally with considerable success for all.

Builders and subcontractors demonstrate an age-old system of co-contracting, which is sometimes adversarial rather than cooperative. The adversarial system requires the main contractor to spend an enormous amount of time and effort checking the work of the subcontractor. The most efficient contractors use tried, tested and conscientious subcontractors so that they can be sure that a good job will be done with a minimum number of checks.

Licensing and franchising arrangements demonstrate cooperation through revenue links. Specsavers Ltd run a franchising operation for opticians in the UK and Holland. They enable trained opticians to set up independently in a large organization by enabling opticians to carry out their craft while the franchiser worries about accounting, premises and optical supplies.

The same kind of cooperation can come through medium or

long-term trading commitments, for example, when arrangements are made for a maintenance contract.

This cooperation can be contrasted with short-term trading commitment such as a specific tender for a specific job.

Lean supply

Co-contracting can reduce the costs of supply, and the lean supply concepts defined by Professor Richard Lemming help to set out the characteristics of efficient supply, as shown in Table 6.1.

Information processing

Information technology plays an important role in supply chain management these days. It is likely to become more important and it can be difficult to keep up with the latest developments. There is a trend

Table 6.1 Characteristics of efficient supply

Factor	Lean supply characteristic
Nature of competition	Global operation; local presence
	Based upon contribution to product technology
	Dependent upon alliances/collaboration
How suppliers are selected by customers	Early involvement of established supplier
	Joint efforts in target costing/value analysis
	Single and dual sourcing
	Supplier provides global benefits
	Re-sourcing as a last resort after attempts to improve
Exchange of information between supplier and customer	True transparency: costs, etc
	Two way: discussion of costs and volumes
	Technical and commercial information
	Electronic data interchange
	Kanban system for production deliveries
Management of capacity	Regionally strategic investments discussed
	Synchronized capacity
	Flexibility to operate with fluctuations
Delivery practice	True just in time with Kanban
	Local, long distance and international JIT
Dealing with price changes	Price reductions based upon cost reductions from order onwards: from joint efforts of supplier and customer
Attitude to quality	Supplier vetting schemes become redundant
	Mutual agreement on quality targets
	Continual interaction and *kaizen*
	Perfect quality as goal

towards integrated systems requiring single rather than multiple entries of data with the entries being made at source. Orders, sales and payments will be made electronically either through proprietary networks (electronic data interchange (EDI)) or via the Internet and there will be transparency of events throughout the chain with information available to levels throughout the chain.

This does not mean that simple methods should be abandoned. Keltec Electronics of Kelso produces printed circuit boards and has won the Small Business Award for the Best Small Company in the Best Factory Awards. Keltec has improved its quality by having simple glass fishbowls into which are put any defective products. The display has resulted in engineers' attention being drawn to the defective items and a substantial improvement in quality as a result of action taken.

Material requirements planning (MRP)

An MRP system is an essential part of any manufacturer's supply chain where customer orders and forecast demand produce a master production schedule which, with bills of material and inventory records, enables the system to produce purchase orders and material plans and works orders.

In MRPII the company can achieve a game plan for planning and monitoring all the resources of a manufacturing company: manufacturing, marketing, finance and engineering. Technically it uses the closed loop MRP system to generate financial figures as well.

There are various sophistications that can be added to MRP. For example, back scheduling can be included, which takes account of lead times and determines when to produce or supply. In closed loop requirements planning, resource requirement plans and rough-cut capacity plans and capacity requirement plans are considered to see if the plan is possible.

Because of unplanned variability in any set of operations it is always necessary to build some flexibility into a plan to allow day-to-day management of those occasions when absenteeism is high or low, or machines are working well or badly.

PURCHASING AND SUPPLY MANAGEMENT

Purchasing and supply has always been an important part of any business. In recent years, with greater automation and more outsourcing, with make or buy decisions often coming down on the side of buy rather than make, effective purchasing has become the major factor in the elements of cost. Yet many businesses have insufficient information about purchasing and inventory.

The five 'rights' are a good basis for evaluating purchasing:

- right price;
- right time;
- right quality;
- right quantity;
- right source.

Companies are now sourcing globally rather than just from within the countries in which they operate. Materials are still distributed by road, rail and water but increasingly fluids are sent by pipeline and products are despatched by air. It all depends on the requirements for:

- delivery speed;
- dependability;
- quality deterioration;
- transportation costs;
- route flexibility.

The decision tends to be based on these in that priority order. In the food business, cool chain delivery is now essential for many products and requires temperature-controlled containers or vehicles.

The negotiation of prices has been developed from an adversarial approach to buying, where buyers challenge suppliers to reduce their prices, to a cooperative system where businesses work with their suppliers to achieve a 'win-win' situation for both sides with lower prices, better service and a better bottom line result.

Warehousing plays an important role in supply management. Centre of gravity calculations can be used to determine the best location for a warehouse together with decisions on how much, when and how to control the inventory system. The layout and organization of the warehouse is dependent on the stocks being held, the methods used for storage and picking and the system used for stock control. Increasingly robots and automatic conveyor systems are used in stores. Widespread use of bar code marking has made automatic control and recording cheaper, simpler and more accurate.

Any control system will take account of inventory costs – the cost of placing the order, price discounts, the costs of stockout, capital, storage obsolescence and production inefficiency. It will be valuable to collect information on inventory profiles to show how inventory varies for products with time or production or sales levels. Using the inventory costs and the profiles it will be possible to calculate economic order quantities (EOQ) for each product and the economic batch quantities (EBQ) for production. From the average inventory level for a product and the cost of a shortage, one may determine mathematically the reorder level and the safety stock that needs to be held, as follows:

Economic Order Quantity (EOQ) = $\sqrt{((2\times O \times D)/H)}$

Economic Batch Quantity (EBQ) = $\sqrt{((2\times O \times D)/(H \times (1-(D/P))))}$

where O = Order cost, H = Holding cost per period, D = Periodic demand, Q = Order quantity, P = Periodic rate of production

These calculations will be built into most computer-based stock control systems.

It is always necessary for there to be a periodic or continuous review of these calculations to take account of changed circumstances and to check actual stock levels to ensure that records are accurate and take account of 'shrinkage'.

In examining the inventory system, the ABC system for categorizing stocks is still valid and important. This is an application of Pareto's principle (see Appendix 1), which states that in many situations, a small number of causes account for the bulk of the effect. In order to use scarce resources (such as management time) effectively, look after the few causes that cause most effect. This is applied in the ABC system so that the A parts or products are those that are most important or have the highest value, while the C parts or products are of low value. The A parts are dealt with in detail while the C parts are looked after with simple, inexpensive systems of control.

The relationship of stock to demand is always going to be an important ratio in judging the efficiency of the inventory systems. By reducing stock levels, capital can be released to increase sales, warehouse space can be released, obsolescence avoided and design changes more rapidly introduced.

PLANNING AND CONTROL OF MANUFACTURING OR THE PROVISION OF SERVICES

Here we look in more detail at the manufacturing or provision of service aspect of the supply chain. Bertrand Faure attributed that part of their success to the fact that they could locate their factory at a site equidistant from Rover in Oxford and Honda in Swindon. Not all companies have the opportunity to do this, but, where substantial advantages can accrue, it is essential to carry out detailed analysis and set out the business's requirements and formalize the evaluation criteria in relation both to the site and to its location relative to other factors such as customers, suppliers, facilities and staff. Mathematical methods can be used to calculate the 'degree of fit' for different sites using both a cost and a weighted points system to evaluate the criteria.

Once the location has been decided, consideration must be given to the layout within the plant or, for services, within the office. It can be valuable to use charting to illustrate the workflow and show the relationships between different operations and enable the distance travelled by both people and materials to be calculated. A computer may be used to evaluate the alternatives and arrive at the 'best' result using the computerized relative allocation of facilities technique (CRAFT).

Consideration needs to be given to the process of manufacture and how far it is going to be possible to automate. Automation has played an important role in the success of the companies that have won awards. However, it has been selective. RF Brookes has been Highly Commended in the section 'Household and General' of the Best Factory Awards. RF Brookes produce high quality food products for demanding customers such as Marks and Spencer. They were able to automate the rejection of diced potatoes that had eyes or other blemishes, but they still quarter potatoes for roasting and extrude mashed potato toppings by hand because these are still the best methods.

Computers enable better and better services to be offered to customers. British Airways, for example, is reported as having the 'vision' of providing individual customers on their flights with their precise needs using information collected from their frequent flier programmes and then being able to offer each individual passenger the newspaper, drink and menu he or she prefers.

Computer integrated manufacturing (CIM) has arrived and companies are using computers in all aspects of their operations. Diamond Multimedia, a San Jose based manufacturer of graphics and sound cards found in personal computers, has installed a product data management (PDM) system which combines computer-aided design with bills of materials and manufacturing instructions – a system well known in motor manufacture and aerospace. Using the Internet, they are able to give access to the database to their subsidiaries elsewhere in the world, enabling manufacture to be carried out quickly, according to the latest design, and allowing the product to be updated quickly to the latest design specification.

United Distiller's whisky bottling plant at Leven in Fife has won a Best Factory Award and CCL Custom Manufacturing's Scunthorpe personal care products and aerosol filling plant has won an Award for Most Improved Factory. Both companies depend for their success on optimized production technology, the principles of which have been described as:

- Balance flow, not capacity.
- The level of utilization of a non-bottleneck is determined by some other constraint of the system, not by its own capacity.
- Utilization and activation of a resource are not the same.
- An hour lost at a bottleneck is an hour lost for ever out of the entire system.
- An hour saved at a bottleneck is a mirage.
- Bottlenecks govern both the throughput and the inventory in the system.
- The transfer batch may not, and many times should not, equal the process batch.
- The process batch should be variable, not fixed.
- Lead times are the result of a schedule and cannot be predetermined.
- Schedules should be established by looking at all the constraints simultaneously.

These principles have helped these companies to increase the capacity of their process lines by working with their staff to reduce downtime and improve efficiency at bottleneck operations.

Just-in-time (JIT) planning and control

Three companies who have won awards for Best Factory use this system of control:

- Krone (UK) Technique, whose Cheltenham plant mass produces precisely engineered, low-cost connectors, including products for telephones, have won the Electronics and Electrical, Best Factory Award.

- Bertrand Faure Seating, whose Stanford in the Vale plant produces car seats, jointly have won the Engineering Industry, Best Factory Award.
- Caradon Mira, whose Cheltenham plant produces bathroom showers, jointly have won the Engineering Industry, Best Factory Award.

JIT aims to meet demand instantaneously with perfect quality and no waste. Bertrand Faure is a magnificent example of this. They deliver to the lines in Oxford and Swindon within a 15-minute delivery window. They have to pay substantial penalties if they are late or if seats are delivered with waste thread not trimmed.

JIT production requires high quality, fast throughput, dependability of supplies, machines and labour and flexibility to adapt to changes in demand. It sacrifices capacity utilization. It can be regarded as a philosophy with a set of tools and techniques. The philosophy is to empower the workpeople and the suppliers and work for and achieve continual improvement. The tools and techniques are designed to eliminate:

- waste;
- final inspection;
- store delays;
- unnecessary motion or transport;
- waiting time;
- over-production;
- process;
- inventory;
- defective goods.

To achieve such valuable benefits there need to be changes in working practices. There has to be tight discipline to see that operations are correctly carried out, yet there must be flexibility to cope with the unexpected. Everyone on the production line has to be treated equally. Everyone has to have autonomy and the authority to stop the line if necessary. Material scheduling has to be done precisely and data gathering has to be meticulous so that shortages do not occur. There needs to be a mechanism, for example *kaizen* or quality circles, to solve problems and achieve continuous improvement. Personnel have to be trained and developed to achieve this and to gain the necessary creativity to produce results.

JIT suits best a cell-based layout, possibly on U-shaped lines, with stations close together and visible, using simple machines with pre-set tools and standard fixtures or jigs with easy loading and unloading. It succeeds if there is total people involvement and there is good visibility of the whole operation. Thus performance measures and stoppages are displayed, as are quality control charts, visible improvement techniques and checklists. There will be displays of one's own and competitors' products – both good and defective ones. There will be Kanban visual control in the open plan workplace.

Caradon Mira implemented Kanban control for their products. A single shower unit comprises some 100 components, some bought in but many plated and polished on site. They decided to use a two-card system, pioneered by Toyota. One card serves as a permit to move products from the point of manufacture to their point of use and the other to control and initiate the movement of piece parts to manufacture.

There is no doubt that JIT works best for simple product structures and high repeatability; thus it can cope well with continuous production (runners) and the batch production of like products (repeaters) and it can provide for the odd, one-off product (stranger).

Project planning and control

To be successful in project management it is necessary to ensure:

- clearly defined goals;
- competent project manager;
- top management support;
- competent project team;
- sufficient resources;
- adequate communications;
- control mechanisms;
- feedback capabilities;
- responsiveness to clients;
- troubleshooting mechanisms;
- project staff continuity.

Any project goes through a series of phases from specification to design, to implementation, to module testing, to integration testing, to delivery. This is so whether one is building a bridge, an aircraft or completing a consultancy project.

Generally control of a project will be through a form of critical path planning and will use a Gantt chart (an example of which is shown in Figure 6.4.) to show the major tasks to be carried out against a time base. The critical path planning shows the relationship between the different parts of the project and how they depend on each other.

Critical path method (CPM)

In the critical path method (illustrated in Figure 6.5) the plan is set out to show that no event can be commenced until all activities leading to it are complete. No activity can start until its tail event is reached. No two activities can have the same head and tail events. From the plan can be calculated the earliest start time, the latest start time and the critical path.

Programme evaluation and review technique (PERT)

PERT can be used to make the critical path network more realistic in that an estimated time is given for completing each activity. This is done by giving three estimates of the completion time – the most optimistic,

Description	Period in days
Drainage	
Roads	
Foundations	
Steelwork	
Cladding	
Interior	
Landscaping	

Figure 6.4 Gannt chart

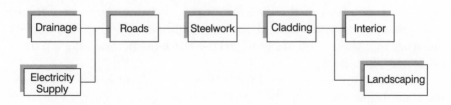

Figure 6.5 Critical path

the most pessimistic and the most likely time. Statistically it can be shown that the likely time for an activity (E) can be calculated as a sixth of the sum of the most optimistic time (O) and the most pessimistic time (P) and four times the most likely time (L).

$$E = (O+4L+P)/6$$

There are sophisticated computer systems now to help with plotting the activities and their dependencies and which can set out the critical path, prepare Gantt charts, indicate the resource constraints, provide cost controls and calculations and set out how a path might be shortened to get an earlier finish time.

Job design and work organization

United Distillers and RF Brookes both show how they believe that their staff working on the job can be the best people to improve the design and work organization of their own jobs. They set improvement targets and achieve substantial benefits.

The original design for the job and the improvement of the methods first adopted require the same questioning approach. Having selected the work for study, a record has to be made of what is done now or, at the design stage, what is required to be done. The questions have to be asked about each aspect of the job:

- What?
- Why?
- When?
- How?
- Where?
- Who?

From this questioning a new method can be developed by asking the further question: If we do this, will it work? The people doing the job need to be involved in the decision process because the most difficult task can be the installation of the new method. This is simplified by ensuring that those who are going to use the new method take a part in its design and selection.

There are a number of tools that a consultant can use in examining methods:

- the principles of motion economy;

- ergonomics with anthropometric data, which gives information about the human body so as to fit the work to the people;
- flow process charting, to enable one to clarify the changes that might be made;
- health and safety standards, which provide limits on acceptable forces or weights, working temperatures, illumination and noise levels.

Behavioural approaches can be used to help determine whether a cell-type production unit is needed or whether a production line would be more effective. Division of labour promotes faster learning, makes automation easier and reduces non-productive work. But it has the danger of creating monotony, causing repetitive strain injury and having little flexibility and poor robustness in that changes cannot be made to a line as easily as to a cell and breakdowns are more likely to occur. Certainly the JIT enthusiasts will consider that productivity levels and quality levels can be substantially improved from the cell structure, which enables job enrichment through empowerment and enlargement.

Rover, the motor car manufacturer, involves its work force in continuous improvement. It has a system of five levels of competence for its shop floor staff, with the level shown by a flag with four sectors, a sector being filled in as the next level is reached:

- Level 1   Just started work
- Level 2   Partly trained
- Level 3   Competent in the job
- Level 4   Competent to train others
- Level 5   Contributes to improving the process

This last category is essential. Lloyds TSB Retail Banking has been the winner of a Unisys Service Excellence Award in the Most Improved Category. The bank has built a continuous improvement loop based on 'Vision, Performance and Feedback' to apply to all aspects of its customer service delivery. CCL Custom Manufacturing have a continuous improvement programme that has already raised output by 25 per cent and plan to achieve almost a 50 per cent increase in output.

Loading, sequencing and scheduling

The loading, sequencing and scheduling operations can be extremely complex. For n jobs on m machines the number of possible schedules is

$(n!)^m$. This means that for three jobs on two machines there are 36 possible schedules and for five jobs on four machines this rises to some 200 million.

A critical cost for any machine is the changeover time. Krone (UK) Technique reduced the changeover times in their plastic injection moulding shop to seven minutes – a great improvement over what it had been earlier. Probably the best example of changeover speed is in Grand Prix racing, with tyres changed and fuel loaded in less than 10 seconds. It shows what can be done and demonstrates that examples can be taken from other industries when looking for improvements to be made in your own.

Many people use simple systems to determine the sequencing of jobs: customer priority, due date, first in first out, longest job first, shortest job first. In fact there are more sophisticated methods for loading machines using Johnson's rule. There is push–pull scheduling where central control provides the push through MRP or the customer workstation pulls work through as in JIT manufacturing. Whatever system of scheduling is used, the design capacity of the machinery or equipment will never be achieved. A planned loss must be expected. This effective capacity (designed capacity minus planned loss) may not be achieved. Actual output can be increased by reducing the 'avoidable losses', so increasing the plant's efficiency.

Determining the total capacity for a plant is crucial for most operations. If too little is installed then customer service will suffer and business will be lost. If there is too much, the plant will operate at under capacity.

Xerox Electronics Manufacturing Centre at Mitcheldean manufactures printed circuit boards and has been Highly Commended in the Electronics and Electrical Category of the Best Factory Awards. Xerox has solved the problem of variable capacity by employing contract labour as a substantial part of their work force. United Distillers attack the problem in a different way by having an evening swing shift so that they can operate the plant for longer hours when it is necessary.

All capacity systems are going to be related to the way in which demand is to be treated:

Level capacity plan	Fluctuations in demand are ignored and capacity is kept steady. This is the way in which airlines, railways and buses work. Scheduled services are of a fixed capacity.
Chase demand plan	Feasible where capacity reflects changes in demand as at Xerox and United Distillers with their flexible arrangements for the labour force.

| Demand management | The producer acts to change demand to fit capacity. Farmers generally have to do this by adjusting the price in order to sell their crop. When the product is in short supply they can demand a high price, as for red roses on Valentine's Day. Professional football clubs and cricket clubs will also manage demand in this way by raising prices for popular matches. |

In determining how capacity will be controlled, forecasting demand will play an important role. Good forecasts of demand will be a major factor in effective planning. (See forecasting in Chapter 4.)

TNT Express Delivery Services runs a transport delivery service and has won the Business to Business Category of the Service Excellence Awards as the Service Excellence Company of the Year. TNT provides a good example that many service companies have of providing a good response to customers. TNT required that their telephone operators answered calls within three rings – down from six rings. Eliminating the welcome 'How may I help you?' achieved part of the time reduction needed.

Queuing theory can also be valuable in service industries to determine the capacity required to provide an acceptable service. This theory was used to change the queuing systems in banks and post offices.

QUALITY

An essential part of operation improvement is quality improvement and Total Quality Management.

There are five approaches to defining quality:

- the *transcendent approach*, where quality is synonymous with 'innate excellence';
- the *manufacturing-based approach*, where the concept is to make products 'free of errors';
- the *user-based approach*, where the object is to make sure the product is 'fit for purpose';
- the *product-based approach*, which views quality as a precise 'measurable set of characteristics' that are required to satisfy the customer;
- the *value-based approach*, which takes the manufacturing approach a stage further and defines quality in terms of 'cost and price'.

Apart from these definitions, there is also the view of quality from operations, which defines quality as being 'conformance to customers' expectations'. Alternatively there is the customer's view, where the customer's perception of quality is regarded as all-important and ideally 'perception should be greater than or equal to expectation'.

With all these definitions there is plenty of room for 'quality gaps' to appear, with differences between:

- customer's specification and the operation's specification;
- concept and the specification;
- quality specification and the actual quality;
- actual quality and the communicated image.

These days the first decision to be taken is which definition should be used when service to the customer is all-important. Clearly the customer view is the most important aspect and in the litigious world in which we live the product-based approach of 'a measurable set of characteristics' may need to be combined with this.

Thus the first step in controlling quality will be to define the characteristics:

- functionality;
- appearance;
- reliability;
- durability;
- recovery;
- contact.

A decision has to be made as to how to measure each characteristic, with variables being measured and attributes assessed. Quality standards have to be set for each characteristic. There are many ways of controlling quality against the standards. For most products or processes some form of statistical process control using control charts showing trends and limits will be appropriate. Sampling will be used to collect information as well as, where appropriate, recording all defects. With that information poor quality can be identified and action taken to find and correct it with the aim of continually improving quality.

Continuous improvement

Benchmarking

Both PHH Vehicle Management Services of Swindon, who offer a full range of services for cars, vans and trucks and has been Highly

Commended in the Business to Business Category of the Service Excellence Awards, and Arjo Wiggins have emphasized how important benchmarking is in making improvements. They use internal, external, competitive and non-competitive benchmarking to establish how their businesses are doing against others and to provide ideas as to how they might improve. Arjo Wiggins has found internal benchmarking against other group companies especially valuable, while PHH has gained most value from benchmarking competitors.

A performance matrix can be valuable for benchmarking against competitors where each factor selected as important to the business is scored on a scale of 1 to 9 and plotted on the matrix. The matrix will quickly demonstrate whether the company is world class or has work to do to improve.

Business process re-engineering

Many businesses are re-engineering their processes, which means they look at their processes, ignoring functions, to reorganize their work around process and make each process as efficient as possible. Companies strive for step change improvements with this technique. Benefits can be achieved by arranging for internal customers to be their own suppliers or putting decision points where work is performed rather than separating those who perform the work and those who control and manage work. The analysis process will include input and output analysis defining inputs and outputs and their requirements. Flow charts (an example of which is shown in Figure 6.6), with rectangles for action and diamonds for questions or decisions, and scatter diagrams can be used to show relationships between the different activities.

Ishikawa diagrams

In this analysis for continuous improvement, cause and effect diagrams or fishbone diagrams developed from an idea by Ishikawa can be very valuable. An example is illustrated in Figure 6.7. On the right-hand side

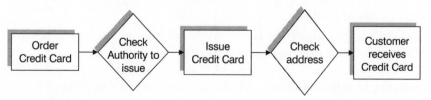

Figure 6.6 Flow chart

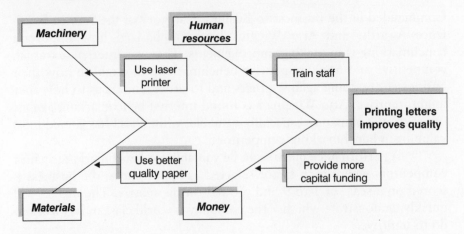

Figure 6.7 Ishikawa diagram

of a large piece of paper a rectangle is drawn and the effect is written in the box. The backbone of the fish is drawn across the paper from this with a number of lines going off it, each to a smaller box in which is written the category of a possible cause. Categories can include machinery, manpower, materials, money. Against the line of each category are written possible causes. The root causes are derived from systematic fact finding and refined through discussion.

Pareto's principle

Pareto's principle is relevant to operations as it is to other aspects of business. (See Appendix 1.) So use it to determine where to apply effort in improving quality or productivity.

Why-why analysis

Why-why analysis is another useful technique used to good effect by both consultants and small children. In this analysis a problem is stated and the question: 'Why did it happen?' is asked. The answers are then further subjected to the question 'Why?' This technique provides a greater depth of analysis.

Keltec Electronics of Kelso produces printed circuit boards and has won the Small Business Award for the Best Small Company in the Best Factory Awards. Keltec provides a good example of solving problems using these techniques, firstly by making the failures evident for all to see and then encouraging operatives and engineers to question why the failures are happening even though they are within the failure levels set.

Failure prevention

For all operations, failure prevention and recovery is an important aspect, whether it be machine failures or process line failures or failures of products in service. In the case of in-house failures, the first task is to detect its occurrence or likely occurrence. Thus there are 'in process' checks and machine diagnostic checks. Product failures can be detected or discovered in various ways:

- feedback from customers;
- point of departure interviews;
- phone surveys;
- focus groups;
- feedback sheets;
- questionnaires;
- complaint cards.

In each case, the cause of failure needs to be investigated. Such investigations range from a full-scale accident investigation into an air crash to maybe complaint analysis or product liability for a product.

It may be useful to carry out a failure mode and effect analysis in which for each possible cause of failure is asked:

- What is the likelihood that failure will occur?
- What would be the consequence of such a failure?
- How likely is such a failure to be detected before it affects the customer?

To determine the relative importance of failure for different products, it can be valuable to use a value system determined by risk priority number (RPN). There are seven steps to using this technique:

1. Identify all the component parts.
2. List all the failure modes – how it could fail.
3. Identify possible effects of failure.
4. Identify all possible causes for each failure mode.
5. Assess the probability of failure, the severity of the effects of failure and the likelihood of it affecting the customer.
6. Calculate the risk priority number, RPN. This number is calculated

from an assessment of occurrence of failure, severity of failure and likelihood of detection of failure, each being scored from 1 to 10 where 1 is unlikely and minor and 10 is very likely or catastrophic. The RPN is then calculated from the product of these scores. Thus a minor failure might be 1 and a major one near 1000.

7. Instigate corrective action which will minimize failure on failure modes with a high RPN.

Some examples of the calculation of RPN are shown in Table 6.2.

Table 6.2 Some examples of the calculation of RPN

Description	Occurrence of failure	Severity of failure	Likelihood of detection by customer	Risk priority number, RPN
Light bulb production	1	10	1	10
Electricity supply	2	10	10	200
Posting to account by bank	1	6	10	60
Technical fault to flight	6	10	2	120

Total Quality Management (TQM)

TQM has been used to good effect in many first-class companies to achieve continuous improvement. Armand Feigenbaum defined TQM as:

an effective system for integrating quality development, quality maintenance and quality improvement efforts of the various groups in an organization so as to enable production and service at the most economical levels which allow for full customer satisfaction

W E Deming gave 14 points for such quality improvement in a TQM environment:

1. Create constancy of purpose.
2. Adopt new philosophy.
3. Cease dependence on inspection.
4. End awarding business on price.
5. Improve constantly the system of production and service.
6. Institute training on the job.

7. Institute leadership.
8. Drive out fear.
9. Break down barriers between departments.
10. Eliminate slogans and exhortations.
11. Eliminate quotas or work standards.
12. Give people pride in their jobs.
13. Institute education and self-improvement programme.
14. Put everyone to work to accomplish it.

L Ishikawa brought in the concept of Quality Circles, where groups of staff from the shop floor and elsewhere meet together to think about ways in which they could improve quality in their particular area.

P B Crosby brought in new ideas of quality costs and zero defects and set up the absolutes of quality management:

- Quality is conformance to requirements.
- Prevention is not appraisal.
- The performance standard must be 'zero defects'.
- Measure the 'price of non-conformance'.
- There is no such thing as a quality problem.

P B Crosby also set out 14 steps to establishing TQM:

1. Establish management commitment.
2. Form interdepartmental quality teams.
3. Establish quality measurement.
4. Evaluate the cost of quality.
5. Establish quality awareness.
6. Instigate corrective action.
7. Form an ad hoc committee for zero defects programme.
8. Supervise employee training.
9. Hold a zero defects day.
10. Institute employee goal setting.
11. Introduce error cause removal.
12. Give recognition for meeting and exceeding goals.
13. Establish quality councils.
14. Do it over again.

Thus TQM puts the customer first and covers the whole organization and provides for service level agreements such that all contribute to quality.

In measuring quality cost and the price of non-conformance, a number of costs are included:

- prevention costs;
- appraisal costs;
- internal failure costs;
- external failure costs.

To help TQM and any quality system, there are the standards set by ISO 9000 and BS 5750, both of which require that there are company quality manuals, procedures manuals and work instructions and specifications and specified detailed methods for performing work activities. ISO 9000 is designed to suit a particular company's needs and therefore, although there are basic standards, generally the quality system can be made as complex or as simple as the situation demands or management requires.

There are Regional, National and European Quality Awards. Entry provides independent assessment of the business against models recognized to deliver sustainable success.

LOGISTICS

A major part of operations is the delivery of the final product to the end customer. This may be delivered direct or may go through a chain including wholesalers and retailers before reaching the final customer. In each case companies these days want to have influence over the best logistics for their particular product. Arjo Wiggins, for example, organizes its transport from the factory not just by the day but at a particular time. JIT deliveries from Bertrand Faure Seating are timed to within a 15-minute delivery window. TNT Express Deliveries has introduced its perfect transaction process, the six components of which are:

- to collect an assignment on time;
- deliver it in perfect condition;
- deliver it on time;
- deliver it with a fully completed delivery note, including the name of the recipient, date and time;
- send an accurate invoice to the customer;
- receive payment at TNT on time.

MAINTENANCE

CCL Custom Manufacturing and United Distillers have both achieved considerable benefits using the concept of total productive maintenance (TPM). In this, maintenance is carried out by all employees who are appropriately trained through small group activities. TPM is defined as 'maintenance management which recognizes the importance of reliability, maintenance and economic efficiency in plant design' and has five goals:

- Improve equipment effectiveness.
- Achieve autonomous maintenance on three levels – repair, prevention, improvement.
- Plan maintenance.
- Train all staff in relevant maintenance skills.
- Achieve early equipment management.

Both CCL Custom Manufacturing and United Distillers have improved the performance of their production lines by ensuring that individuals on the line can carry out simple maintenance tasks themselves and recognize when things are likely to go wrong or have gone wrong and so pre-empt larger problems. They have considerably reduced time to repair and time between failures and so achieved a reduction in total downtime.

SECTION THREE

DEVELOPING INFRASTRUCTURE AND RESOURCES

CHAPTER SEVEN

Improving Business Information

John Dempster

Many years ago Peter Drucker wrote a book about the 'Age of Information'. Currently there is an explosion of information: some 30,000 new books are published every year; we shall soon be able to view hundreds of different TV channels; newsagents stock hundreds of magazines and with the Internet, there is a further boost to the exponential growth of information, with millions of pages accessible from a simple PC. There is no shortage of information but there are opportunities for improving the way information is selected, stored and published so that it will add value to the business. This chapter considers how a consultant would think about this.

INFORMATION AUDIT

Any consultancy study has to start by determining the current situation. The mission statement and the objectives of the company or organization must set the background of such a study and all the subsidiary information must be slotted into these prime requirements.

The audit should start at the top with the Board and be directed in the light of the Board's responsibilities and objectives. Questions include:

- What information does the Board receive and issue?
- Where is it stored?
- How is it presented?
- When do members receive or issue it?
- Who produces it?
- What is the cost and the value of that information?

There will be a mixture of written, oral and pictorial information. There will be circumstances when Board members receive a wad of papers 10 cm thick and others where there is just a single-sheet agenda and all information is given to the Board verbally or visually. The right answer is the one that enables the information to add the greatest value to the business.

The audit should be carried out with the Pareto principle in mind. This implies that 20 per cent of the information is likely to add 80 per cent of the value. Thus time can be saved by examining closely only those items which are likely to have most effect – for example, information about sales, costs, staff, cash, capital investment, business opportunities and threats.

Such an audit should then be cascaded down through the organization from the Board to Board members and the staff in their departments. At each level it is necessary to ask the same questions as were asked of the Board, but it can be helpful to express the question as one of need. Who needs what information, why, how, where, when and at what cost, and what benefit will the business or organization receive?

Even a cleaner needs information about what to do, how and when and to what standard of quality. The information does not have to be written but the cleaner has to be able to confirm his or her understanding.

When John Reeve joined Willis Corroon, an international insurance broking company, as executive chairman he said that he spent hours trying to draw inferences or trends from the first set of reports he received but found they were 'a wall of numbers'. He was receiving pages and pages of numbers in which important information was buried. He needed a more focused, visual commentary with bullet points warning of adverse trends and raising issues and questions. He needed to be aware not of what had happened but what was likely to happen so that the Board could act to seize opportunities and counter threats.

It has become almost a cliché that data are not the same as information. But – despite being a cliché – it is true.

Sometimes management information systems are – instead – called decision support systems. This is of value, because it encourages information to be valued in terms of its function rather than simply its existence.

IMPROVING THE UTILIZATION OF INFORMATION SOURCES

Internal network

Most information used regularly in an organization comes from internal sources. Much of it is well known to all staff but it is surprising how much can be hidden away secretly from colleagues, not necessarily deliberately but rather because 'nobody has asked'.

The first objective should be to improve the use of this internal information network, for example by the following.

Signposting/information maps

An information map describes where information of any kind can be found. It can be single level with sources of all information listed or it can be multilevel with access restricted to certain levels for security reasons. The map can show where information is stored in all its different forms, from books, data sheets and computer data to individual people.

Gatekeepers

These people have the task of acting as pointers to the information. They know where the information is kept and how to access it. Sometimes, they themselves will be the repository of the information. The informal system of 'gatekeepers' is used by many companies in preference to the more formal information map. Any successful company will have a mixture of both.

Audit trail

Anyone who has used a computer or filing system knows how files can get lost through misfiling. The audit trail, which shows what has happened to documents or books, can assist this. It may be as simple as booking items out to individuals and keeping a record of that fact.

Intranet

Computers can make the internal information network even more effective through increased access, searching capabilities and links between related areas.

External sources

The internal network will also provide guides and links with the external network that is available through publications, books, magazines, newspapers, television, radio, teletext, etc. Currently there is an explosion of information available on Web sites and through digital radio and television. Information providers such as libraries have made searching for books easier by cataloguing their stock on computer. Specific information on companies can be determined from Extel, Reuters and Dun & Bradstreet or from the company's own Web site. These sources will be useful for carrying out desk research internally. Specialist research companies are available to provide information quickly from specialist databases, eg Companies House, patent searches. Several professional organizations provide a specialist search service free to members on their management information database, as do several other societies, business school libraries and universities.

Conferences and exhibitions

Information can also be obtained from attending conferences or exhibitions, which can provide an efficient means of keeping up to date through meeting and listening to experts and establishing contacts that can be added to the external network as a source of information.

Internet

More and more people are now using the Internet as a source of information. It has the advantage of enabling searches for the precise information to be done from one's desk. The various search engines enable worldwide searches of databases. Specific sites related to newspapers and broadcasters give up-to-date and past news sorted for a specific topic. Many companies and organizations have their own sites, which can be readily checked for information about a customer, supplier or competitor. It requires expertise and practice to use this service efficiently but it is undoubtedly the important source of information of the future.

IMPROVING INFORMATION STORAGE AND RETRIEVAL

A major decision for every manager in an organization is what should be kept and how. Looking in any organization's filing cabinets or computer files, copies of the same document will be found filed in many places by different people. A memo sent to four people will be filed by the sender and the four recipients. Papers sent out to a committee will be kept by all the committee members. Enormous savings of space can be achieved by having easy central access to files. One example is the government in Guernsey, where considerable savings were made through the establishment of a central archive service, which stored all archive material and offered a 24-hour retrieval service. Most departments were pleased to pass files to this service, which sorted them for duplicates and backed them up on microfiche. Substantial storage space was released and files 'lost' for years became available again and were securely stored.

Computer storage and retrieval can provide central storage and rapid access for much filing currently done manually. This can only happen if all staff have the same access to the system that they do to their filing cabinets and they have a positive attitude to using the computer. Enormous amounts of paper can be produced if each user insists on printing documents for easier reference. The further benefit from computer storage is that the system is regularly backed up so that records are not lost. The cost of computer storage is reducing as better optical storage becomes available and hard disks hold more data, and it can be envisaged that the need for paper files will steadily dwindle. A reliable computer system is needed if staff are to have the confidence to relinquish paper files and rely almost completely on computer records; some finance businesses have already achieved this.

Any system of filing, whether in libraries, filing cabinets or computers, has the same characteristics. It provides a cascade of categories going from the general to the particular until it identifies one specific item. The larger the number of people using the system, the more formalized it must become. Thus the ISBN system for books is used by libraries, bookshops and publishers internationally although each library may supplement it with its own catalogue system.

Because the objective of any filing system is to be able to retrieve material readily, it must be designed to suit the prime user. Usually it will categorize by main, sub and further subsidiary categories. In designing the system it is necessary to include a simple way of adding new categories at any level and for archiving material. Some systems just archive all files at the end of the year and start new files. This is simple and cost effective but it does mean that old files that may not be needed are kept. On a computer system or in a manual file it may be valuable to note the 'life' of the document on it when it is filed. This enables documents to be removed from the manual or computer system readily by junior staff as a matter of routine.

Where masses of information are stored, inevitably information will be lost, often through misfiling or because the searcher is not using the right categories – looking for Van Gogh instead of Gogh, van. Data mining, using fuzzy logic, can help to find lost information filed on computer and it is possible to search for words in documents or document titles or for keywords. This is an added advantage of filing on computer – retrieval can be more efficient.

Finally, the best information is that which is clearly visible. A pile of finished stock, a fishbowl full of defective parts, an empty storage bin, all give information efficiently, as part of the job, and more effectively than any stock record.

IMPROVING INFORMATION ANALYSIS

Many tools are now available to assist with the analysis of information.

Databases

Databases can be rapidly designed for collecting together numerical data and written information in a form which enables, for example:

- a list to be prepared of the articles available on 'information' giving not just the title, author and publication but the article itself;
- a list of all the salesmen and their sales for the last month;
- the number of people of a certain age who buy a particular product.

Many of the databases can be purchased 'off the shelf' for specific purposes such as accounts, daily diary, personnel records. These can also be modified to suit a particular need or a database program can be used to design a tailored database.

Most consultants will use databases to help in the collection and analysis of information.

Spreadsheets

Spreadsheets have developed into a powerful system for analysing numerical information and preparing 'what if' scenarios. They can be used simply for adding up a matrix of numbers or for more complex calculations since they allow a full range of mathematical, statistical and financial functions to be used. A simple use might be for product costing. The current costs are set out on the spreadsheet and can be added automatically to give the sub assembly and total costs. By including, in the sheet, a factor for each element of cost relating to inflation, it can be possible to adjust the total cost for inflation by altering just the inflation figure on the spreadsheet. Different inflation figures can be introduced for labour and materials or the calculation can be more complex depending on the situations expected.

A spreadsheet can be used for budgeting and forecasting for the financial results of the business as a whole so that profits or cash flow can readily be calculated for different levels of sales and cost.

Graphs

Both spreadsheet and database programs allow for the calculation and presentation of information in graphical form. It is easy to produce bar charts, pie charts and simple graphs from the data available – see Figure 7.1 for examples.

Although computers can readily produce graphs, there is psychological benefit for team working to arrange for the team leader to draw graphs by hand as new information becomes available. This can strongly reinforce the sense of progress.

Charts

There are a number of computer programs that enable charts to be produced and presented in a very acceptable form. These include

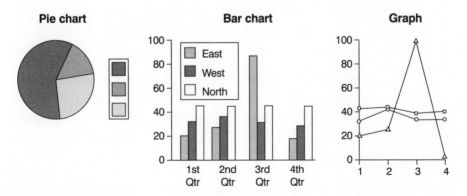

Figure 7.1 Graphs

organization charts, network diagrams and flow charts. These can be valuable to the consultant in understanding, communicating and analysing systems and processes when carrying out business process re-engineering, work study, method study or value analysis.

IMPROVING THE PRESENTATION OF INFORMATION

Information is collected and analysed for control, decision or development. Unless it helps in these applications it is useless.

Overload

Most managers currently suffer from information overload. It has been estimated that over 60 per cent of mail, faxes and e-mail are junk – unsolicited mail or information that was not needed. Thus managers have become skilled at recognizing what could be valuable quickly and rejecting the rest. The best examples of this come from the media. Journalists receive hundreds of press releases and can only publish stories based on a few. Thus in writing a press release to attract the journalist's attention, it is important to ensure that the title is clear and eye-catching and that the first 25 words set out the story in brief. It should be the same for managers. Information should be presented with a clear title and brief précis of the nub of the contents. Such presentation can ensure that the communication is understood and, if valuable, read.

Information cascade

Information can best be presented as a cascade with a brief summary at the start supported by more detailed information if it is needed and further detail as required. In many cases it may only be necessary to present the brief summary and allow further information to be called for if needed.

Thus for control purposes a one-word report 'OK' may be adequate as the summary. For sales, a graph will be better than figures for reporting a trend. A photograph will show off a new model better than a description.

Timeliness

Information for control or decision needs to be issued in time to have effect. Feedback for some information can be immediate – machine breakdown for the machine minder, today's sales for the salesperson – but it can take longer to provide the same information to managers. Providing rapid feedback is a matter of organization. Accounts for the month can be issued the day after the end of the month providing entries are made daily, books are closed at the end of the month, and there is a standard report with few comments required. In achieving speed, one may have to sacrifice some accuracy since there is unlikely to be time for minor corrections.

Timeliness of accounts was benchmarked in 1998 through the Coopers & Lybrand Pan European benchmark study. This showed that the top performers achieved the following:

Time to produce monthly accounts	1 day
Time to produce period end performance reports	<4 days
Period from start of budget preparation to final budget approval	<1 month
Period from year end to finalization of audited statutory accounts	<1 month

Decision making

Most decisions have to be based on incomplete information either because the information is not available or there is not time to collect it. It can also result from the attitude: 'I know what I want to do, don't confuse me with the facts!' The Pareto Principle can be applied effectively in this decision process which should ensure that:

- the information is available that will have the most effect on the decision;
- as far as possible it is known what information is missing or incomplete;
- any estimating system used is mathematically, logically and statistically sound, eg a sampling method.

Where decisions have to be taken at meetings, careful planning is required for the best decision to be reached. Members of the meeting need:

- *To understand the subject on which they are asked for a decision.* To achieve this may require no more than a statement of the subject matter in the agenda, but it may require a report or even a series of reports, meetings with experts or meetings on site. Even then members of the meeting will have different perceptions of the subject. Pictures, graphs and charts will be valuable aids to understanding most subjects.

- *To understand and agree the objectives of the decision.* This may be defined in the objectives of the organization or may require detailed written definition. It may be easy or may be impossible to agree the objectives, and meeting members may have 'hidden agendas'. The attempt should nevertheless be made.

- *To appreciate the range of possible decisions that are available.* Usually the range can be narrowed to three or four options. These should be spelt out in such a way that it is possible for the meeting to amend the decisions if necessary. This requires careful drafting of the original options.

- *To select the best decision.* The best decisions are usually made where the meeting accepts as a whole one of the options proposed. This assumes that the options have been carefully thought through before the meeting.

At some meetings decisions are made on the basis of the views of one or two people who are supported by the rest as 'people who know best'. Sometimes at such meetings the expert 'who actually does know best' keeps quiet.

The chairperson plays an important role in ensuring that options are fully considered, all members take part and the final decision is agreed by the meeting and is workable.

IMPROVING ACCOUNTING

Presentation of annual report

Annual reports showing the accounts and the achievements of the company over the past year are vital for influencing all the communities of concern to a company or organization. A single report can never be expected to satisfy the whole audience. At least three can be required:

1. *The main report* which is directed at the major shareholders and major lenders. This will include the accounts detailed in accordance with the latest statutory requirements and a narrative which sets out the achievements of the company over the past year and the trends over five years. It should also give a forecast of the future for at least one year ahead with the objective of encouraging

major investors and lenders to have confidence in the company's future.

2. A *summary report* which is included in the main report but should also be able to stand alone and be sent to all minor shareholders with the option to request the full report. The summary should best be presented so that the first page shows the major facts.

3. A *report for local communities* should present how the business is benefiting the community through providing employment, assisting with social programmes (arts, sports, charities etc) and improving the environment. This requires a separate report with emphasis on those matters that are of interest to the community rather than on the financial accounts. All organizations can benefit from support from the local communities they serve. At worst they can attract a higher standard of job applicant; at best it may mean that a planning or grant application is received favourably.

The annual reports should be designed to reflect the image of the company. A glossy booklet may be appropriate for a bank but not for a small charity. It should include pictures, especially of the people in the organization who will be of interest to the reader and of any major new projects or successful programmes. Results should be presented graphically as well as in figures.

IMPROVING FINANCIAL CONTROL

Much of the information in a business is on financial matters. The provision of finance is discussed in more detail in Chapter 10. In this section we consider financial information and some of its uses.

Processing sales and purchases

The majority of businesses and organizations, even small ones, now use computers to process sales and purchases. Most are able to use 'off the shelf' programs, many of which will now accept electronic input and provide electronic output that is acceptable to debtors or creditors. Greatest efficiency is being achieved by those organizations that are able to use e-mail or electronic data interchange for input, output and processing. The best examples of electronic input come from retailing, where bar codes are read automatically, an invoice is made out, payment is registered, cash received recorded and data collected for invoicing credit card companies and banking cash. The system is also connected into stock records so that purchasing can be managed as well and some systems connect into suppliers.

Greater efficiencies achieved in this area enable stocks and stockouts to be reduced, so increasing return on capital and raising sales volume, apart from the reduction in overhead costs from increased efficiency in dealing with sales, purchases and stocks.

Credit control

There is legislation to ensure more prompt settlement of debts. It might be thought that this would solve the problems of late payment. At present every firm has the option of including payment terms as part of the sales contract which is enforceable by law. Many firms already have, in their contracts, arrangements for discounts for rapid payment or penalties for late payment. Most companies honour these contracts but some do not. Some organizations, as a matter of policy, always take discounts and never pay charges for late payment. Because such companies are large and valued customers, no supplier takes action even though the matter could be dealt with, in many cases, as a petty debt. In such cases, is action going to be taken under the law?

There will still be a need for good credit control and proper action to collect debts. Many small businesses neglect this area. There are simple rules that can make a big difference to cash flow:

- Check out the creditworthiness of potential customers.
- Agree terms and conditions of business in writing.
- Give extended payment terms reluctantly.
- Maintain accurate records.
- Send invoices out promptly.
- Send monthly statements out to arrive on the first day of the month.
- Send reminders of payment automatically to arrive on the day payment is overdue.
- Have a clear, automatic system for chasing late payments.
- Develop relationships with customers' staff.
- The request for a decision to take the matter to court should be raised by staff automatically so that the appropriate person can decide the action to be taken.
- Having decided to start court action, arrange for the solicitor to send a letter and carry the matter through to court, if necessary, to obtain settlement.

The worry of credit control can be transferred to another company by factoring debts. The charge made by the factor covers the cost of collection and interest on the sum involved. Debt factoring releases capital which may be very valuable for an expanding company with a high level of profitability. Professional help in collecting debts can be obtained from a business such as the Credit Protection Association (CPA) which offers a range of debt recovery and credit management services. One option is to sell the debt to them for 85 per cent of its value.

Credit checking can be done through a number of agencies, eg Dun & Bradstreet, Standard & Poor's, a clearing bank or businesses that trade with the customer.

Control of assets

Many companies have worthless assets on their books that cost money to maintain and also have valuable assets that are not earning their keep. A regular survey of the organization's assets is needed on the 'ABC' system, where important, valuable or expensive assets are classified as 'A' and reviewed frequently and in detail and the cheap, least important assets are reviewed at regular intervals with a simple system. Thus washers in manufacturing, postcards in a museum shop and copy paper at a bank may be reviewed annually by the local manager while the buildings, any rental and maintenance costs will be checked at least annually by a director.

Take-overs occur because assets are not being fully used and a full review of assets can enable the current management to realize unused assets or examine ways in which they can increase the return on the assets they retain.

An asset which management sometimes seem to ignore is cash. A business that holds a great deal of cash is inevitably ripe for a take-over since most business people would expect to be able to achieve a greater return than can be gained from holding cash on deposit.

Interpretation of accounts

Accounts have to be examined in the light of any qualifications by the auditors and the notes given to the accounts. Note should also be taken of the purpose for which the accounts have been prepared: management control, annual financial return, tax, and the accounting system used: FRS3 or SSAP6. Each is likely to give different results which are appropriate to the purpose or rules.

Important ratios used in interpreting accounts are shown in Appendix 1.

MANAGEMENT ACCOUNTS

Improved control

Budgets

Budgets not only provide the opportunity for closer control of the business but also the opportunity to give greater freedom to managers and empower staff. The process of creating the budgets gives the key to empowerment. Budgets should be built up by a reverse cascade based on general instructions given by the Board, starting with junior staff whose budgets are approved by their supervisors before being consolidated for presentation and approval by their managers and so on to Board level. These budgets are then reviewed by the Board and revisions that are needed fed back to staff so that they can amend their budgets accordingly. Ideally this iterative process will produce an agreed budget to which all are committed and within which all staff have the authority to operate.

Budgets can be fixed or variable. Fixed budgets generally relate to those costs or incomes that are unlikely to vary during the period, such as most overhead costs and rental income. Variable budgets may be set for items that are likely to change, such as costs and income directly related to sales.

Zero-based budgeting

Zero-based budgeting is a valuable approach for all costs but especially for overhead costs. In this approach the assumption is that the cost could be eliminated (reduced to zero) and any budget for a zero-based item must be justified afresh. There is always a tendency in all budgeting systems to take last year's figures and add 'something for inflation'. Zero-based budgeting attacks this unquestioning approach and has been adopted by many award-winning companies.

Controllable costs

Managers will have some costs that they can actively control – controllable costs – and others which are outside their control – uncontrollable costs. An objective of any organization will be to structure itself such that all costs are controllable and a manager is designated to have responsibility for controlling each cost. Many organizations will spread overheads arbitrarily over departments so that – for example – a sales manager is allocated 20 per cent of the central cost of computing. This may be valuable in ensuring that this cost is included in calculating the sales price but from a control point of view it is not valuable unless the sales manager can buy the computing from the central service and is able to refuse their offer of supply and buy elsewhere. For this reason, and the problem of finding and retaining skilled staff, many companies are now looking to outsource their central computing so that managers can actively manage their use of central resources.

Non-financial measures

Accountants tend to concentrate on the financial aspects of control. However, it is valuable to include in the armoury many non-financial measures such as 'quality', cycle time, productivity, customer satisfaction etc. Management accounting information tends to be backward looking, telling managers what has happened rather than providing clear indications of what will happen. Some of the non-financial measures can be effective indicators of the action that needs to be taken to avoid a downward trend in financial results. Measures of customer satisfaction and quality can be valuable for many companies.

John Reeve of the international insurance broking company Willis Corroon told *Management Today* that a full array of non-financial indicators might show, for example, that productivity in sales is tailing off. He said non-financial measures let you get behind the numbers more explicitly so that you can get on top of problems earlier and take action to overcome them.

Balanced scorecard

A 'balanced scorecard' is the combination of financial and non-financial figures. This defines what management means by 'performance' and clarifies whether or not the desired results are being achieved. It takes the mission and/or vision statements and translates them into a comprehensive set of performance measures that can be quantified or objectively appraised. Generally the measures will include:

- financial performance, including, for example, sales, costs, return on capital, cash flow;
- customer performance, including, for example, market share, customer satisfaction, customer loyalty;

- internal business process performance, including, for example, productivity, quality, timeliness;
- innovation performance, including, for example, percentage revenue from new products, employee suggestions, index of improvement;
- employee performance, including, for example, morale, turnover, use of best practice.

Building a balanced scorecard takes the following steps:

- Establish the organization's vision and strategy.
- Identify the performance categories to link the vision to results, for example the categories given above.
- Develop effective measures establishing both short-term milestones and long-term targets.
- Ensure acceptance of the measures across the organization.
- Create appropriate budgeting, measurement and reward systems.
- Collect and analyse performance data and compare actual with target.
- Take action to close unfavourable gaps.

The balanced scorecard should include critical success factors, which are measures that management considers must be achieved for the organization's vision to be attained. By defining these separately, management's attention can be focused on the most important results to achieve.

Improved basis for decision making

Evaluation of capital projects

There are several approaches to evaluating capital projects. The most commonly used are payback, accounting rate of return (ARR) and discounted cash flow (DCF).

Payback
This system is popular in Japan. It has the advantage of letting management be aware when the cash flow from the investment is likely to have covered the company's expenditure on the capital project. It is useful for seeing when capital will be available for further investment.

Accounting rate of return (ARR)
The payback system deals with cash flows but the accounting rate of return deals with profit and therefore calculates a return on the investment which

can be compared with the company's accounts to see that the return will improve or reduce the business's return on capital. This is valuable information for the shareholder

Discounted cash flow (DCF)

This mathematical approach to assessing capital projects is a popular way of providing justification for an investment decision. It takes account of the value of money over time. It provides a single figure, internal rate of return (IRR) or net present value (NPV), which enables widely different proposals to be compared or for a proposal to be compared with a standard IRR set by the company. It must be remembered, however, that the calculations of the single rate depend on many uncertain assumptions about investment costs, profitability levels and future income and cost flows and inflation rates. Sophisticated approaches to DCF allow uncertainties to be built in. Most spreadsheets provide for DCF calculations, making the system readily accessible.

Cost–volume profit analysis

A graph showing the sales and costs plotted against units produced can be useful in understanding and communicating the variation of profit with volume (Figure 7.2). The graph can be plotted as a break-even chart where costs and sales are plotted as two separate lines against volume: the break-even point is where the two lines cross and the fixed costs are shown where the cost line cuts the vertical axis. Alternatively the graph can be plotted as a profit–volume graph where profit is plotted against volume: the fixed costs are shown as a negative amount

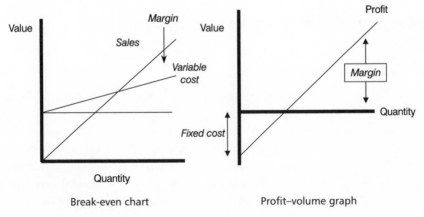

Figure 7.2 Plotting break-even and profit–volume

on the vertical axis and the break-even point comes when the line crosses the horizontal axis.

Both graphs are valuable in assessing the sensitivity of profit to volume changes and the effect of variation in fixed or variable costs or price.

Absorption costing

In absorption costing, the costs of products are calculated from the direct costs to which are added the overhead costs allocated (on a fairly arbitrary basis) in proportion to the labour hours, the material cost or the production area used in the manufacture of the product. Pricing decisions can then be based on the 'total cost'. This system has the advantage that it covers all the expenses of the business and ensures that the income covers total costs provided the volume of sales is achieved. If this system is used alone for calculating prices, it can result in products being under- or over-priced. This is because overheads have not been allocated accurately to each product.

Marginal costing

Marginal costing calculates the cost of producing one additional unit. This can be valuable in determining the minimum cost at which a product can be sold to provide a contribution to overheads. The assumption is made, however, that overhead costs are fixed. In fact if production increases substantially then overhead costs are also likely to rise. Marginal costing is valuable for an expanding company which can increase sales and profits by reducing prices.

Activity-based costing (ABC) and activity-based management (ABM)

Activity-based costing (ABC)

In activity-based costing the components of cost and the drivers of cost variability are identified. It is used to: 1) determine how cost can be reduced by decreasing the cost of an activity or decreasing the number of activities per unit of output, and 2) re-price products and optimize new product design, since managers can analyse product profitability more accurately through the combination of activity-based cost data with price information. Understanding cost drivers allows the design of new products to be optimized.

To carry out activity-based costing it is necessary to work with staff who incur the costs to:

- establish the key activities performed – for example, materials handling, machining, order processing;
- establish the cost drivers for each activity – number of parts for material handing, number of pieces machined, number of orders;
- group overhead and other indirect costs by activity and identify drivers;
- collect data on how the demands by product and customer affect activities;
- assign cost to products and customers based on their usage of activities.

Because the system requires managers to look at their work and break it down into several activities, costing is carried out in more detail. By defining drivers that really do correlate to the activity, costs are determined more accurately and managers can see more clearly how costs may be reduced through eliminating activities or by product redesign.

Activity-based management (ABM)

Activity-based costing forms the basis for activity-based management and links into business process re-engineering. By defining activities, it is possible to reorganize management to ensure that individuals have control over particular activity costs so that one person can be responsible for continuous improvement for an activity. Using the greater detail available, operational planning can be improved to achieve a greater return from the available resources.

As well as cost for each activity, one calculates the performance for each activity in terms of quality, elapsed time and human resources.

Substantial improvements have been made by some banks through the use of ABM to look at whole processes from the customer's point of view. An analysis of mortgage applications, for example, showed that applicants were required to write out their address several times and even asked seven times for their account number. Customer satisfaction was improved by rewriting procedures to avoid asking for the same information twice.

At one time it took one bank 10 days to replace a lost credit card. The ABM analysis was completed and the bank asked why a job that takes three minutes to do took 10 days to perform. The elapsed time of 10 days has now been cut to overnight.

The simple task of answering letters was analysed and it was determined that three of the four days required to answer a letter were taken up by the Post Office. Saving a day on posting gives a significant improvement. Fax or e-mail would be even better.

Step change improvements can come from both ABC and ABM, which both seem still to be in their infancy.

CHAPTER EIGHT

CONSULTING APPROACHES TO INFORMATION TECHNOLOGY

David Jefferson

Why is it that some organizations use computing and communications technologies to great effect and others don't? Some organizations just seem to know how to recognize the opportunities, avoid the pitfalls and get the best from the information technologies on offer. Others don't. Why? This chapter is about helping you to bring IT success to your organization.

Companies both large and small have been using IT for many years. Case studies of successes and failures form interesting patterns. In organizations which have experienced significant IT failures there may be many causes, but most interesting is the fact that in the management team there are abnormally high levels of fear, uncertainty and doubt on the subject of IT. Not a surprise? Possibly, but what about the successful use of IT? In companies that succeed with IT, it is not in a particularly elevated position and there is little reverence for systems. When you study management attitudes to IT in these businesses you find understanding, comfort, acceptance. There is also a very positive attitude towards a future of continuous and sometimes uncontrolled change that comes with a high level of dependence on IT.

So why should companies seek the help of a consultant on this matter of using IT? In most cases they understand their business well and manage all its resources successfully. They probably manage their IT resources on a very professional basis as well. Perhaps the top team becomes aware that they are some distance off the mark in using the emerging information technologies to best effect. Perhaps they need help in identifying what needs to be on the IT agenda.

Perhaps the top team are also seeking someone who can manage a project, marshal the appropriate resources, bring along the latest knowledge, inject examples of success formulae from previous clients, and establish the vision of how IT should be used in the business.

If you are to provide consultancy support in the area of IT, you might help an organization by:

- identifying where IT might be best applied – ie what should be on the IT agenda;
- ensuring the technology used is appropriate, and the budget adequate;
- enabling the implementation of that agenda within the context of the business.

These are different tasks, which in large organizations might be handled by consultants with specialist expertise in each.

In this chapter we will explore each of these areas in turn. We should be clear that we are discussing business issues and tools for enabling your organization to handle the matter of using IT effectively. We are not attempting to cover material on the management of an IT department nor what systems or technologies are particularly good investments. Any statement we might make in these areas would be out of date by the time it was in print!

For most organizations, technology is not the problem, but the danger is that the complexity of information technology obscures the real issues. As with any change, you need a vision of how things might be, a means of creating a state of readiness for the change, and the resources to make it happen.

DEVELOPING AN IT AGENDA

The IT agenda derives from both remedial and developmental imperatives. The remedial agenda is about 'keeping up'; the developmental agenda is about utilizing IT to achieve significant competitive advantage.

Remedial agenda

Changes in IT, other technologies, and markets will present the organization with opportunities to change its systems, or upgrade existing systems. In IT, for example, there may be greater functionality on offer, or more efficient operation that can justify the expense of making the move to a replacement system. There will be an expectation that the benefits of installing a new system will show a net return. Straightforward cost–benefit justifications are to be welcomed, but much IT change is less clear-cut. These might arise as follows.

Functional

The organization is developing its business and finds that an IT application is no longer capable of handling all the tasks required of it. Something new is needed, perhaps with different and probably greater functionality. A failure to make the replacement will constrain development.

Technology-driven

A system meets the need, but the developer brings out a new version of the software with better performance and functionality, or computer or communications hardware is announced giving better performance. The system is therefore technically obsolete but continues to meet your needs, while a replacement system would do so at a higher standard of performance.

Supportability

The organization is using a system that has been superseded some time ago, but newer versions have added features that would add nothing to the business. The developer has declared that the obsolete system will no longer be supported. Using an unsupported system may have business risks, but they are very difficult to quantify. Companies with mature IT experience generally do not allow themselves to remain dependent on unsupported system versions.

Speed and efficiency

The system is performing to your requirements but new releases promise improved processing.

Old-fashioned

The systems have not received regular investments and the latest equivalents have a new look and feel. There is evidence that staff are uncomfortable with out-of-date systems, and have become concerned that the organization is not providing the most appropriate systems for their work.

Developmental agenda

The remedial agenda leads to areas where IT will contribute to better performance and profitability. Efficiencies and slightly improved systems will change the business in modest ways, and the benefits are worth the investment. But the key to securing major gains or competitive advantage is only to be found in some completely new activity or a major restructuring of activities from the present organization. The developmental agenda depends upon the construction of a new vision of the business.

Success stories

There has been considerable change in IT since the mid-1980s when it began to emerge as a driving force in its own right. New technologies and new economics of systems use made new ways of working possible. Sometimes the old ways became obsolete without warning. Companies with no noticeable IT problems suddenly lost out to a competitor who exploited some new technologies, created new opportunities, and established new ways of working. One company's obsolescence is another company's success story. The sad thing is that the losers are unaware that the battle is lost on the day they discover the battle has started. This pattern has been repeated throughout the 1990s.

Devastating changes in competitive position have been known and are the legends of management consultants' presentations. Typically they work for one type of business and at one point in time. The successes themselves do not generalize well except to serve as a lesson that IT is changing the economics of many types of business processes. In general, huge opportunities are there for the innovative and the courageous driven by an entrepreneurial insight.

The competitive advantage applications exist, but you need to be ready on the day. Being in the right place at the right time plays a big part in this sort of dramatic success. Success stories are told and retold with different emphases depending on the point of view of the raconteur. For the 21st century, management must retain the clear view that these are examples of business insight and business success, not simply IT success.

Making your own luck with IT

If yesterday's success stories are anything to go by, the luck was on the side of management teams with an experimental attitude to IT.

Companies not likely to see much luck may be in stable businesses with little competition and little need for IT. Where that is true today there will be a solid basis for management believing that nothing important is happening in IT which is relevant to them. That security can be shattered by an IT change exploited by a competitor. An organization that is continuously looking at its industry and the IT elements of its business will walk into the opportunities.

So making your luck means being 'out and about' in your thinking and in your business contacts:

- What are the latest success stories?
- What are companies in your industry doing?
- What is the typical IT spending level for your competitors?
- What do IT suppliers recommend you should buy?
- What success stories do suppliers share with you?
- What are clever users of IT talking about doing?
- What technologies are just a little bit too expensive?

Relate this back to your business and regularly work to visualize what would happen following a major economic movement in IT kit prices. Find some budget to experiment with the opportunities that aren't quite there yet. That's where you will find the key to the transformation of your business.

Formulating a developmental agenda

The key to real competitive advantage lies in doing something the business has never done before. The inspiration for this probably lies outside the traditional business framework.

Consultants often have an advantage in moving the systems thinking 'outside the box', as they are not emotionally attached to existing ways. A consultant has no desire to maintain the status quo, preserve jobs of favoured employees, or make assumptions that whatever has been done for years must be good because it has stood the test of time. When you seek new solutions outside the box there is a need to build a new kind of open-mindedness into your search.

This means both challenging conventional wisdom and assumptions about the business, and understanding what current information technologies can do. In practice, you can do this by bringing together a mixed team, setting terms of reference so that this is seen as a business visioning exercise.

Visioning exercises should become a regular part of your business thinking processes. Pose a question like: 'Where could you find a new revenue stream and develop it using a transformation of the present organization?' With this start point a study group can explore, synthesize a vision and report back. Another starting point might be: 'How can our cost/value structure be changed to give a better gross margin?' It will take many exercises before anything major arises. Senior management needs to manage the focal point of each exercise by posing a question or brief. One such question, which did produce results, was: 'How can we change the product so that the customer is locked to us for subsequent purchases?'

SUPPORTING THE IT AGENDA

Maintaining the IT agenda

Once formulated, the IT agenda must be regularly reviewed and kept up to date.

At the very least the organization will need one person charged with maintaining a general awareness of progress in relevant IT sectors. This is likely to be a senior person in the IT function. A second observer role should be assigned to management to report on activities of competitors or organizations in similar industries.

At the time of the annual planning cycle, IT resources should be specifically reviewed in relation to the reports of observers. Projects should be set out for the following year with terms of reference and budget.

Planning IT change

Organizations need not react to each and every aspect of IT change; a selective response when major changes occur may be sufficient. This could result in an overall lower cost of IT than that experienced by organizations which unnecessarily respond to each new IT opportunity.

But there are dangers in being purely reactive. IT strategies of this type are at best survivalist in thinking and defensive in attitude, and with the present high rate of change and innovation, they should be considered risky. Organizations following reactive strategies are unlikely to discover applications that have a major impact on their competitive position. There are other related problems, too:

- Reactive organizations often have a low capacity for change. As the rate of change in the environment exceeds the ability of the organization to adjust, it will enter a state of partial obsolescence as a business entity. The risk is that a competitor using a different business model and innovative systems enters the market and is more competitive.
- Policies of minimal change tend to foster attitudes in the management and staff that the organization should stay very much as it is. When change does become necessary it is disruptive, since it runs counter to people's desires and expectations for stability. More time will be needed before staff will work effectively on a change project.
- During periods of change there may also be a high level of intolerance for errors, since the impact of any such miscalculation could bring significant discomfort to some members of staff. If change is being inflicted on unwilling staff, they may be unforgiving when their abilities to do their work are hampered by the teething problems of new systems.

Traditional step change

A more effective strategy than gradual, incremental change is therefore the step change.

This process fits well with consultancy assignments since it has a limited time horizon. It is also ideal where there is negligible environmental change. The new system can be bedded in and then allowed to run for some relatively long time without much further management involvement.

This is how it works. The organization maintains a cursory awareness of the IT environment and its relevance. Projects designed to address specific problems will provide in-depth knowledge in selected areas. This ideally will be sufficient to make the step change in one area and secure the benefits.

The learning value of projects needs to be captured and shared with senior management as each project is completed. These learning projects may be the only input senior management receives on the developing IT environment.

Change management

By contrast, the traditional management consultant's approach to change management occurs in several stages. To appreciate what this means it is necessary to see the procedures of the organization as normally fixed and frozen. The change management process is used to implement new procedures in such a way that they then become the new normal ways of working. This is necessary because people experience great discomfort when trusted elements of their working lives are changed.

1. The first step is to enter into discussions with the staff and indicate to them that there are good reasons for changing the currently established patterns of work. (A consultant would advise working with staff to identify areas where change may have become necessary.) This gives them permission and a framework within which to change procedures that would otherwise remain frozen.
2. The second step is to work with staff to discover and define new and more effective procedures. This second step may take some considerable time and resource. When the second step is nearing completion, the new procedures or systems, or application packages, will be selected. They should then be critically scrutinized before being agreed and implemented.
3. The third step is the process of bedding-in the new procedures, and this may involve modifications. When this is complete, the closing down of the change process can begin. At this point procedures are documented and finally accepted for sign-off by management. They again become frozen and are no longer subject to modification.

This change process can be as easily led by a manager as a consultant. It is, however, important to consider carefully how the learning stages are managed and what provision you make to support it with special studies, projects, training courses and full staff involvement.

Financing the IT agenda

Budgeting

With a planned level of response to technology-driven change it is possible to deal with IT on the basis of what is affordable. For companies needing to maintain IT expenditure at a minimum, a level of between 2 and 8 per cent of turnover can be expected. Management needs to set this level and monitor how it constrains IT investments. The progress of the organization will be constrained as a consequence. This constraint issue is the one to keep in front of management, and a consultant's report would highlight this.

IT as part of the planning process

When your organization began its use of IT, it is very likely that your first exploratory project was an extraordinary item on the business agenda. Perhaps it was a computerized accounting system or your first investment in word processing. You may recall the problem of justification that this raised. In many companies the early IT investments were fraught with difficulty as there was no budgetary provision for IT items of any magnitude. This has resulted in many projects going ahead under-funded. Management may eventually complete the work by cutting corners. This was acceptable in the past when badly managed IT was something an organization could tolerate without adverse consequences for the business.

A few years later, other IT investments made sense and again were handled as projects, or perhaps as capital items, but still looked at by senior management as matters requiring special attention, but then to be retired from the agenda of the top team. During these years the IT budget might have been as little as 1 per cent of the turnover of the business and IT assets might have had a life of 5–7 years. Businesses that make a strategic commitment to IT in order to gain competitive advantage may be spending as much as 10 per cent of annual revenues on IT and expecting to turn over the investment every 3–4 years. Some very simple arithmetic will convince you that this latter situation is not possible without a complete restructuring of the whole financial and trading structure of the business. If this is your business it will be easy to see that your IT strategy is key to your longer-term survival. As a resource management issue, IT now takes its place in the planning process.

Finding the budget for competitive advantage

Wherever you are in your use of IT and your experience of the real costs associated with doing things properly and professionally, you will probably be unhappy about the amount you are now spending. Many companies regard IT as a cost that needs careful control and threatens to erode profitability. While these views prevail, your organization will never find the will to be successful with a competitive advantage investment. Companies struggling to become confident and comfortable with high levels of IT spending sometimes need to employ a management consultant to assist with the planning process. Visioning is an example.

You have discovered a competitive advantage IT application. If you can get it right you put your competition behind you for several years. If you get it wrong you could be out of business. How do you explore this dangerous territory?

Here is a consultant's thinking device for helping a management team find the will and the confidence to reach a decision. Begin by building a model of the business as you expect it to be in five years from now. Build it honestly (assuming success) so that it is a realistic vision of what the business will be when all the problems you now face have been resolved. Position yourselves and your planning team as top management in the new company of your vision. This means making a mental leap to a point where you can accept that you are actually running the business as in the vision. From that vantage point, look back at the journey that brought you to that position. From your position of success, review the problems you have overcome. List them; investigate them; explore how they were solved; identify the most worrying periods and document how the business 'survived'.

Consultants use this method of vision modelling to free the minds of a management team from the debilitating thought of failure. It's a simple device but needs some careful senior management direction. There are many dimensions to this process, and one unfortunate by-product can be the discovery of individuals who may find it difficult to make the journey.

When you return to the world as you know it today, you will have a substantial agenda to work on and you will have some idea about the resources that you will need to make the first steps in a competitive advantage change in the business. When your team can see that the investments are substantial and success in IT is just as important as success in each of the other major areas of the business, the budget will be found.

DEALING WITH THE TECHNOLOGY

Out of the business needs analysis and planning processes comes a statement of areas where IT could be important to the business and possibly give competitive advantage. Before you can begin investing it is necessary to state your plans in terms of systems, technologies and products. It is important to have a good understanding of what is possible in IT.

Building an appreciation of the relevant technologies, matching systems to business needs, and planning the new IT vision is how the task begins. This is your IT strategy. Bringing new assets into operation, and managing system asset integrity and availability are the tasks that realize the benefits for the organization. These are the dimensions of a consultant's approach to assisting a company to take advantage of IT.

An IT overview

The technology issues are rightly seen as the focal point for any IT strategy, and indeed a solid understanding across the board is vital. A problem which most organizations face is acquiring knowledge of what is happening to the thousands of information systems products and technologies. Many of the technologies could have a direct bearing on your organization, but which ones? One might be the basis of an application which brings you major business advantage, but will you be able to recognize it when you see it? How should organizations address such an immense knowledge acquisition task? Few people in the industry are able to cope with the whole of this technology spectrum; it's too big and moving too fast, so what chance do you have?

Let's begin with a few basic ideas. In this overview we will explore how the technologies are evolving, and the management significance of what is happening. It is not our purpose here to attempt to teach you the substance of the technologies themselves. This overview and statement of general trends will give you a starting point. You should then engage in your own learning projects to bring these ideas up to date. One of the key consulting techniques is to focus a learning project on an area which is of genuine importance and do it in depth. Your team can do that too. This will begin a process of maintaining a general level of awareness across the board with in-depth knowledge in specific areas.

General trends

Here are the starting points for understanding this market.

Price/performance

System products, both hardware and software, are offering better price/performance than ever before. In many areas the prices have fallen in absolute terms in recent years. For most companies this means better affordability of systems they need to run their businesses. This is partly technology-driven and partly market-driven. The technology race and the competition that drives it will continue to improve price performance. When new products come out they will be priced high, assuming a conservative uptake. In a buoyant economy the volume of sales will increase as new customers discover that the economics apply to them and prices will ease off a bit. You will hear people advise you to wait until the price comes down. The time to buy is the first point at which the business economics make sense. Waiting for a rock-bottom price will leave your business one or two generations behind.

System deployment economics

The economics of deploying system solutions are changing. The trends are towards better affordability in off-the-shelf systems. In many product sectors there is, however, a proliferation of products. You need a system that will work, and you want to avoid the products that will be withdrawn from the market next year. The products that achieve global-scale marketing are the ones that will be able to deliver the best value offering. Learning which ones will meet your needs takes time, and is expensive. The installation costs may be reasonable but training staff to use the systems properly is not. With increasing costs of skilled staff, the total deployment cost will have only a small systems component. Most of the cost will be in people-related expenditure. This trend is strengthening with increasingly complex systems.

System availability

In the past you may have been comfortable planning to purchase systems, have them installed, and expect them to work without further intervention or investment. Now there is a much higher complexity of the systems in your portfolio and higher levels of sophistication and functionality in the systems you install. This brings with it a cost of staying operational which is going up at an alarming rate. This is the cost of technical support, maintenance, and systems integrity.

In simple terms it is the cost of maintaining your whole IT infrastructure in a state of readiness and full effectiveness. The cost of this on top of operational systems is a significant per-person overhead – it may be as much as 20 per cent loading on the cost of a person at a desk. This is an unavoidable cost one way or another; if you decide not to provide the resource to guarantee availability, you could waste far more while people wait for someone to bring the network back when it falls over.

Half-life of IT knowledge

The attrition pattern we see in the body of IT knowledge occurs in other areas. The concept of a half-life has been very useful in understanding such phenomena and enabling people to formulate strategies to deal with them. The half-life of the body of IT knowledge is the time it takes for half of it to become invalidated. The half-life of IT knowledge gets shorter as the pace of development increases. The disturbing fact is that during the 1990s the half-life of IT knowledge dropped below four years.

What this half-life concept means in practical terms is that you need to somehow re-learn half of what you know about IT every four years! This is difficult because there is no easy way to keep track of which elements of IT have been invalidated. In practice it will mean that you will need to revisit all your areas of IT dependence annually and possibly commission learning and investment projects to assess and possibly replace or upgrade at least 25 per cent of your whole IT investment each year. And this percentage will increase as the half-life of IT knowledge drops.

The learning resource will be a significant IT cost which no organization can afford to disregard. This is a matter of the personal obsolescence of your IT experts and advisors, as well as the attrition of your organizational knowledge pool within the management and staff team. As this latter process takes place, decision-makers will become less comfortable spending money on IT, and your organization will lose its will to maintain the pace of progress. With a half-life of IT knowledge below four years, the budget for constant learning activity and resource will be significant.

Realizing benefits requires management commitment and effort

There is a level of spending that is required in these emerging IT cost areas. There is significant potential benefit in making the investments and operating the systems but management must ensure that the systems are used with discipline and commitment so the benefits are realized in practice. The benefit is the business source of the renewal funding to maintain an appropriate rate of progress. It is inadvisable to drop the full benefit to the bottom line and ignore the future.

Software

Business application software off the shelf is now addressing most areas of system needs. A few years ago, word processor, spreadsheet and accounting packages were the only options, but now the choice is huge and increasing. Prices are affordable and dropping. Boxed products sold on a global scale are likely to have high functionality and low cost. National and regional packages usually have to be sold at higher prices and usually give lower functionality. Smaller developers, however, may be able to offer features that the global market does not require and which are not found in the global product. There may also be the option to commission modifications to suit requirements that are unique to your business.

Two packages with virtually the same functionality may do what you need, one a global package and the other in a customized format. The economic choice will be the boxed product and the trend is to accept what it does or even fit your procedures around its functions. Customizing a system can result in large expenditure and considerable delay. The end result may include special features that access benefits in your operation. Because of the large person-day component in customizing, few organizations can justify the higher (perhaps 200×) price.

Developing software specifically for your needs is not a good investment. This is a statement which has great importance but about which there is some debate. You may have some difficulty reaching consensus in this matter in your organization. Being your own consultant, you may need to facilitate some learning projects.

Finding people who are able to talk openly about their experiences of software development in the real world is difficult. Most business people who advocate bespoke development have the opinion that it is worth paying almost any price to have a system which suits every element of the way you do business and all of your established office procedures.

A feature of today's business is that software packages will define application areas and boundaries. This is a problem for many companies that have evolved an organization based on historical activity groups and possibly the personalities and skills of senior managers. Occasionally there will be implementation problems or even package selection problems arising because there are inherent threats to business divisions as documented in the organization chart.

These issues will need careful senior management handling, especially when the business need analysis indicates certain application functionality groups, and suggests function boundaries which are inconsistent with the packages which happen to be on the market. A common answer from the senior planning team is that the software must be commissioned from the company's IT function or from an outside supplier. Looking at the overall business effectiveness, a consultant would counsel a serious attempt to get the organization to discover the benefits of structuring around the systems that can be purchased and installed rapidly.

Plan your company's IT future

Translating business needs into systems terms is an important process. Start by discovering the real nature of the business; how it is, and how it might be different. Use functional, organizational, value chain, process, and financial models to guide your exploration (as discussed in earlier chapters). Build a portfolio of systems assets and applications, and then design an infrastructure of IT resources needed by your applications and organization as a whole. Note areas of the business where high IT impact might result in high corporate value contribution.

The *applications portfolio* is the documentation for a continuous process of systems asset management. It will be the focal point for system acquisition, maintenance/renewal, and life-cycle management. Initially it may be as modest as a prioritized shopping list. It will grow. This is an extremely powerful thinking and management tool. It provides the documentation and thinking structure for reasoned and realistic investment planning in an uncertain IT world.

When you have drafted your applications portfolio you can begin to think about equipment you will need to run the applications. This is your *IT infrastructure*. This is the 'architecture' of your whole investment in IT resources, showing locations and interconnections.

Few companies start with a blank sheet on these matters. Probably there is old equipment and there are systems which are adequate but which you might not choose today given an unlimited budget. The way forward will be punctuated by problems of compromise.

There may also be questions of providing budget to satisfy all business needs and create the whole IT infrastructure and applications portfolio in one project. Sometimes this is a good investment in order to have the whole infrastructure working together. Mixed infrastructures tend to need more management and may fail unpredictably for undetectable reasons.

The applications portfolio

Each application is an asset, either planned or installed. A typical asset in this portfolio might be the accounts system. Out of the business needs analysis comes a statement of requirements for systems in major functions of the business. Out of the IT marketplace come system possibilities. There will be a need to define the boundaries of the application with reference to the features required by the business, and then in relation to various system options available. Where there is a fit, the asset can be documented.

Such areas where a good fit is likely may come from this list:

- accounts: general ledger, debtors ledger, creditors ledger, order processing, asset management etc;
- budgeting and fiscal planning;
- human resources management, training, staff development; payroll;
- stock management, warehouse, finished goods;
- materials management, stocks;
- manufacturing planning;
- engineering maintenance; vehicle fleet management;
- sales systems, customer database, prospect database;
- e-commerce, quotation systems;
- marketing planning and modelling, campaign management;
- R&D, lab systems, statistical analysis.

Each organization and industry will have its own list, perhaps different from the above, but certainly based on the main sectors of the organization. These applications will be the main information engines of the business. In smaller businesses PC applications will be the norm. For large companies there are likely to be more areas where IT investments might pay back because of scale.

The e-commerce subject requires some enlargement here because of the lack of hard evidence on how to get good returns. This is a competitive advantage area that cannot be ignored. Companies face two types of threat. First, they may invest large amounts on building an e-commerce application and discover that there is no significant trade in their business area (yet). Alternatively, they may decide to avoid the Web unknowns and later discover that someone's e-commerce presence has made a previous business structure or customer-value proposition obsolete. Companies should be clear that e-commerce is not 'optional'; it's a question of 'when?' and 'how?'

There are also applications that go across all functions of the business. When a corporate standard is in place, it is easier for different parts of the organization to work together. Typical applications are:

- word processing;
- spreadsheet systems;

- electronic mail;
- diary and personal organizer/productivity systems;
- fax systems;
- interactive data/information access;
- decision support systems/executive information/MIS;
- graphical/publishing/management report presentation tools;
- telephone systems;
- Internet access;
- internal functions provided by intranet;
- project management, knowledge management;
- network operating systems.

You should compile a list for your organization. Where you have an operational system, you can provide very detailed information about functionality, areas of the business using the system etc.

As you prepare to document your portfolio of existing systems it will become evident that systems themselves are defining boundaries and areas of work. Even departments can be defined in this way. This is natural and sensible where there is a group of activities and data that cannot easily be separated for systems treatment without creating enormous data handling and data ownership/administration questions.

The IT infrastructure

It is tempting to miss out this stage and move straight from business needs analysis to strategic application investments. It is understandable for companies unfamiliar with IT to be impatient to make decisions about buying hardware. It is true that having some hardware standing in a room does give the impression of progress and is good for morale in the early stages. Later in the process you might discover that your ideal system needs hardware you don't have, or you may be faced with some significant unplanned waste. The lesson that emerges from the applications portfolio stage is that the business need is the driver, second comes system application, and finally, hardware/infrastructure appropriate for the whole corporate job.

New systems investments

The make or buy decision has always been a difficult question for the management team. It is true that developing bespoke software is recommended by many consultants, experts in software houses, and vendors of programming languages and rapid development systems. On the basis that there is more work for them to do in this situation, their advice should be given critical consideration. Likewise, a management team can be expected to opt for bespoke development if it feels threatened by changes in working practices following the implementation of a package system.

Someone needs to step back and balance up the issues. In simple terms, the package requires functional and organizational compromise, but works from day one and delivers predictable benefits. Looked at equally simply, the bespoke solution will cost more than planned, will take longer than planned and will not have the functionality planned, but when it works it will be a better fit to the original specification than the package. In theory, a higher benefit stream several years in the future is the realistic expectation. Neither option is a clear 'winner'.

Application compromises

In order to build the first draft of the applications portfolio you will be well advised to state business needs in such a way as to fit within the functions defined by packaged systems that happen to be available and affordable.

This is an important starting point and although it may worry some members of your top team, it is truly a realistic and sensible planning statement. The compromises in some areas may be very large, and the team may find it difficult to commit to achieving proposed savings and productivity gains if an inappropriate system were to be installed. It is important to remember that the applications portfolio is a decision clarification model, and not a specification.

At this stage a consultant might need to bring some outside knowledge and share it with the planning team. This would be in the nature of discussing the management issues surrounding bespoke software development projects and the history and experience of real-world success expectations and achievements.

Organizations whose total staff number less than 250 are probably too small to find the resource to manage bespoke developments or earn back the potential benefits in improved performance. Companies with between 250 and 1,000 need to proceed carefully and those with more than 1,000 employees are probably mature IT users, have experience of many development projects and know what to expect.

As a thinking and planning exercise, however, it is also useful to explore what it would mean to change the way the organization works in order to make an exclusively package-based IT procurement strategy work. Construct your applications portfolio on that basis and then begin the documentation of each application project. As a planning task, this means providing sufficient analysis and thought to enable you to decide which applications to implement urgently and which to leave for a time. Purchase decisions are for later and will be the result of more in-depth investigations and package search.

But, before you order a bespoke system . . .

There are many ways to develop systems that meet specific needs and many claims are made for more recent development methodologies designed to speed up the delivery cycle. There will be occasions when the payback is overwhelming and the need is something that no other business has experienced. The odds, however, are stacked against success. Let's look at the issues:

1. Bringing the system in on time and on budget: There are no statistics, only horror stories.
2. Writing the specification: How do you go about writing the specification? Who has the knowledge? Who has the ability?
3. Securing benefits, savings, paybacks: By what mechanism will the system deliver returns? Will it happen? Who will commit to deliver the payback?
4. The business environment is changing rapidly. If the payback stream starts in 24 months, will the investment be paid off before the system is obsolete?

These are the four issues that have dogged IT projects for years. In recent times item 4 has been the most punishing of the good intentions of clever designers and management teams. In IT it is difficult to predict the conditions that will prevail in three months, never mind in years when the theoretical payback stream completes the cycle.

There are problems arising in specification:

- Current staff who might use the system are using manual procedures and have a tendency to ask for the new system to replicate the way they work now. The specification becomes very elaborate.
- Technical people are usually keen to show their development skills and are inclined to accept the requirement at face value.
- The payback mechanism may never have been tested in an IT

environment so is, at the early stages in the project, a theory. It may not be well understood by either staff or specialists.

- Neither group is well placed to devise new and more effective ways of working based on problems and exceptions they have never seen.
- The specification writing process takes longer than anticipated, with amendments and poor communications between IT specialists and operational staff.

And there are problems in the system delivery process:

- Discussions and clarifications between users and developers cause the specification to evolve as the development stage proceeds. Changes in the environment also force specification changes.
- When the system is delivered, new requirements are recognized which could not be seen at the original design stage. Mark I of the system meets specification but is unworkable.
- Rapid reaction by developers addresses the new specification. Mark II is adequate and is implemented, but the environment has moved on by 12 to 24 months.
- The payback mechanism has changed and new features are built into the system. They work and meet the real needs of users. Mark III is an operational success and payback starts.

This is the sad profile of a project that falls prey to the very human problems of optimism, difficult communication, and cultural differences between builders and operators. It is a difficult situation to avoid.

Selection of an application package

There will be many package selection projects. Given the problems and the long time-scales suggested by a strategy of bespoke development, it's important not to kill the benefits of buying a package by overly elaborate system selection projects. It's important to understand the marketplace in order to guide and manage the selection project as an up-to-date IT consultant would.

The package market encompasses a wide spectrum of prices, package sizes and supply options. The lower priced packages do not have much supplier margin so you can't expect much time with the salesperson explaining and presenting the product. Certainly you will not get enough time to take you through all your decision issues. In this situation the strategy is to short-list the top products and buy one or two to test. Get to the in-house testing stage as quickly as possible. This is an important learning experience.

Budgeting for the IT infrastructure

Sharing information and data around the enterprise and storing it safely is a corporate responsibility; the resources, an infrastructure cost.

Accessing shared corporate data may be part of an applications package (in relation to that subset of the whole data asset of the company), but increasingly companies are turning to corporate solutions for managing and accessing all of the company's data assets. This is an infrastructure issue with an MIS (Management Information System) payback.

Providing the data networking to link desktops and data sources is an infrastructure issue.

Communication amongst employees by e-mail is on the surface an internal infrastructure issue. In fact the issue must be defined more broadly in order to address the real scope of the matter. Communication is now about seamless desk-to-desk communication from each individual employee to any other communication point in the global business community with which you expect to interact. This includes e-mail, fax, data transfer, video conferencing and certain types of voice traffic. It also includes the whole of the Internet issue and e-commerce.

Communication infrastructure for some organizations, particularly with a number of sites, will mean the merging of data and voice.

E-commerce will take hold in the form of a series of customer-facing activities. This will need significant capacity for data transfer and the handling of live customer-oriented communications. There will be a new non-geographic shaping of 'interest based' communities of potential business targets. The scale of the business opportunity will determine the appropriate level of participation and budget and risk.

Some companies will host e-commerce applications within their office networks and connect to the Web through high capacity links. Some e-commerce applications may be hosted close to the communications 'backbone' of the Web. In either case corporate communications needs will have an increasingly large off-site and extra-organizational component.

IT infrastructure in the recent past was as simple as a linking mechanism between desktop PCs and servers, or possibly mid-range processors/servers. The data traffic generated by such configurations was small in relation to the capacities that will be needed when e-commerce develops. The rule with communication, as with desktop processing power, is to be generous. Working to an under-specified architecture today means running the risk of being forced to rebuild before your first investment has paid back.

The skills to handle IT infrastructure and particularly communications matters are often not within the spectrum of knowledge of computing or business applications specialists. The area of communications products and services is a relatively new subject with its own learning curve. Although you may be planning to be your own project manager, you may need to budget for a certain amount of specialist advice on the design and specification of your IT infrastructure.

CONCLUSION

Bringing together the major features of the IT marketplace and knowledge of your trading environment equips you to look at alternatives.

The business imperative that your research will give you is that of the financing and re-financing of the whole IT asset. This will be a key corporate issue for the foreseeable future. It is not an IT issue. Do not delegate it.

While being your own management consultant in this area, concentrate on your business knowledge, organizational, motivational and management strengths. Like a professional management consultant, recognize your areas of weakness or ignorance and don't be afraid to seek specialist advice.

In your IT application investments, seek rapid deployment and rapid payback wherever possible. Be very cautious about longer-term payback arguments.

In your IT infrastructure investment you may find it impossible to discover a simple payback process. Without the enabling infrastructure the business will not be able to function. An act of faith at board level may be the only way to release the investment and maintain the commitment.

This is an issue of corporate-level business strategy and the IT contribution will be along the lines of how best to invest what the organization can afford. It will never be enough. That is normal.

CHAPTER NINE

MANAGING PEOPLE EFFECTIVELY

Peter Jones

By definition, a consultant does not have executive authority in the client organization, and so he or she has to work *through* the client management structure. In a similar way, managers have resources at their disposal – people, finance, equipment, materials etc – and they have to deploy these to best effect. One definition of a manager is 'someone who is responsible for more than their own efforts'.

A key resource for managers is other people, and when people are managed well, it means that the organization is effective. But if not done well, then organization performance suffers. In this chapter we therefore consider how a consultant would look at the task of managing people. Most managers see their jobs as covering a wide range of responsibilities and tasks. Their role is about how they manage to juggle all these tasks to achieve a reasonable level of performance. As a consequence, they are always very busy, always doing lots of different things, moving from one operational activity to another and coping with unexpected issues and problems. In such circumstances it is very easy to lose sight of the key task of how they lead and manage their people. Managers need always to ask themselves the questions: 'Am I doing a good job in performance management and improvement?'; 'Do my people know what I expect of them and do I give them good and regular performance feedback?'

Rather than doing things themselves, managers need to emphasize the real business benefit of focusing on how others can do those things for them – and probably better than they can do them themselves.

MANAGING PEOPLE TO IMPROVE PERFORMANCE

Performance management, improvement and achievement are essential tasks for managers engaged in leading and managing groups of staff of any size. Achievement is a function of the efforts of all their people, not just managers themselves, and a key task of a manager is to help their subordinates achieve high performance. Once managers start doing tasks that should more properly be delegated, they are stealing responsibilities from somebody else and they are giving the wrong message; other people will copy them and start taking on tasks which they should leave to their own staff. It is a vicious circle with which we are all familiar.

How can managers avoid this pitfall? The key is the ways in which they set objectives for people, including themselves, and then review progress and performance with their colleagues. They need to break out of close operational management and concentrate on those jobs that they are best placed to do:

- setting the agenda;
- defining the objectives set for people;
- dealing with interference around the boundaries;
- coaching staff;
- telling people how they are doing.

Improved performance will follow because everyone will know what is expected of them and know where to seek help if they meet problems and obstacles. Set out below are the questions you might ask to see if people are being organized effectively.

Setting the agenda

All work consists of a mixture of routine and non-routine tasks. Routine tasks consist of such things as responding to enquiries, preparing reports, paying bills and so on. Non-routine tasks may be concerned with rectifying problems, introducing new systems, or appraising the need or otherwise for elements of the routine work.

The 'agenda' is simply a way of defining what these non-routine tasks should be. Obviously there is a limit to the amount of non-routine work that can be undertaken at any given time – there is a limit to the capacity of an organization to absorb it. (When this happens, it is called 'initiative overload'). So the agenda needs to capture the priorities that need to be addressed in the short term.

These priorities can only be set in the context of the business as a whole. People need to know:

- What are the organization's business plans?
- What must be achieved over the relevant business period and beyond?
- What are the measures of success?
- Are potential problem-areas known?
- Does everyone understand the implications of the business plan on their jobs and the changes expected of them?
- Can we help every team and individual to see where they fit in the whole plan?

Defining objectives

Having set the agenda (the tasks to be accomplished), these need to be converted into objectives:

- What are the key tasks for each member of the organizational unit?
- Do they know what their colleagues are concentrating on so that they can both help and avoid inadvertent obstruction?
- Are the objectives set out in terms of current roles as well as improvements, both organizational and personal?
- Are some objectives shared because they need cooperation from several people working together?
- Are they agreed rather than imposed so that people *really* feel committed to them?

Managing interference

- Who is keeping an eye on changes in the external and internal business environment which might cause plans to need revising (rather than continuing with irrelevant activities just because we started off agreeing that they were important)?
- How do we manage events on the boundaries so that they contribute to successful achievement?
- Who makes sure the resources are available to help the unit achieve its plans? (That is where the manager has an important job to do.)

Coaching staff

Managing people should be like coaching sports stars, whether individuals or teams – they can keep getting better with help. Coaching does not imply that they are 'bad'; it offers the opportunity for them to get even better.

- Do people feel OK about asking for help because they are confident that their manager will support rather than blame?
- Are managers receptive to being coached by their own staff, who know them best, as well as by colleagues?
- Are feedback and coaching valued in the organization?

Reviewing progress

Is this done informally over a cup of coffee (and key points not mentioned or forgotten) or as a significant event in its own right where two partners talk through progress, what they have learnt, what is difficult, what is going well and also what is not going so well – to make sure that everything is on the table? Annually is not often enough; at least quarterly is about right because the progress reviews must be seen as important. Then managers can feel comfortable that there will be 'no surprises' for them or their colleagues when they finish the performance review and move on to pay.

And what about pay? Surely that's the element that really makes a difference to individual performance? The accepted view is that people are motivated by pay and the annual pay increase and that is what brings about performance improvement – except there is no strong evidence that this is true! And there is evidence that people work effectively without the incentive of pay increases. Obviously people do expect appropriate rewards in terms of pay, and low pay, however defined, is a demotivator.

It is sensible to have pay increases based on *recognition* of performance and contribution. But it can never be a substitute for effective management, for clear objectives, coaching and feedback – so that people know how they are doing and for people to feel motivated to take on personal responsibility for high performance. Most managers would be insulted by any suggestion that they can improve their performance through having some monetary incentive. Are other people in the organization any different? Remember the words of caution expressed by Jeffrey Pfeffer: 'most merit-pay systems share two attributes – they absorb vast amounts of management time and make everybody unhappy.'

DECIDING ABOUT THE CULTURE

We are all impatient to make an impact and to make changes in the ways that things are done in our business. We 'know' that change will bring about something better than we have now got and we all like to talk about the kind of culture that we want – but do we know what that word implies? Caution followed by careful thinking is essential. Before changing the way things are done in their organization, leaders need to understand the current reality – and also understand that people will have different interpretations about what that reality is. Next, leaders need to consider the kind of organization they want to become in place of the one they have at the moment. This will raise a number of critical questions:

- What are the longer-term objectives of the organization, which the new culture is to help achieve?
- How much should our ambitions be limited by the existing culture and the constraints on possible change?
- How do we develop plans for business strategy and culture in parallel so that they support each other?
- How do we integrate the strategies, culture, systems and policies in effective pursuit of our chosen goals?
- How do we resolve the differences, whether of principle, opinion, style or preference, of the different members of the organization?
- What kind of behaviours, by individuals and groups, will characterize the new culture?

When we talk of integrating business strategy, culture, systems and policies, we need to remember that culture is qualitatively different from the other concrete features. We may have to balance marketing priorities against those of finance but the analysis and conclusions within one discipline will not be affected by those of the other. Our cultural approach, on the other hand, affects every decision we take. As well as being an important item on the agenda, it also governs the process by which we tackle the agenda.

Inevitably, therefore, as we discuss how to plan and introduce a new culture we are using an approach and methods that are part of the currently existing culture, even as it changes. This point is not just an intellectual curiosity. It explains *the* major difficulty in making and sustaining large-scale cultural change. It is notoriously difficult to accomplish because, by definition, cultures are self-sustaining.

The keys to consider when looking at cultural change are:

1. working on the vision for change – what it will be like, to make sure we have the map to bring together collective and individual progress;
2. winning support for change – mobilizing and getting commitment to make sure that change is both accepted and properly implanted;
3. making change happen – the actual implementation to ensure that we succeed.

Jumping over these stages, from vision to implementation as an example, will likely cause significant problems. Many multi-million pound IT projects have failed because insufficient effort was put into helping people own the project – an awful and expensive lesson. And the stages do not necessarily follow in a simple time sequence; sometimes we have to take a step back and think about our learning before we move forward.

And we have to remember the present too. Life goes on as we change. We cannot stop all competition and operations whilst we get on with changing things. So, current reality calls for:

1. working on the vision for change – whilst valuing what we have and what we have done;
2. winning support for change – whilst maintaining morale;
3. making change happen – whilst managing existing processes.

What kind of culture?

What kind of culture does the organization want to develop? There are some norms in place from an early stage – the features that make the organization what it is and describe the 'ways we do things around here'. Newcomers want to learn them as soon as possible so that they do not make, in their view, silly mistakes. Established employees may not think consciously about the norms because they fit with them already. Managers need to think about them consciously to ensure that they have the kind of culture that they want – and that they can change what is no longer appropriate.

Many organizations have drafted mission and vision statements which try to set out their preferred culture and describe their general aspirations, what they want to achieve and their relationships with their customers, suppliers and employees. Visions seek to set the general map of why the organization exists, what it does, how it plans to grow and develop. They lead, inevitably, to descriptions of the kinds of behaviours that individuals should aspire to and seek to develop, thereby recognizing (sometimes implicitly) that the organization is a community which depends on positive behaviours to achieve its objectives, and which will not do so if the behaviour of individuals is inappropriate. US companies have found it easier to address this issue of behaviour; British companies have often found it difficult to do so, almost as if asking for changes in behaviour involves undue interference with individual freedom or is not the kind of thing which should be discussed openly. The American practice of openness seems more sensible. Behaviour, corporate or individual, does have a clear impact on performance and achievement. The 'old' British behaviour of strict job demarcation led to inflexibility; the 'new' behaviour of teamwork both contributes to business success and creates a more positive work environment. Open discussion of appropriate behaviours is more likely to lead to changes than pretending that such debate is not necessary.

There are some critical elements that can be identified in terms both of the responsibilities that can reasonably be expected of employees and the rights that they can expect in return. The culture is not just about what staff can expect from the business; it is also about what they can and should be contributing. Setting out these rights and these responsibilities provides the road map so that everyone knows 'how we do things around here'.

The *responsibilities* of staff might be expressed as follows:

- *commitment* – accepting positively a duty to contribute to the best of their abilities and putting in the effort needed to achieve the organization's goals;
- *performance* – being prepared to work to their best, flexibly and without unnecessary restrictions and demarcations, using skills to the full to contribute to the business's needs;
- *learning* – taking personal responsibility for developing skills to increase effectiveness at work – in current and future roles;
- *respect* – working with and helping each other at work on the basis of positive cooperation and mutual respect;
- *well-being* – protecting the health and safety of themselves and of others in physical, mental and emotional terms;

- *coaching* – giving appropriate feedback to others, to help improve performance and relationships, and seeking and welcoming such feedback about their own performance and contribution.

These responsibilities apply to everyone – not just the managers.
The *rights* of staff could be as follows:

- *being treated as individuals* – through responding to their particular needs and wishes rather than enforcing some conformity with common but inappropriate standards;
- *performance feedback* – given appropriately so that they can improve their skills and overcome any shortcomings with their manager's support;
- *dismissal being a last resort* – by ensuring that all practicable steps are taken to ensure that dismissal is used only as a final sanction and that fair procedures are followed to ensure the fairness of decisions;
- *objective employment choices* – between people regarding appointment, promotion, pay increase and all other employment matters, whether before or during employment;
- *fair pay* – acknowledging the right of people to be paid at a fair and equitable level in relation to their skills and responsibilities and also to the external labour market;
- *personal life* – recognizing and supporting the right of employees to a reasonable personal life outside work and not intruding upon the privacy of their home life nor making excessive work demands which deprive them of time for it.

There is a business case for these rights. In some cases, it is very straightforward. For example, it is the most sensible business course to avoid unfair discrimination in selection, because in that way the employer gets the best person available for the job. In other cases, it is more indirect. Particular forms of behaviour may also be or become unacceptable to society, which may express its disapproval clearly through legislation (as in the case of health and safety) and impose sanctions for certain acts or omissions. Society's disapproval may be less specific, so that certain actions damage the employer's reputation and its sales or its ability to recruit. Of course, society includes suppliers, customers, current staff and their families and potential staff. They can all have a major influence, for good or for bad, on how successful an organization is.

And that is where the manager must consider the values, and indeed the ethics, involved in managing any kind of business. Rushworth Kidder of the Institute for Global Ethics set out some key reasons for 'doing it right' and assuring business success too:

- Shared values build trust.
- Predictability helps in crises.
- Customers care about values.
- Partnerships need common values.
- Consistency helps planning.
- Companies are as good as their people.
- And shareholders care too.
- Giving responsibility inspires loyalty.

There is indeed a virtuous circle, but it depends on effective management of the culture.

Use the lists above to consider your own organization. Is the culture one that supports the business and its future? Is it one that brings the best out of your people? Do the answers to these questions point to the need for changes in culture?

DECIDING ABOUT REWARD

Belonging to an organization has its own rewards – the opportunity to exercise and develop personal skills, to socialize, and to achieve success. But the reward that is most communicable – and an essential part of the contract between the employee and organization – is pay.

There are many practical issues to decide about pay, but first managers need to think about the objectives of their pay system and the ways in which it fits with and supports the objectives of the business. Managers who have thought through these issues will then find that they have answered most of the detailed policy points about their pay structures. Some of the important issues to consider are set out below.

Organizational and personal performance

The overall objectives of the business, people's tasks and how well they perform them, and the reward they get for doing them well, should be related so that all staff:

- understand the organization's purpose;
- know what is expected of them individually and together;
- can see the relationship between that overall purpose and the ways in which they are managed and rewarded.

These are all part of the same overall approach to people management. They might mean that it is appropriate to have incentives related to individual and corporate performance so that staff understand the relationships and links between what they do and the success of the whole business.

Messages to staff

Employers send messages, intentional and otherwise, to staff by the ways in which they manage pay. Are those messages the positive ones that managers want their staff to receive or are they suggesting that the organization is unclear about what it wants to achieve in pay terms? Does the organization, for example, encourage teamwork and cooperation but have an incentive scheme that rewards individual performance? Frequent changes in reward systems will suggest uncertainty in management about how best to motivate and reward staff. Good communication about the intentions of the reward process will encourage staff to believe that their management has given these issues careful consideration.

Common terms and conditions

Providing common pay and benefit arrangements for all staff from the most senior to the most junior provides a powerful message about the organization's values. Any differences in approach and payments must be open and justified on the basis of market or other competitive reasons. Trying to keep them secret will cause different problems.

Simplicity of structures

Can the organization develop as simple a reward system as possible with the minimum of allowances and special payments for overtime etc? Can it aim to provide an annual salary in return for which staff do the work expected of them and improve their performance with no other pay complications? Simplicity has the virtue of telling people that their pay is being dealt with appropriately and they can then get on with improving their performance. It allows managers to concentrate on meeting the aims of the business rather than answering questions and explaining how the pay structure works.

Market comparability

Competitive organizations have to maintain an appropriate measure of comparability within their market sector, particularly in a sector where key people can be very mobile. What does comparability really mean, how can it be measured and what does it cost? What does being an 'upper quartile' payer mean – and does that describe basic or total pay? Market information is rarely easy to match or to interpret, whereas internal relativities may be much clearer and have more immediate impact. How and by what rationale can a balance be struck which meets the business needs? Market considerations will also be affected by cost-of-living factors. There is no right to a pay increase because the cost of living has increased – that can lead to inflation and salary budget problems for the organization. And both market comparisons and the cost of living take some control of pay away from the organization's managers. People can be very aware of what they think is fair and unfair in how and what they are paid – but 'felt fairness' is impossible to measure.

Job structures

Are job structures best designed to cover all jobs in the same way through a minimum number of grades, if there are to be grades? Can they encourage staff to build and widen their responsibilities without necessarily expecting a grade promotion? What should be the criteria for promotion – staff taking on greater responsibilities for themselves or formal job promotions? Changes in responsibilities are likely to be constant features of an organization's life and the maintenance systems need to recognize change fairly quickly. And they should ensure that people do not expect a pay increase every time they take on extra tasks.

Job evaluation

There needs to be some basis for determining relationships between jobs in the organization and ensuring equity of treatment. Formal job evaluation provides a practical means towards achieving these business and people management ends; it is not an end in itself. The system used needs to be credible, robust, relevant, comprehensible, fair and seen to be so. It must focus on the work done or expected as distinct from the characteristics and performance of the jobholder. And transparent fairness is essential. Staff themselves may be the best people to decide the relative size and rankings of jobs; that will give them real ownership.

Incentive pay

What kind of incentive or bonus payments does the organization want to provide on top of basic salaries and what is its justification for doing so? Does it want any performance-related pay to be geared to individual or team performance? What are the minimum standards to be achieved before incentives are paid? Does everybody know what he or she has to do to earn and continue to receive incentives? Is everyone involved in the incentive plan; and is that plan geared to ensuring that the business objectives are achieved?

Staff development

The links between pay, current performance and future development may be forgotten. How do the performance review arrangements link with pay, if at all? Are performance review discussions just about current performance or do they also consider issues of development and continuous improvement, in current as well as future roles? Do pay and development discussions take place at the same time? If so, is there a risk that people will become defensive about performance because they are concerned that their pay will be affected?

Organization culture and desired behaviours

The organization's values must be reflected in declared behaviours that it wants staff to display in the ways that they work. These, in turn, must be reconfirmed through the ways in which performance is recognized and rewarded. These are not prescriptions and staff will need help and support in recognizing their relevance to their roles – and see that reward systems reflect these behaviours. If, for example, teamwork, cooperation and mutual support are desired values, then the pay system needs to be in tune with them rather than just emphasize individual contribution.

Some myths about pay

There are some well-established myths about the impact of pay and labour rates on business performance. Jeffrey Pfeffer identified the most common ones in a 1998 article in the *Harvard Business Review* and managers need to think hard about them.

Myth One   Labour rates and labour costs are the same thing

Confusing them leads to management misunderstandings and mistakes. Labour costs are a calculation of how much a business pays its people – and how much they produce. Labour rates just record straight wages, with no regard to levels of productivity.

Myth Two   Labour costs can be lowered by cutting pay rates

To get labour costs down, businesses need to address productivity levels rather than just actual rates. Lowering labour rates can sometimes increase labour costs because of the impact on organization and morale.

Myth Three Labour costs are a significant proportion of total costs

Yes, but not always. The proportions vary from industry to industry. They may be easy to manipulate and change. But that does not mean that they are the biggest expense.

Myth Four   Low labour costs are an effective and sustainable competitive weapon

Better to get it through quality, customer services, product and service innovations. Everyone can cut labour costs; only the most effective can do something about those other elements.

Myth Five   Individual incentives improve performance

They also undermine teamwork, encourage a short-term focus, lead people to believe that what their manager thinks of them is what's important.

Myth Six   People work for money

And also for some meaning in their lives. Bribing with pay does not lead to loyalty and commitment – look at recruitment and retention experiences in the financial services and the IT industries where, despite high pay, people frequently move job.

COMMUNICATION – YOU CAN'T CHANGE AND IMPROVE WITHOUT IT

Tasks may be clear, the culture healthy and rewards satisfactory, yet still an organization may be operating sub-optimally. The next thing to look at is the quality of internal communications.

Communication is the life-blood that circulates in all areas of the business. It needs constant attention and improvement. We all accept this as a universal truth – but in our actions do not always practise it. We are too busy; there is a crisis to deal with; we will tell people later. Communicating really well must be a priority for everyone. In changing business environments, it is critical to commitment and performance. In the words of the CEO of a major US corporation: 'If I could go back and change one thing, it would it be the way I communicated with my colleagues.' Good communication enables:

- *Shared direction*: People need to know how their efforts fit into the whole. When things are moving fast, a shared view of the target holds the change effort together.
- *Commitment*: Every piece of research about what gets people committed has emphasized that involving them in the decisions makes the difference to successful implementation.
- *Informed decision making*: Effective performance at every level depends on smooth and speedy information that flows up, down and across the organization. Downwards alone is not good enough!
- *Morale:* People need opportunities to discuss their personal concerns about change – so that they continue to feel good about the organization and their place in it. They also need encouragement by acknowledging and publishing successful progress.
- *Learning in individuals and teams and between people across the organization*: There is a need to share experiences, good and bad, from previous change initiatives and to help others to learn from each one as it evolves. There's no point in learning alone; profit lies in learning from one another for continuous improvement.
- *Business integration across the organization and to 'focus on the customer'*: Most change depends on communication across organizational borders and the customer ideally only wants one interface. Multiple change initiatives across the organization also need to be integrated to avoid duplication and to maximize their impact.

How to communicate effectively: four answers

1. Actions speak louder than words – behaviour is the key

Senior executives need to present a consistent view of the future as they see it. Their behaviour will be watched more closely and have more credibility than the latest corporate video. So, for example, if the new corporate vision is 'The customer is king', front-line employees will soon become cynical about managers who, for example, push old stock when it doesn't match customers' needs or indulge in parochial, 'stove pipe' thinking. The vision will wither on the vine. Employees will follow the example set from the top.

2. Face to face is best

Communication immediately conjures up visions of corporate videos and newsletters. But research suggests that 75 per cent of companies using such media believed them ineffective. Of course there is a need for some corporate communication. The source of information that employees really trust is their immediate supervisor or manager. They need to be primary targets for clear communication and support – particularly in times of change when they may feel vulnerable.

3. Real listening as well as talking

Communication is a two-way process. Open channels upwards are just as important as open channels downwards and across the organization. Groups and individuals need opportunities to give managers their reactions to what's going on; to know they will be listened to without defensiveness or fear; to feel their contribution is valued and respected.

Senior managers need to appreciate and take advantage of the reality that those closest to the customer – and the day-to-day work – may know how best to improve performance. They need to understand the practicalities and impact of change through listening to those views and acting on them.

4. Plan it, manage it, keep it flexible and evolving

The best examples of major and radical transformation include significant plans for communication and involvement. The plans cover the total workforce and a significant investment is made in them. So communication is not just about expensive and flashy launches or even the activities for the first 100 days. To be effective, it requires a sustained programme which keeps the message constantly in front of people – on the agenda of routine meetings; formal briefings; videos; newsletters; e-mail; notice boards; senior executives walking about talking to people and so on.

IMPROVING PERFORMANCE

A consultant's efforts are not only remedial – helping to rectify something that is not working as well as it should – but also developmental. What needs to be done to identify areas for improving performance in managing people?

Key to that are the design and operation of performance management review systems. These focus on improving performance – at the individual, organizational unit and corporate level. The processes used and the paperwork systems should be directed at that aim of improvement. They are not about carrying out post mortems on what has gone wrong in the past or assigning blame. Nor should they be about assigning grades and marks. The evidence of past performance must be used as the basis of future improvement.

The key points that managers must think about and try to implement in their performance management systems are set out below.

Shared ownership

The individual employee and manager must 'own' their performance review. It is not sufficient for managers to tell individuals how they are doing for good or bad – that requires no particular responsibility or ownership by the individuals, who probably know best how they are doing and where they need help. It is the most significant formal communication between the individual and employer and both must take responsibility for ensuring that regular and appropriate reviews take place so that everyone knows where they stand. The manager has more than one employee to manage and review, hence the need for each individual to share some of the responsibility.

Emphasis on improvement

Performance reviews and appraisals are about seeking and making improvements – for the organization, the unit and for the individual. Information about past performance and relationships provides the material to identify and agree areas for improvement, both those where the individual needs to overcome weaknesses and become more effective, and those where he or she needs to move forward because of new work requirements. What has passed has passed; its value is to provide some of the raw material to look ahead and plan together for improvements.

The emphasis on improvement takes over from any previous concentration on problems and failings. The review system should be a positive process for looking forward using recent evidence as its foundation. Individuals will then become more willing to identify concerns and weaknesses and seek help to resolve them – and then take responsibility for doing so. Separating the performance review from the pay review in time and also in policy will encourage open discussion rather than defensiveness.

Collecting feedback

There are several people who can help the individual review performance – the manager, colleagues, members of staff who work closely with the individual. All have contributions to make and useful feedback to provide. Some of this useful information will be missed if the process is only two-way between individual and manager.

It is worthwhile collecting comments from some of these people – certainly the manager, one or two colleagues, one or two members of staff. This information is best collected in a relatively informal (but written) way rather than through complicated assessments.

This approach can supplement formal paperwork systems. And it does not need complex 360-degree assessment processes for the shared feedback to be valuable. Too much information can confuse; a little and often is more likely to be acted upon.

Agreeing objectives

The performance review fits in the context of the organization's overall plans and the expectations of the individual and the unit in which he or she works. An individual's objectives need to fit with those overall plans and those for the unit – and also with his or her development needs.

It is often helpful to identify three categories of objectives:

- *doing the job*: why the particular job exists and the basic requirements which need to be met for the individual to contribute to the aims of the business unit;

- *developing/improving the job*: the objectives which will bring about improvement – producing information and reports earlier than usual; looking at different and more effective ways of carrying out a standard process;
- *developing the skills of the individual:* what the individual is going to do to develop/build his or her skills – these may be formal training courses or they may be coaching from the manager or working alongside other employees.

Too many objectives will confuse everyone about what the real priorities are. Two or three in each category with appropriate time-scales are more likely to be achieved and the individual and the manager can then agree some more.

Describing objectives

Objectives must be clear, tangible and understood in advance by the parties involved. Employees must know what they are committing themselves to; managers need to be clear in their expectations.

A useful process in defining objectives is to ensure that they meet the definition of being SMARTI objectives. That means:

S *Specific* so that no one can misunderstand what has been agreed
M *Measurable* so that progress and success can be seen
A *Achievable* so that individuals feel that they can actually deliver their objectives, even if some will stretch them
R *Realistic* in fitting with the needs of the business
T *Time-related* so that there is a finishing point
I *Integrated* and consistent with other people's objectives.

(Sometimes the I is dropped, and slightly different words used – eg see Chapter 13.)

Reviewing progress

Managing people and helping/coaching their progress is the key task of managers. That cannot be done just through an annual discussion of performance. There needs to be a regular review to identify what help is needed and what things may have changed.

Managers should have an objective for themselves of meeting formally and regularly with their staff, say quarterly, to check on progress, change objectives that are no longer appropriate and provide helpful coaching. This will encourage and help people see that the appraisal process is a 'live' one, which changes as necessary. And they will regard their manager as being a help rather than a check on what they are doing in their job.

Performance ratings and pay

Rating systems at the end of a performance appraisal are unhelpful and lead to defensive behaviour at a time when the aim of the performance review/improvement process is openness, feedback and dialogue. The most effective appraisal systems record the key points covered and provide an overall picture with no sectional or overall ratings. Ineffective performance is dealt with outside the appraisal process, whilst using some of the issues which have been discussed.

Performance does have an impact on pay, however, and performance appraisal and pay review are best dealt with as separate but connected events. The performance appraisal process leads to an agreed record between the individual and manager of the key points, often prepared by the individual, with a mutual recognition that there will some implications for pay at a later time.

WORKING TOGETHER IN TEAMS

How do we describe a team? At the basic level, a team is:

a group of people with a common goal, which they are dependent on one another to achieve

At a more descriptive level, and recognizing that team members want other things than just objective goals of performance:

an energetic group of people who are committed to achieving common objectives, who work well together and enjoy doing so . . . and who produce demonstrably high quality results!

Most people work in groups with others with whom they need to cooperate. That does not make them a team – they need to work at being an effective team together. There is significant evidence that individuals and groups perform more effectively when they do work at being a team as well as doing what their individual jobs require of them. Good sporting teams do not just happen; they work at the skills of the individual members and also their skills in working together and supporting each other. And they do not stop working at these skills just because they have done well. The football club that wins the Premiership will get back to work pretty quickly to meet the needs of the new season. They know that they need to work at their skills and improve them even further if success is to be repeated; just doing the same as they did in the previous season will not be enough. The same requirements apply to teams in other businesses too.

The work of business teams

Groups working together in organizations need to consider these questions – and keep reviewing them on a regular basis:

● What are we here to do?
● What are the key things we need to do for the business?
● How shall we organize ourselves?
● Who is in charge?
● How do we review progress and measure success?
● Who cares about our success?
● How do we settle problems?
● How do we work with other groups?

These are not easy questions, though groups can come up with simple answers. Teams need to consider them regularly and often to ensure that everyone has their say and expresses their views on the team – both positive and negative. And the team must have a process for dealing with differences and problems. Teams that do not ask themselves these questions about their problems may fool themselves into thinking that they are effective because they do not have problems and disagreements. Effective teams, on the other hand, talk about their problems as well as their successes. The team leader has a key role here in encouraging the members of the team to talk openly about the negatives as well as the positives. It is not a case of wearing a hair shirt for the satisfaction of doing so. Rather, it is all about looking at how to improve – and keep on improving. Celebrate what has been successful – and keep on working at getting even better!

From form to perform

Teams are organic; they have a life and character of their own. And there are often similar phases of development. These have been usefully summarized in four phrases by Scholtes as:

1. *Form* – Members are tentatively exploring the issues involved in working with a group of new and different people. Behaviours include attempts to find out 'what needs to be done' and to check out acceptable ways of working with other group members.
2. *Storm* – This is probably the most difficult stage of team formation. Once the initial euphoria has died down and the reality and scale of the task in hand loom large, feelings will include frustration at lack of progress and fear of not being listened to. The behaviours will include arguing among members and a fair amount of defensiveness and competition.
3. *Norm* – If the team members can 'ride the storm' then it will become apparent that the competition and frustration are not productive. This gives the opportunity for redefining the work to be done and the processes to be used. Cooperation is seen as a positive alternative. Feelings will include relief that the corner has been turned and tentative optimism. Behaviours include stating criticism in positive and constructive ways and working with rather than in spite of others. Team members begin to work out their differences and they now have more time and energy to spend on real work.
4. *Perform* – Now that the team have developed an agreed focus and ways of working which they are 'comfortable with', they can begin to make significant strides towards the achievement of their work. There is now some unity of direction, effort and will which enables the team to move forward in confidence and the expectation of achieving their goals. Feelings at this stage include a growing understanding of the importance of group process and an acceptance of other members' strengths and weaknesses. Behaviours will include ability to work through or prevent group problems, and helping other team members with their tasks if the need arises.

There is a clear sense of purpose, members look forward to working together and are moving steadily towards achieving their goals. If some untoward event occurs which pushes back their achievement, then this is dealt with in a positive and constructive way and the team is quickly back on course.

The 'A' team

Is there a perfect team? Ray Charlton suggested some of the dimensions that the leader should aim to achieve. Not all are attainable but his definitions provide an excellent model. The team needs to be:

- *aware*: with everybody knowing the team's purpose and goal;
- *aligned*: with everybody sharing the same direction;
- *attuned*: with rapport and team commitment of the highest order;
- *able*: with every individual in the team having the required skills for the purpose;
- *achieving*: with all team members knowing its progress, which is measured by clear objectives/plans in 'bite-sized' chunks;
- *acknowledged*: with the team and individuals' contributions being openly recognized;
- *accountable*: with the team acting responsibly and legitimately to meet the needs of the business;
- *adaptable*: when the team is always responsive to changing environments and needs;
- *alive*: when people are switched on, have fun and overcome all setbacks.

MAKING CHANGE SUCCEED

Change is covered in more detail in Chapter 12. Suffice to say that there is increasing evidence that change projects, major and minor, succeed or fail depending on the involvement of the people who will own the outcomes of the project: the new ways of working, the new processes, the new expectations – particularly of each other within the organization.

The following checklist (from ideas developed initially by Roger Plant, 1987) identifies some of the key points that are generally associated with successful change attempts. Managers need to assess the changes that they are considering in terms of these measures of progress and success – and make any improvements that could increase the chances of successful implementation:

- *Realistic goals*: Are the change objectives sufficiently clear and realistic? If not, how can they be improved?
- *Quick wins*: Can benefits from the change be seen quickly? If not, what might they be?

- *Visible completion*: Are there clear milestones for completion and an end product to the change and each of its stages? If not, what should they be?
- *Management commitment*: Are managers demonstrating their commitment to the change? If not, how should they do so?
- *Involvement*: Do those responsible for implementing the change feel involved in making the change a success? If not, how can they take real ownership?
- *Competing pressures*: Are other projects and pressures reduced sufficiently to free energy for attention to the change? If not, what needs to be stopped or delayed?
- *Rewarding new behaviours*: When people try to behave in new ways, are they recognized, rewarded and encouraged? If not, what new behaviours need to be introduced – and recognized? Are the old ways of behaving discouraged?

Like all such questions, a Yes/No answer is not enough. Think hard about what other people will think, not what you think that you already know.

And why do so many change projects fail? There are many reasons, but some of the most common are about the involvement of and communication to the people who will make the project succeed or fail. They include:

- misunderstanding what the project is all about;
- insufficient planning – because managers forget the process and concentrate on the result;
- goals being too far in the future;
- quick fixes instead of quick wins;
- fear of failure;
- the 'not another change' attitude;
- employees', and especially middle managers', resistance and fear.

Remember these obstacles, plan how to deal with them, and the prospects of success improve. Involve all staff so that they know what is happening and their concerns are allayed early and the prospects of success increase even further.

CHAPTER TEN

FINANCING THE BUSINESS

Chris Edge

What do you use finance for? Do you need to borrow money for the day-to-day running of your business? Do you want to borrow money to buy capital equipment or premises? Or do you want to organize the profit you are making to maximize the use of your surplus funds? Whatever your need, you must control your finances and this chapter suggests how to do just that.

MANAGING THE GOING CONCERN

The best tip anyone can give a business is to ensure that you have adequate control over your finances on a *regular* basis. The meaning of regular will vary according to the type of business and could be:

- minute-to-minute control for a business dealing in shares;
- daily or weekly control for a manufacturing operation, restaurant or other catering operation;
- monthly monitoring for a construction or other business with less controllable variable costs.

Many businesses fail due to the lack of control; some even lack knowledge whether the business is making a profit or loss speedily enough. One business owner, a drainage construction company in the UK, could not accept that they had made a substantial loss for the prior year, some six months after the year-end! The signs were all there – cash flow had started to get difficult, the bank was continually rejecting direct debits and standing orders were not being paid on time. After the initial shock the decline came very quickly – the bank appointed a receiver who eventually took the director's home to satisfy the personal guarantee and second mortgage.

Practical strategies can be adopted for many situations but nothing can be better than to gain and retain control over the finances of the business. Experienced management accountants to help, whether employed or retained on contract, can be worth their weight in gold! Often auditors lack the commercial awareness and experience of dealing with management accounts, tending to concentrate on the annual statutory accounts.

For example, a restaurant needs to control its gross profit almost on a daily basis to enable it to enact corrective action, perhaps reducing the amount of food or staff overtime costs in line with seasonal variations or a downturn in business. However, a daily physical inventory can often be impractical, but a weekly check is probably vital. A physical check, whilst time consuming, can also offer added value by ensuring produce about to become out of date can be used in a 'special' menu. If foodstuffs are kept in a central area and drawn from stock as required daily, it might be possible to obtain 'flash' or quick daily management accounts along the lines shown in Table 10.1; note the contingency for stock losses.

Table 10.1 Daily flash report for restaurant business

	Gross	Ex VAT* (£)	Percentage of sales (%)
Cash takings	£1,175	1,000	100
Food and other items taken from Central Store, say		200	20
Contingency for stock losses		50	5
Gross profit		750	75
Staff wages – Restaurant		150	15
Staff wages – Kitchen		200	20
Employer's NI & other fixed costs, say 25% of staff wages		88	8.8
Contribution towards overheads		312	31.2

*Assumed 17.5% of sales

Similar 'flash' profit and loss reports, or indeed balance sheet or cash flow reports, can also be developed for other businesses; remember the main aims of a profit and loss flash report are to:

- provide rough financial information, not 100 per cent accurate final accounts that take weeks to complete;
- show that there is adequate contribution towards overheads on a regular basis;
- enable management to take prompt corrective action if required.

If a business consistently fails to make an adequate contribution towards overheads then something is wrong either with the accounting or the business itself and help may be required.

WHEN MORE FINANCE IS REQUIRED

There are five main uses of cash and resources that should be planned for:

- *Meeting current day-to-day financial obligations*, eg purchase of stock, payment of bills and wages. This item of expenditure is unavoidable. An inability to meet these cash outflows is likely to lead to the downfall of the business.
- *Repayment of loans.* This is also unavoidable expenditure, vital to the survival of the business.
- *Purchase of fixed assets.* Initial expenditure on fixed assets is unavoidable – production relies on it. Further upgrades or replacement of fixed assets can often be timed to coincide with periods of high cash balances, but should not be delayed so that continuity of production is threatened.
- *Giving a cushion against expenditure.* A cushion must be regarded as necessary, to cope with the inevitable unforeseen variances in the assumptions underlying projections.
- *Taking advantage of investment opportunities.* Although projections are unlikely to highlight such opportunities, spare cash is a valuable resource and there should be a return on it at all times. This could range from bank deposit interest in the short term to investing in employee training to help the longer-term well-being of the business.

What to do if you are in difficulty

What can a business do when it is in real difficulty? The first step is to review the financial position – draw up as quickly as possible:

- a profit and loss statement;
- a balance sheet;
- a projected cash flow for the next six months and longer depending upon the business.

Have your financial staff and/or accountant review the above and help you decide what course of action to follow.

A key question in these circumstances is to ask yourself: is the business worth saving? By worth saving it does not mean that the owner or directors *want* to save it, or that you want to preserve it for the employees, but is it *really* possible. Tactics to consider in this situation might include voluntary arrangements with creditors, an Administration Order, or as a last resort liquidation or bankruptcy. If there is more than one business it might be a sensible tactical move to liquidate one business to save another – but make sure you pick the right one!

When there is only a little money, which creditors should be paid first?

Before taking such drastic action, see if you can extend your creditors. A business should not generally give preference to creditors; indeed this can be illegal or make a director personally liable for the debts of a company in certain situations. Nevertheless some creditors should be paid in advance of others:

- Priority creditors should always be paid more or less on time – these include VAT, National Insurance, PAYE, Corporation Tax and Uniform Business Rates. Repeated failure to pay these creditors on time may result in progressively larger fines, not to mention many government agencies having draconian rights to investigate your business – not a helpful matter if you are struggling anyway!
- Bank or other mortgages, loan repayments, hire purchase or lease payments should be maintained on schedule or negotiate a change – don't just ignore it. Failure to pay may result in a quick repossession of the business assets at a critical moment – in addition, directors may have signed a personal guarantee for these types of debts.
- Utility, fuel and telephone charges also need to be settled promptly – if your lights and telephone are turned off, your customers will soon realize there is a problem and cease dealing with you.

Other creditors to settle promptly will include those suppliers who provide you with urgent supplies or services for which you are unable to locate a suitable replacement quickly. This will clearly depend upon the type of business, but from a tactical standpoint you might like to ensure, where possible, there are at least two suppliers for key requirements.

Credit contol is vital but many businesses take negative approaches to credit control and only enact any control when a customer has placed them into a difficult position. The government has introduced changes allowing interest to be charged by small businesses on late-paying customers. But why add interest onto a debt paid late by a customer – the chances of collecting this are very unlikely even with the new law. Instead, consider increasing your prices and offer a substantial discount if payment is received in an agreed time-scale. Clearly some businesses will be unable to adopt this approach due to contract arrangements; perhaps others feel it would cause damage to customer relationships. It is, however, worth trying – it is hardly surprising that people will take advantage of you otherwise. If you don't ask, you won't get – and you may earn their respect by asking!

POSSIBLE SOURCES OF FINANCE

The business may be in good order, and you may want further finance. You need to think why and if you want finance. A cash flow forecast will help determine if and when further cash will be needed, or whether there is surplus to invest. The first place to look for funding for future projects is from the profits of the business – reinvesting for growth. If these are insufficient, you will need to investigate alternatives.

There are many possible sources of finance, some of which are listed here. Not all these are considered in depth here, but are all worthy of consideration; they have been categorized below:

Extracting finance from the business

Cash flow can be helped by arranging: 1) extended credit with suppliers; 2) prompt payment by customers.

Factoring can help with the latter. Factoring companies, in effect, buy invoiced debts from the supplier, who receives immediate payment of all invoices – although this will not be 100 per cent of their value – without having to wait 30 days or more.

The benefits of factoring are often underrated and misunderstood. Once seen as a panic measure for companies with cash difficulties, it is now considered to be an appropriate way of funding a growing business, neutralizing the effect of late payment. Factoring can help companies excluded from bank lending. Apart from the cost, however, one drawback with factoring is the impact on your customers, who will need to settle their invoice directly with the factoring company. This can be an irritant for customers who may get confused whom they should pay.

Invoice discounting is a similar tool, but the owner controls his or her own ledger whilst receiving an agreed percentage, say 80 per cent of the total debt. The customer pays you, then you refund the monies to the factor. The main benefit of this as opposed to normal factoring is that the customer does not know you have discounted the debt.

Providing finance yourself or from personal contacts

If you believe in yourself, invest in yourself. But providing finance from your savings means that you run the risk of putting all your eggs in one basket – your capital savings as well as your income are dependent on the success of the business.

Selling shares to business partners or to employees means that you share the risk and the profit, but the same risks apply.

Family members are also a good source of funds, but you must always be confident that they will get a good return; you may hide from investors but you cannot lose your family.

Getting finance from outside lenders

Look to see whether there are grants available; these sometimes involve lots of paperwork, but could be worthwhile.

You can also use the assets of the business to raise capital, by mortgaging buildings, or arranging a sale and lease-back of other assets. Similarly, you can raise a mortgage for financing building.

Hire purchase is a useful way to buy equipment, spreading the cost over a period of time. The downside is that you do not legally own it until the final payment is made; miss one payment and you can lose all your money and equipment. Lease purchase and lease rental are also ways of avoiding high capital costs.

Your bank can be a source of finance, by using a bank overdraft for covering day-to-day running costs, or a bank loan for medium to long-term investments.

Other sources of finance include venture capital funds (which will lend to a potentially risky business but expect high returns in the medium term) or business angels, who are individuals who operate in much the same manner.

Beyond this is offering shares in the company, perhaps through private sale (to, say, a pension scheme; the company pension scheme might also be an investor in your company) or more generally through stock listing on a stock exchange.

EFFECTIVE METHODS OF RAISING FINANCE

The most effective method of raising finance depends on a number of issues, which might include:

- the reason for finance, eg short, medium or long term;
- the tax implications, eg use lease rental rather than overdraft for financing capital expenditure to reduce short-term tax bills;
- the projected cash flow of the type of business (eg a retail food chain with high initial capital investment, but with cash customers, will differ from a firm of solicitors);
- the ability of the owners to self-finance and their past experience and credibility;
- whether the business is in a development area with possible grants available;
- the risk of the business sector and geographical location;
- the general economic climate and lenders' perceived attitude to investment;
- the rate of return on investment.

Professionals to help raise finance

Unless you are competent to do it yourself (remembering of course the old adage 'if a lawyer handles his own case then he has a fool for a client') specialist advice should be sought to help obtain any external finance. Professional help will enable you not only to reduce the effort, but also add credibility in your case.

As well as the usual professionals (eg bankers, accountants and other financial advisers), consider the many other institutions that are set up to advise businesses on sources of finance.

Information required

Most sources of business finance will need basic information for all ventures. Typically this would include:

- *Resumé of key personnel*, detailing their career, education and qualifications. Some mention of their family status and outside activities is also helpful, as is the age of any children. The precise details would vary according to the type of business; for example, for an engineering business clearly more emphasis would be on the professional engineering qualifications of the key personnel, but the fact that one or more may also have legal or accountancy training would be very useful.
- If an existing business, the *history of the business* including any milestones. This should include both positive and negative. For example, if the business has had a major financial crisis in the past, but managed to trade out of difficulty, then this is a positive thing, but even if negative the financiers may find out and wonder what else you have to hide if you do not include it! Certainly nothing should be hidden from professional advisers; let them decide what to include or not. They may decide to leave items out of any written submission, but to mention it verbally.
- *Existing finance* should be shown in detail, including any security. Security might range from a personal guarantee of the directors or a relative, to a fixed and floating charge on the business assets.
- Copies of the *last three years' accounts* should be included. Additional past years' summary financial information may be appropriate, especially if long-term investment is required, to show the longer-term growth. Graphs with percentage increase in turnover and profits against government indices might also help your case.
- *Insurance coverage* for indemnity or third-party liability if appropriate.
- *Business plan* and projected cash flow.

A final word: look at it from the investor's point of view. Is the information that you are providing demonstrating a convincing case for the benefit of investing in your business?

INTRODUCING AND IMPLEMENTING CHANGE

CHAPTER 11

INFLUENCING OTHERS

Mike Kearsley

Management consultants are often called 'agents of change' and when we work with organizations, we make recommendations that could often lead to significant change. Not uncommonly, however, these changes are not implemented, or not implemented to the planned extent. This may be because circumstances have changed, now negating our intervention, but very often it is because the changes we planned did not have the support and concurrence of enough of the client's employees. Sometimes assignments go sour – and the cause very often is a personality clash, not technical incompetence.

What can we do, then, to influence people so that they will support the changes we have proposed and work happily with us?

AN OVERVIEW OF THE PROBLEMS OF CHANGE

Our first problem is that it is often perceived that our primary reason for being in a client's organization is to change things. It could be argued that change in an organization simply means changing the patterns of recurring behaviour within it. Shepard (1970) argued, however, that cultures are maintained through the operation of self-validating processes. Changing a culture requires interventions that invalidate old processes and conditions that facilitate the creation of new self-validating processes. Smith and Beck (1986) considered that changing the behaviour of an organization is 'nearly impossible'. Organizations, they argue, are not meant to change; they are a form of social life that is meant to endure. Cannon reasoned that when a group of people work together they tend to develop justification for behaving in the way that they do and these could be called the organization's 'norms'. Once the justification for behaviour is internal to a group, it is very difficult to change it.

> *Two management consultancies in the same specialist area merged and their training groups were then asked to operate together. The first consultancy was twice the size of the second but its training group was only half as large. The first consultancy's trainers were predominantly male, the second's were all female. The first group saw itself as primarily providing what people asked for, the second saw itself as supporting a cultural change to the values that they were promoting. The first group worked as individuals, the second as a team. On the surface the two groups were doing the same job, but underneath their ethics, values and approaches were very different. This caused some problems of integration.*

Many organizations are thus apprehensive about change and Smith and Beck provide some perspectives on change, which, they argue, if taken cognisance of, would ensure the maximum opportunity for survival of the change and minimal disturbance to the organization. These are:

- no one likes to change;
- when people want to change, it is because they see the new behaviour as being in their own self-interest;
- people change most easily with things they feel they need rather than being told what they need;
- people change most easily when they have a say in the change;
- resistance to change is a healthy reaction which maintains predictability and reliability;
- it is more successful to view the social setting for change as a whole, not just selective aspects of it.

They argued that selected change could be brought about without observable resistance but certain dangers could result from this. One is that if resistance is too costly for members of the organization, they may change but only so long as controls are imposed. When controls are lifted, behaviours will revert. Another danger is that a change in behaviour may spill over to areas that were not originally intended. A third danger is that new behaviours are adopted but without real commitment. Thus, new behaviours are accompanied constantly by informal complaining and other subtle resistances. One form of resistance, of course, is overt refusal. Most organizations will seek to avoid this, perhaps because they fear that they cannot cope with such resistance in a productive way, and, as a consequence, the consultants may be blamed and dismissed.

Lewin (1952) is credited with providing the first basic theories for organizational change. He argued that before any change process begins, life is going on in a dynamic field of forces. This could be described and measured, and individuals within the organization would know and live by the norms, the unwritten acceptable code of behaviour for that group. The organization experiences forces that encourage change and forces that resist change. This balance is linked and supported by values, customs, rationale, rituals and other activities, collectively called 'culture'.

The forces for change are often trying to improve the organization and its effectiveness but the restraining forces constantly raise questions of stability, predictability and of changing too quickly from tried and proven ways which have protected the organization and often allowed it to survive. Most of the daily work of organizations is restraining and most training in an organization is aimed at teaching the standard required skill which is, in fact, intended to tell individuals what is expected of them.

This activity is required for every organization and will function well until a new force that cannot be accommodated intrudes. Change takes place when the field is reorganized into a new state that incorporates the new force. Lewin argued that the period of change when an organization is unfreezing and refreezing is a critical one. If it is unfrozen too long it disintegrates. If it refreezes too soon, no new behaviour will occur and it will revert to what it was before. For organizational change to take place, then, many people must complete the change process and in the appropriate timeframe.

The marketing department of a major electronics group wanted a comprehensive competency-based development programme to support its appraisal and management development system. A consultant was brought in and conducted in-depth interviews with a cross-section of staff to define all their needs and wants. A detailed development plan was created which would cover all staff over a 2–3 year period over a number of key areas. The plan was presented to the staff and was received with great enthusiasm – so much so that a new training manager was to be employed specifically to implement it. The consultant was not kept on but contacted the group a year later for a progress report, only to find that the new manager had never become involved in the project and implementation had been shelved until 'the appropriate moment'. Two years later the moment had still not arrived.

Ottaway (1980) suggested three kinds of change agents. These were:

- change generators (unfreezers);
- change implementers (changers);
- change adopters (refreezers).

Management consultants are often brought in as change generators. In essence, their function is to highlight that something is not working and that some change is necessary. They may be directed by the earlier beneficiaries of change from within the system, who are often the most senior people. We therefore need to ask ourselves: 'Do we have the support of the most influential people in this organization? Who else needs to be involved in the evaluation of change? What are the unwritten rules and the political forces that are operating within this organization?'

Often this early dominant group will form a coalition for change simply because they are obvious stakeholders in the benefits that will ensue. Their position and authority may be enhanced. They may see their role as internal change agents but they may wish to ensure that the change operates under their guidance and for their benefit. Often the organization's benefit and their own future benefit are strongly linked.

The exact nature of change may not yet be defined. This group, having accepted that change will occur, is likely to be open to the many supportive problem-solving techniques which consultants may bring to the organization. Techniques such as force-field analysis, cause and effect analysis, nominal group and Delphi techniques, pairs comparisons, and quest techniques (quick environmental scanning) will all be acceptable because they support the development of change with the appearance of objectivity.

Once the organization realizes a need for change, however reluctantly, change implementers surface. External implementers may be invited in, often to provide quick solutions. These may not be the original consultants who defined the need for change. The external implementers cannot proceed successfully without the support of internal implementers. Internal implementers are often selected from the personnel function, the training department or the planning department. These will then be charged with the specific and long-term task of implementing change.

This can cause conflict, as these individuals are part of the system with responsibilities both to maintain and now change it. At this stage, trainers may be attempting to train people into adopting a new behaviour that is not yet transferring to the work situation, where old habits prevail.

> *The managing director of one organization suggested that much could be learned from individuals admitting and detailing mistakes that had been made. He persuaded a fellow director to be the first to detail in writing a major mistake he had made, what it had cost the organization and so on. Far from allowing others to feel comfortable about revealing their own mistakes, the director found that ranks closed against him for his 'failure'. No one else admitted to their mistakes and within 12 months the director had left the organization.*

For change to occur, the new behaviour has to be adopted into the day-to-day behaviour of the organization. This is the task of the final group of change agents – the adopters.

The first adopters try the change in their own areas or groups. It is important for success that the change agents accept the change for themselves and it is important for organizational change that the early adopters are well regarded in the system. Lewin felt that it is not until those who run the organization on a day-to-day basis commit to change that the system refreezes. Often, there is still a low commitment to change and a high commitment to old behaviours. Once the change is adopted, a further group (perhaps the organization's clients, customers or suppliers) will also need to approve and support the change for it to continue.

There are, thus, many stages in the development of a successful change programme. Many consultancy initiatives fail because they do not successfully consider all of the forces that are involved. Let us consider these by reviewing the points made by Smith and Beck.

WHY CHANGE IS DIFFICULT

No one likes to change

Consultants are often in the difficult position of working with individuals in an organization to attempt to establish the parameters of change without being able to discuss with the individuals involved what change may or may not occur. We may be working in the strictest confidence and reporting to a single individual. It is difficult, however, to get people to deal with you when they are fearful of the future and, for many, our mere presence creates suspicion, questions, doubts and uncertainties. It is important, therefore, that we are able to tell people exactly what we are doing and what we hope to achieve from it. It is important, too, that in our day-to-day activities we fit in as well as we possibly can and do not alarm or offend people by our behaviour. This is particularly important if the organization does not have a history of using consultants or if the influence of previous consultants has been seen to be negative.

Self-interest

A great deal of consultant activity may be taken up with convincing or supporting the dominant group of the viability of a change programme. Often, however, the direct recipients of this change within the organization are given much less attention.

One IT vendor needed to dramatically increase its poor sales in order to survive competition. An attractive incentive scheme was designed for all sales managers. Over a period of time one sales manager achieved outstanding results through tireless determination and effort. The MD realized that this sales manager was now in the position of earning far more for the year than himself. The sales manager was also being seen as the saviour of the company. Not only was the full incentive commission not paid, through minor technicalities raised by the MD, but the sales manager was accused of having held back potential sales in order to undeservedly earn more. The sales manager was head-hunted by a competitor within three months.

As consultants, we might begin to ask ourselves whether we have established the benefits at all levels and for all employees. Further, have we in fact communicated these to all the individuals involved? Of particular concern will be the damage that our proposed change will inflict. The fears of redundancy, of changing roles, of lost status or importance, are all genuine fears and we need to be able to manage these. It is not usually possible for everyone to benefit when some change is planned. It might be interesting, however, to consider some of the competing motivational theories which might help us to understand why people might accept change.

Vroom and Deci suggested five different motivation clusters:

- *Response or behaviourist theories* suggest that organizations can be quickly programmed into behaviours through a system of punishments and rewards. The ultimate punishment is, of course, separation from the organization, although there may be certain legal implications involved with this.

- *Drive and instinct theories* suggest that we are all driven by strong cyclical urges such as survival, power and the avoidance of pain and that if these are brought into play they will move most people to action.
- *Goal theory* suggests that if the individuals within a group can be encouraged to buy into a desired future state, then they will acquiesce to the need for change. Thus the promise of future promotion or salary increases are all examples of future goals.
- *Psychological theorists* such as Maslow suggest that individuals seek to maximize their potential and will thus agree to change that will allow them to move to higher levels.
- *Social theorists* link motivation to the influence of social behaviour and acceptance by the group. Thus if most people see change as beneficial, the rest will accept it.

In today's complex organizations, no single motivational theory will adequately cover all the individuals involved; indeed many consultants would not see the motivation of an organization's employees as part of the consultancy brief. They may refer to the organization as the client but, in reality, the client may be one or a group of powerful individuals within that organization. Time taken to discuss how change might be regarded and implemented is, however, productive. The IT world, for example, is quite accustomed to the cost of implementation being far greater than the cost of the initial purchase of a system. This may not be the case with other consultancy projects and clients may be loath to consider and thus pay for the details of implementation.

People respond best to what they feel they need

It is the nature of most organizations that the individuals in it will become immersed in their own immediate tasks and responsibilities. In order to ensure a successful change programme, however, it may be necessary for us to widen the picture so that all individuals understand the need for change and the benefits that this will bring.

The benefits must be personalized to the individual or the immediate group and we must consider how these might best be presented. The structured logic that is relevant for board members may not be appropriate on the shop floor. Can we, for example, provide the latter with examples of other organizations where change has occurred and detail the effects of this for the people involved?

There is a danger, of course, in over-presenting something and thus magnifying out of proportion the implications of a relatively small piece of change. Consultants should consider the appropriateness and extent of communication as well as the level of formality or informality that this may take.

In many organizations, there are individuals who do not care at all what the organization is planning. If it does not suit them, they will leave. Some individuals whose skill lies in their professional or technical ability may be capable of easily transferring to another organization. There is thus the danger of losing expertise or transferring it to competition.

People want a say

Our Western approach to management and to change has tended to be a top-down, authoritarian approach. We have traditionally seen that senior management decide what needs to be done and then impose it on the organization. At this point, they are faced with justifying their decisions to their workforce. The quality circle approach, espoused by Deming, takes an alternative view where the workforce is involved in the need for change and the manner of that change right from the start. This process is often based on formal suggestions from the shop floor as to how every facet of the organization's activity can be improved. It has been shown that workers can be very creative when they understand what the problem is and are given the chance to express their views.

This approach, of course, implies that we accept the need for a process of communication, that individuals communicate in different ways, that disagreements at a senior level tend to stop communication, and that some individuals and groups seem to have a need to communicate more than others.

Increasingly, the major consultancies influenced by Deming and by the various aspects of process consultation (see, for example, Schein's book, 1969) are seeking to have this kind of relationship with their long-term clients. Most of the major consultancies, however, do not yet themselves operate internally in this way.

Resistance is healthy

Consultants can often become very committed to the defined change activity. They are, after all, the experts, and in many cases the clients are insistent that we strongly defend our proposals. Alternative views and resistance are thus not welcomed by the consultants themselves. They see this as a hindrance rather than a warning sign where there may be implementation problems. As highly educated professionals, they are also reluctant to discuss their proposals with the organization's employees, who might nevertheless provide some interesting insights. Professional firms such as consultancies are not noted for changing themselves too quickly. Perhaps we need to put ourselves into the shoes of others. The reasons why we have a difficulty with this are discussed a little later.

View change as a whole

Often, as consultants, we are dealing with only one small part of an organization and the changes that we make there might be successfully implemented without affecting much else. Time taken in the early stages and throughout to evaluate how this might affect other groups and, particularly, how other groups might be informed of the change activity might be productive. We need also to consider, of course, that the organization we are working in also has suppliers and customers. These may also need to be considered and consulted if a successful change action is to take place. Their comments may support or negate many of the actions that are being planned.

We may also need to consider our proposed change set against the background of developments in the client's industry and sometimes in the economy in general. It is unfortunate, however, that many clients do not see the need to widen the consultancy scope to incorporate this kind of discussion.

Thus far, we have considered influencing others within the context of organizational change theory. Much consultancy activity, however, ultimately comes down to the interaction between two individuals and it is our success in presenting ourselves and developing relationships that effectively ensures our success. We operate on a day-to-day basis with individuals and while they may be comfortable with our ideas and the change programme, they may not be comfortable with us as a person – specifically, with our personality.

> *One professional firm allowed a senior manager to be increasingly involved in practice development (i.e. sales activity) because no one else liked doing it. The manager was seen to be more gregarious and energetic than others. Eventually he was completely involved in sales activity, bringing in work for several groups, and was allowed to operate with almost complete autonomy. In a general downturn of business throughout the firm, senior management decided that any individual who was billing their time for less than two days a week was to be made redundant. The senior manager was, therefore, let go and none of those who benefited from his efforts sought to speak on his behalf – they argued that he was now too independent and had too much freedom.*

INTERPERSONAL SKILLS

Aspects of personality

The desire to understand other human beings and thus influence them is as old as civilization itself. Throughout history, we have attempted to classify or group human characteristics into a workable system that we could use to interact better with others. There are a vast number of personality or psychometric tests available on the market today. Many of them are variations of an earlier four-quadrant approach to personality which positions people in one of four groups, dependent on whether they are more task or people focused and whether they are extrovert or introvert. LIFO is an example of this approach. It classifies people according to whether they are extrovert or introvert, and whether they are more interested in people or the task in hand.

Each of the four quartiles demonstrates markedly different behaviour. The *task/introvert* is methodical, precise, likes data, is cautious, pessimistic and seeks to avoid problems. *The task/extrovert* is driving, entrepreneurial, a risk taker, bullying and demanding. The *people/introvert* is caring, sharing, supportive and group-centred. The *people/ extrovert* is gregarious, talkative, social and entertaining.

Each group is considered to be better suited for certain roles – for example, accountant, entrepreneur, social worker or salesperson. These divisions are, of course, very simplistic and they can be criticized in a number of areas. Firstly, they are not contextual, and we can accept that under different circumstances an individual may exhibit all four characteristics. Secondly, they are not time based – our behaviour and attitudes an hour before winning the lottery may be somewhat different to an hour after winning it! Finally, they do tend to lump all traits together in one classification when this may not be supportable.

Consultants, as a group, are often considered to be task-centred. The nature of engineering, accountancy, information technology and many other process-driven professions may support the view that these are task-centred introverts. The more dominant and outspoken task-centred extroverts may go on to become the senior managers and partners of their organizations. Ultimately, they may create their own consultancies, but an obvious difficulty is that many consultants are more interested in achieving the task rather than pleasing the people involved.

It is salutary to read descriptions as to how task-centred individuals are likely to behave. They may, for example, 'analyse, interpret and provide factual and logical analysis of problems and proceed towards a solution in a very methodical manner'. They may 'become set with their own views or opinions and become less open to those of others'. They may be 'comfortable in changing situations and may strongly push for needed change'. They may be 'intolerant of the ideas or opinions of others'. They may like 'dynamic presentations', 'clear-cut actions', 'long-range, in-depth planning', 'keep power to themselves', 'appeal to reason'. They may 'compare against an ideal model', 'set high standards for themselves and others', 'not reveal their own position', 'require structure, agenda and methods'.

It can be seen that this approach may come into direct conflict with other individuals who approach life in a different way. In short, we tend to get on best with people who are like us, but we tend to have problems with people who are not like us. As the consultant – a stranger to the client's community – it is surely up to us to make the adjustments to fit in. One of the greatest difficulties we have is when we encounter task-centred extroverts. These people are usually dominant, energetic individuals who will be clear in their demands of us. Many consultants do not like to be told what to do and how to do it, and how they will be held accountable.

The power struggle that this involves can be particularly difficult for the most senior consultants and partners. It becomes increasingly acute if the consultants perceive the client to be less educated, less intelligent or less competent than they are. The client, for their part, of course feels that they are more knowledgeable about their own business and their business environment. Young, less experienced consultants may also experience this difficulty.

The central issue in all of this is that each of us has developed patterns of behaviour which suit us. Some of us need more information than others; some are slow to make decisions, others act more quickly. Some require great detail, some need group approval, some want to be in charge and others want to have fun. The moral is that we as consultants need to recognize these traits in our clients and endeavour, as much as possible, to present ourselves in a manner and style which suits the client group. If we do this, they will feel comfortable with us and are much more likely to become committed to our proposals. Some consultancies have applied personality testing to their own and even client personnel, particularly their team preferences (see Belbin's works for more on this). This can be of importance where teams from the consultancy are interacting with teams from within the client community – sharing responsibilities and implementation.

A further issue with personality is for the consultancy to recognize the various facets of the group culture of the client. There may, for example, be regional or national characteristics and the same company may operate in slightly different ways in two different locations. Overseas-owned companies often experience a culture problem and the owner's ways of doing things are subtly altered to suit the national traits.

Building rapport

There are a number of strategies that have been suggested in order to help people to develop a better relationship and rapport with clients. One of these is NLP – Neuro Linguistic Programming – an approach which developed from the therapeutic world in the 1970s. They present strong arguments for mirroring and matching – that is, behaving in a similar way to the client even down to the kind of language which is used. There is much talk in NLP of representational systems (whether people are visual or auditory etc) and of observing eye movements. If nothing else, a study of NLP forces the practitioner to observe closely the people they are dealing with. This alone will provide a remarkable number of signals which can redirect conversation and behaviours.

NLP began by modelling three well-known therapists in order to ascertain what it was that made them so successful. This process can itself be useful. Within every consultancy, there are consultants who appear to be much better at influencing clients and getting on with them. It is valuable to observe and question what it is that they are doing (or not doing) that helps them to be successful.

> *The regional branch of a major professional association for HR profession-*
> *als always invited guest presenters to its monthly meetings. Average atten-*
> *dance could be well over 40 and so the presenters often saw this as an*
> *opportunity to develop contact with new prospects to gain new business.*
> *On two occasions presenters spoke about their in-house work for develop-*
> *ing good relationships and enhancing personal rapport. Each was from a*
> *different 'school' of training but both managed to totally alienate most of*
> *their audience with their confrontational behaviour and immoderate com-*
> *ments. Each, however, was convinced that they had succeeded in challeng-*
> *ing and stimulating their audience to higher levels of awareness – they*
> *seemed completely unaware of the strong negativity against them. Both had*
> *failed to practise what they preached or to achieve for themselves the out-*
> *comes they assured for their audience.*

LAB profiling

NLP practitioners consider meta programmes to be the main traits or
drivers of an individual's behaviour. One attempt to classify these was
the LAB (Language and Behaviour) Profile. Through a series of questions in a normal conversation, a number of these traits are revealed.
For example, if you ask someone how they know something (for
example, that they are good at a certain job or that something is valid),
they will tend to respond in two different ways.

The first (external) will cite all the external evidence which supports their view. These could be reports, assessments, monthly figures,
feedback from the client or their manager etc. Others (internal) will tell
you that they 'just know inside' when something is right. You can immediately see the implications of this. Externals will listen to outside information and, indeed, will need it in order to feel comfortable. Internals,
however, will only accept something if it fits with what they feel inside
already. It is very difficult to convince internals if they have already
made their mind up about something. Many professional people, inci-
dentally, including management consultants, tend to be internals and
their professions often encourage them to become even more so.

If you ask people what they look for in something (for example,
a job, a consultant or a computer system) they will begin to tell you
their criteria for success. These are not always put in the order of
importance nor are relative importances always revealed. Further questioning can establish this. What they are telling you is the criteria by
which success, and therefore the consultancy assignment, will be

judged. As consultants, we would do well to listen to what they say and try as much as possible to follow what they want.

> *It is reported that when Renault and Volkswagen were competing in the prolonged negotiations to buy Skoda, the two offerings were eventually remarkably similar – but Volkswagen's offer also included an understanding that there would be a position on their board for the incumbent CEO of Skoda. Although they also had detailed discussions with the CEO, Renault did not include this in the offer. Skoda was eventually sold to Volkswagen.*

If you highlight a number of these criteria and explore why that is so important to them, you will begin to see a pattern emerge which will indicate whether these criteria enable them to gain something or whether it protects them from something. You could call this the greed- or fear-driven traits. LAB profilers refer to this as *towards* or *away from*. It is quite important because many consultancy offerings are presented either in a 'towards' or 'away from' manner – that is, you will do something better and make more money or your business will not suffer and you will not be punished by the tax inspector. Management consultants are often 'towards' people whilst accountants, tax advisers and the like are often 'away from' people. Thus there may be a mismatch between consultant and client in both approach and manner.

Perhaps one final example will suffice. If you ask people to describe to you when they did something successfully, they are quite likely to describe to you how they prefer things to be done. If you listen carefully, however, you will hear them describe how much inter-relationship they require. Some people will describe how they had complete autonomy and power in the situation, and as a result, the conclusion was successful. Others will present how they worked in a group but each had their individual responsibilities. Others will describe how they worked completely in a team role, making group decisions and under group approval. What they are telling you is whether they prefer to be independent at one extreme or cooperative at the other. Many management consultants are, in fact, independent and are happy to work under their own control, motivating and accountable to themselves. There are some obvious problems with this as when, for example, they need to interact with more team-focused, cooperative clients.

What LAB profiling is trying to achieve is that we understand other people better, that we adjust our behaviour to suit the ways they seek to interact, that we present ourselves more successfully in situations and that we become more aware of the various facets of our own makeup.

CONCLUSION

This chapter has only scratched the surface of what is available in the study of influencing other people. It is a fascinating area and there are many approaches to it. If it is made a lifelong study, it might help to fight against the human tendency to become fixed in our ways and to believe that the way that we like to do things is the right way. This is particularly the case if we have been brought in as the 'expert consultant'.

Many surveys have shown that the most preferred and the most successful ways to develop new consultancy business are by recommendation, by referral and by repeat business from existing clients. All of these are directly influenced by our ability to integrate into a client's organization and develop a good relationship with the individuals in them. An understanding of organizational behaviour, of personality and of influencing techniques is a crucial factor in our long-term success.

CHAPTER TWELVE

CHANGE AND PROJECT MANAGEMENT

Graham Johnson

The management of change covers two areas:

- Projects, where formal methods are used to implement a tangible deliverable such as a building or computer system. This aspect focuses on the tasks required to produce the deliverable, and is concerned with what you see your typical project manager do. He or she will have a good, solid, robust plan, risk analysis and have the project mapped out with clear deliverables.
- Changes that involve culture change or a change in people's attitudes. The methods used in these cases are less formal and are people related, and are concerned with managing the people, aspects of the change, handling hidden agendas, smoothing the way by selling the ideas behind the project, building a team etc.

Of course, projects involve change, and change needs project management, so in this chapter we will provide a unified method and set of tools and tips for you to address both aspects.

The project or change lifecycle that we use is based on the steps in Figure 12.1.

UNDERSTAND WHY YOU NEED OR WANT TO CHANGE

The first thing to consider before embarking on a change programme or project is why are we changing and what it is we are trying to change. What is the 'new situation' you are trying to get to?

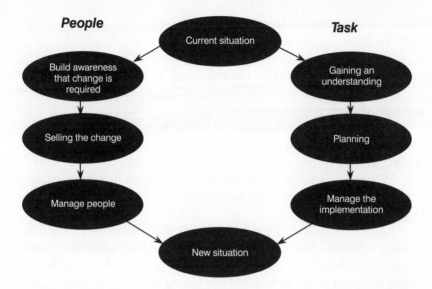

People   **Task**

The new situation then becomes the current situation ready for the next change

Figure 12.1 Project and change lifecycle

Some projects may be justified on pure financial grounds such as an increase in profitability. In other situations, you may feel that things need to change but you cannot explain why. Things just don't seem to be as productive as they should; there are lots of arguments. It doesn't feel like a good place to work.

Change can be initiated on two bases: 1) remedial – putting something right that is not going as well as it should; 2) developmental, which is about moving the business along.

In some situations, a financial business case can be made: 'If we do not improve productivity, we will lose business to the competition' (remedial) or 'We need to develop a franchise operation in China' (developmental). In other cases, there may be good reasons to introduce change, but the business case may be difficult to quantify, eg compliance with new regulations (remedial) or improving the working climate (developmental).

There is also a limit to the amount of change that can be absorbed by an organization at any one time, which will depend on several factors such as:

- your organization's attitude to risk;
- the strength of the drivers for change, for example how much better your competitors are doing than you;
- the attitude of senior management to change.

Many organizations go through an iterative change loop as shown in Figure 12.2.

Typically the outer loop generates small projects which generate small benefits. After a time, if the expected benefits are not being delivered, fundamental questioning begins which is likely to create a need for bigger change programmes.

So where are you in this process? Is it appropriate for you to start fundamental questioning or are some smaller changes a better option?

Once you have worked out an idea of what needs to change and your organization's propensity to change, you then can start the process of change itself.

The first step is to gain a detailed understanding of the current situation, what needs to change, and gauge people's likely acceptance of the change. Your work here can start to get people's buy-in to the change, which is to prepare them for change itself.

PROCESS OF CHANGE

Gaining an understanding

One of the common techniques used by consultants is the fact-finding interview with questionnaires to gain understanding of a situation.

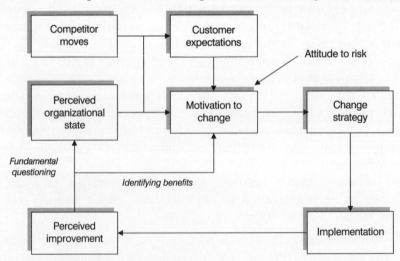

Propensity to change

Figure 12.2 The iterative change loop

These can be used both with senior and junior members of staff. The staff at lower levels will generally have a more detailed focus than senior executives. Consequently, investigating topics which are specific to the area involved is an excellent way of identifying detailed issues. Commitment to the change is increased through consultation at all levels.

Once you have collected the information, you are able to start to formulate outline solutions. There are three approaches you can use with staff to develop a way forward for the project:

- The *expert* model of consultancy is used where you tell the staff what to do based on your expertise in the area. This model is generally used by specialists such as IT consultants who are experts in their field.
- The *doctor/patient* model is used in situations where you are expert but require specific knowledge of an organization to identify the best way forward. This model works in exactly the same way as a doctor/patient consultation. The doctor asks you about the symptoms and he or she comes up with a diagnosis and treatment.
- Schein (1987) developed an alternative approach known as the *helping* model. This involves helping people to come up with their own ideas of the best way forward. This involves the consultant facilitating their ideas. This approach generates more commitment to change as people feel that the ideas are theirs and they are therefore more committed to them.

The most appropriate approach for you will depend on:

- *the people you are working with*: if they expect to be led, the expert model might be most appropriate;
- *you*: your standing and personality will lend itself to one of the approaches;
- *the culture and structure of the organization*: an organization that is aggressive will not readily accept the helping model as people may see you as weak.

When you have decided which approach to adopt, having collected your information, depending upon the people you are dealing with and the subject matter, it might at this stage be appropriate to hold some workshops. The purpose of these would be to highlight your thoughts and findings from your discussions and to discuss the various options that might be available.

But whichever approach you take, the end result from this first phase should be:

- you have a detailed understanding of what needs to change and why – a vision to aim for;
- you have built a relationship with the people who are likely to be affected by the change such that they appreciate that change is required;
- you have an outline of a basic approach;
- you have identified the high-level risks – things that may cause project failure.

Selling the concept

Your next challenge is to 'sell' the change to the key stakeholders – the people who will make the decisions and are most affected by the change. There are several methods to do this, one of the most common being need satisfaction selling (NSS). It is a similar approach to the helping model, except that you are now 'selling' the project. You have worked out what the project should entail; your aim is to obtain the authority to proceed. You use NSS to help you obtain agreement to this. It works as follows:

- Explore the needs of the people involved.
- Understand the need.
- Explain how the change helps to meet their needs.

For example, when meeting senior members of staff, you would talk to them about what is holding them back. When they have stated this, you would explain how the change would help them succeed and do better. Sounds simple, doesn't it – it is and it is a highly effective approach. The next time a car salesperson asks 'What are you looking for in a new car?', bear this in mind!

A key point here is that it is not only the overt objectives that should be considered. It is also the covert as these are often more important to the individuals concerned. Covert objectives include such things as the size of the department a manager controls, or whether a manager can be seen to be better than their peers in front of the CEO.

The structure of your organization should also be considered. It will often dictate the amount of work involved in 'selling' the vision to senior managers. For example, if a company is controlled by a single person who owns and runs the business, it may only be necessary to convince him or her. In a larger organization, where work is arranged on a functional basis with separate finance, marketing and other functions, it may be necessary to sell the vision and seek agreement to the vision with the different heads of department.

They may have very differing backgrounds, aspirations and views on the way that the business should be run. This can make the job of persuading difficult. For example, the head of the marketing department may wish to be innovative, and be open to taking risks, while the finance director may wish to adopt a more cautious approach.

Balancing the needs of the various managers and obtaining an agreed way forward that will give benefit is sometimes difficult. If you get stuck at this stage, you could hold a workshop and thrash out the issues. Whether this works depends heavily on the people and their relationship with each other.

Alternatively, you can apply incremental steps to your change, as shown in Figure 12.3.

In essence, you embark on a small change that leads you logically to the next stage etc. At some point you may find you change direction as a result of other external factors or as a result of learning from an earlier change.

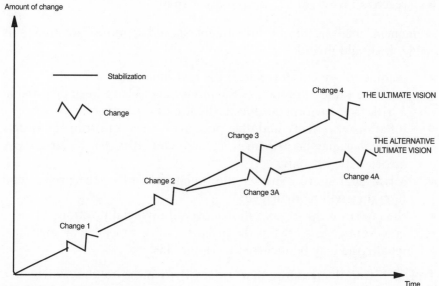

Figure 12.3 Incremental change

An example where this approach has been particularly success-ful is in organizations with a low risk culture. There is little point rec-ommending radical change in a risk averse organization, as the organization would be unlikely to be able to cope with it. In these cases, the policy of incremental change is more appropriate.

BUILDING A BUSINESS CASE

When you have identified what needs to change and how you are going to go about it, and you've sold the idea and approach to senior man-agement, you may need funding and you will have to justify the expen-diture.

In some cases, there are tangible benefits where the financial return is clear. In these cases, you can use the standard methods for cal-culating financial returns, which are described below.

Tangible benefits

When the financial benefits are clear, you will probably be investing for one of the following reasons:

- asset replacement;
- cost saving;
- expansion;
- reactive investment to keep market share.

A financial analysis of the investment should demonstrate that it is viable. It should include:

- income forgone as a result of the investment;
- the time value of money, as the money could have been invested in a 'risk free' investment during the life of the project;
- inflationary effects and the potentially disproportionate differ-ences that may be present in income and costs, particularly those associated with staff;
- a risk analysis to consider the potential risks to the project and how they will be managed;
- the effect on the organization's overall financial position;
- crawl-out costs so that if the project is to be cancelled at any stage, what costs may be incurred by doing this.

Typical financial measures that are used to measure the worth of a project are as follows:

- payback;
- accounting rate of return;
- net present value, NPV;
- internal rate of return, IRR;
- discounted payback;
- profitability index.

Make sure that all the relevant costs are included in the analysis. Opportunity costs are often overlooked, such as the income that could have been received from the alternative use of a facility.

Sunk costs, which is expenditure that has already been committed, should be ignored in any analysis going forward as it does not affect the return now available. The money is spent and, irrespective of whether you proceed with the change, this money is gone. It is important to establish this, otherwise an emotional reaction, 'good money after bad', can mean that perfectly good projects are not progressed even though they offer a good return on their investment.

Balanced business scorecard

In some cases where the benefits are intangible (such as increased customer satisfaction), financial analysis will not work, so a different approach is required.

The method to adopt in these cases is to attempt to quantify the intangible as well as the tangible benefits by using an approach such as the balanced business scorecard, described in the *Harvard Business Review* (Kaplan and Norton, 1992). The method is used to measure the performance of a business, but it can also be used as a framework to assess and measure the benefits of a project or change to a business.

The approach acknowledges that people's behaviour is shaped, to some extent, by the way they are measured. Classic accounting measures, by contrast, do not support innovation.

The scorecard technique is based on measuring the following factors:

- How do customers see us? (the customer perspective);
- What must we excel at? (the internal perspective);
- Can we continue to improve and create value? (the innovation and learning perspective);
- How do we look to shareholders? (the financial perspective).

The scorecard has the following benefits:

- It brings together in a single place the disparate elements of an organization's competitive agenda.
- It guards against sub-optimization as it forces senior management to consider all the important operational measures together.
- It highlights that by gaining in one area you may be losing in another (for example, cost savings at the expense of customer service or innovation).
- It allows for experimentation, by having innovation as a measure.

The way that you use the scorecard is to apply all of these factors to your proposed change. You should then be able to show that there is benefit to the business using a widely accepted business model.

If senior management won't accept this and insist that there has to be a financial payback, a way around this is to calculate the required uplift in sales that will be required to pay for the project. You can then gauge whether the improved customer satisfaction is likely to generate this level of sales, thereby justifying the project. This can only ever be an approximate method as there are many external factors that can affect sales figures, but at least the method can provide a feel.

In summary, in situations where there are clear financial benefits, classic financial measures can be used. In a situation of uncertainty where the benefits are intangible, the balanced business scorecard can be used. If senior management dislike the scorecard approach, the financial case can be worked backwards to show the required improvement to justify the project.

Project documentation and assessment

To bring all of this together, the project can conveniently be documented on a project definition report (PDR). In principle, this contains the following sections:

- the vision statement;
- an analysis of the benefits of the project, be they tangible or intangible;
- a high-level view of the tasks required to meet the vision;
- staffing requirements, including an organizational breakdown;
- an outline of how the project will be managed, with information on reporting systems;
- high-level risks.

Managers from different departments are required to sign to state that the project should proceed. This is important because it signifies that the proposed change fits business need from several perspectives.

Risk analysis is undertaken to identify those things that might cause project failure. Sensitivity analysis is included so that decision-makers obtain a feel for the effect on profitability of an adverse change in circumstances.

Figure 12.4 shows an example of a standard form that can be used when undertaking this type of exercise.

As you can see, the back-check form in Figure 12.5 mirrors the project assessment form. This helps ensure that the project is assessed against the original justification. You can use this arrangement to demonstrate to senior management that you are confident that the project will deliver the stated benefits.

WHAT HOLDS YOU BACK

You've now reached the point where you have justified the project and got the necessary buy-in to the change. You can now start to move the project forward. So what will hold you back?

A quote from George Bernard Shaw provides a good illustration: 'The reasonable man adapts himself to the world: the unreasonable one persists in trying to adapt the world to himself. Therefore all progress depends on the unreasonable man.'

In other words, you have to be unreasonable to elicit a change from where your organization is today. Don't accept that you cannot change – keep asking, 'Why not?' If people say, 'because we have always done it this way' then it's about time to change. You must be the champion of the change; a major part of your success is tied up in your ability to convince everyone that the change should be made. Your task is to create a force or momentum for change.

People will complain it's too difficult. But in the vast majority of business cases, the changes aren't attempting to put a man on the Moon or build a Channel tunnel – both of which have been done – but to implement something much more simple. So assuming that you have the resources to undertake the work, the main thing holding you back is you and your people's attitudes. So start with a 'can do' attitude and instil this into your team – lead by example.

Politics, covert objectives of managers and hidden agendas will hold you back. Typical overt objectives of managers are to decrease the amount of administration work, thereby increasing the performance of their staff. A covert objective might be to increase the size of their

PROJECT TITLE:

OBJECTIVES:

AIMS OF THE PROJECT:

SCOPE

LIFE OF THE PROJECT

IMPLEMENTATION:

BENEFITS:

PROJECT TYPE

OTHER OPTIONS CONSIDERED

	REASONS REJECTED
1	
2	
3	

CONSEQUENCES OF NOT PROCEEDING WITH THE PROJECT:

DEPARTMENTAL PRIORITY

RISK ASSOCIATED WITH THE PROJECT

	EFFECT ON BENEFITS
1	1
2	2
3	3
4	4

RESOURCING AVAILABLE

CORPORATE STRATEGY FIT

COST-BENEFIT ANALYSIS

	Predicted	Target
Aftertax internal rate of return (IRR)		> 20%
Pre-tax ROCA for first 5 years		> 30%
NPV at 20% discount rate		> 0

Investment plus first 5 years' running cost

Cashflow payback

SENSITIVTY ANALYSIS

BACK-CHECK DATES:

SIGNATORIES

Project Sponsor
Name:
Title:
Date:

I confirm that the project is required to further our business.

Signature

Project Manager
Name:
Title:
Date:

I confirm that the project timescales and budgets are realistic, and that their resource is available.

Signature

Finance Manager
Name:
Title:
Date:

I confirm that the financial calculations are correct.

Signature

Strategy Manager
Name:
Title:
Date:

I confirm that the project has passed the strategy assessment.

Signature

To ensure that project managers are focused on meeting the agreed objectives, organizations carry out back checks at appropriate times. Below is an example of a back-check form which could be used where financial benefits are measurable. A similar version can be used for intangible benefits

PROJECT TITLE:			AIMS OF THE PROJECT:
OBJECTIVES:			SCOPE
PROJECT TYPE			
COST–BENEFIT ANALYSIS	Actual	Target	
After-tax internal rate of return (IRR)		> 20%	
Pre-tax ROCA for first 5 years		>30%	
NPV at 20% discount rate		> 0	
BACK-CHECK DATES			

BENEFITS REALIZED	(Y/N)
IF NOT WHY NOT	
Signed:	Project Manager
Date:	

Figure 12.5 Back-check form

department so as to obtain more authority and power in the organization for the manager's own ends. Endeavour to understand the covert objectives as well as the overt objectives. The covert are often more important to them than the overt objectives.

There will be other things holding you back which will be project specific, such as a lack of expertise in a certain area. A technique to help understand and manage all of these issues or drivers is called force field analysis (see Appendix 1).

This can be used in a workshop where you would get the people to identify the forces for and against the change. To be effective, you should endeavour to include both covert and overt objectives.

The next stage is to work out those things that you can do to maximize the impact of forces for change and minimize those forces that are hindering the change. Following this, you can assign actions to staff involved to do this.

Another thing that may hold you back is your own personal authority. According to Handy, the principal sources of power available to you are:

- *Position power*, where as the project manager you can state that you have the backing of senior managers. This can only be used rarely, otherwise you lose credibility.
- *Resource.* If you control the project budgets you are able to utilize the budgets to ensure that money is available only for those tasks which fit with the project vision.
- *Personal skills.* The management of change requires expertise in interpersonal skills to persuade people to do things for you.
- *Expertise.* If you are perceived as successful in this role you will be treated as the leader. In a technical area, expertise in the particular technical area works in the same way.

Use these sources of power wisely.

You've now come to the point where you understand the change that is required and what will help and hinder you getting there. The next step is to plan what you are going to do, which is vitally important as many projects fail as a result of poor up-front planning. For example, with insufficient planning, you may not have sufficient resources to undertake key tasks or tasks will be carried out in the wrong sequence etc.

FORMAL PLANNING

When planning, it is important to bear in mind that you are striking a balance between:

- the time to undertake the tasks;
- scope of the work;
- quality of the deliverables;
- costs of provision.

For example, you may sometimes have to reduce the scope of a project if costs are higher than had been predicted. Or if you need higher quality, it may take more time and cost more. However, you can cheat the equation. One aspect that is often neglected is the people working on the project. If the staff are highly motivated, the paradigm can be shifted such that increased quality does not automatically equate to increased cost or time. You can do more with less!

Milestone identification

The first stage in planning a project is to identify the major deliverables from the project. This enables the production of the milestone list. From the milestone list, the major pieces of work that are required to produce the deliverables can be identified.

A key thing to bear in mind here is that a milestone should not be an activity. It should be a measurable deliverable. So, for example, in an IT project a milestone would be a signed off specification for the system, not the *task* of writing of the specification.

The milestone list can be used to generate the first-cut task plan using a work breakdown structure.

Work breakdown structure (WBS)

The WBS is a method of breaking the project down into manageable tasks. You have to consider how you will deliver each milestone – what are the tasks that you will undertake. What is the sequence of the tasks, in other words what are the dependencies between tasks, such as software that has to be written before it can be tested? All this must be well understood and built into the plan.

Priorities of the milestones and priorities of the tasks must be set, and do bear in mind that each task should have a clear start and end point.

Once you have established the tasks that need to be undertaken, you will need to assess how long they will take and who will carry out the work. You must build resource availability into the plan so that whenever staff are unavailable this is incorporated into the plan. Build contingency time into every task to allow for the unforeseen.

Ensure that each task has an owner. This makes the staff accountable and it helps to motivate them, as they feel responsible. Also, make sure that all the staff who are named on the plan agree that they will complete the tasks in the time-scales shown. Get their buy-in to the plan.

The plan can conveniently be shown on a Gantt chart. There are many software tools for helping with this. With these types of product, you are able to break the WBS down into different levels such as phase, activities and tasks.

These products have the facility to incorporate dependencies and resources. When things change, such as a task starting or finishing on different dates from the planned dates, or a member of staff becoming unavailable, the software can automatically calculate the effect on the plan and draw a new plan. The products represent the plan as a Gantt chart. An example is shown in Figure 12.6.

When planning and indeed managing the project, the sequence of tasks that take the longest time is known as the critical path. As project manager, you take a great interest in these tasks and the staff working on them as these tasks define the time that the overall project takes.

Another popular aid is the network diagram. Networks are diagrams of the relationships between tasks with dependencies. There are software packages, too, that you can use to display network diagrams.

Project staffing and organization

Work streams

The complexity of the project dictates whether the plan is 'owned' by

ID	Task name	Resource	Duration	17 Sept '01	24 Sept '01	1 Oct '01	06
1	Analysis of system	GJ	5 days				
2	Write specification	GJ	2.5 days				
3	Write software	SB	7 days				
4	Test software	CM	5 days				
5	Sign off deliverable	GJ	1 day				

Figure 12.6 Gantt chart

the project manager at a high level with sub-projects set up at the more detailed level which are owned by work stream managers, or whether there is one plan.

Once you have identified the first-cut resource requirement, the need for work stream managers can be formulated. At this stage, it is useful to choose the work stream managers on the basis of their expertise. This will include parameters such as:

- their ability to manage teams;
- their technical knowledge;
- their leadership skills.

In large organizations, it is standard practice to establish a contract between the overall project manager and the work stream managers. The purpose of the contract is to highlight what is expected of each party, such as the deliverables from the work streams and also the support the project manager will give to the work stream manager. This contract can take the form of a written agreement such as a role acceptance form or similar.

Staffing

There are several options for staffing a project. The main alternatives are: 1) second staff to the project; 2) use staff in their normal operational roles working on the project in parallel.

Both options have their benefits and disadvantages. For example, secondees are often viewed suspiciously by other operational staff. This may decrease their effectiveness, particularly if cultural change is involved and staff are concerned for their futures. The quality of secondees may not be the best; operational managers may choose to release their less skilled and competent staff as they have targets to meet and consequently will wish to hang on to their best staff.

Staff working in a dual capacity will often have conflicting requirements upon them. This may take the form of a balance of work between their normal work and the project. More serious is the case where an operational manager may instruct staff to work against the project aims to meet some covert need.

In general, research has found that the most effective arrangement is for staff to have dual roles. However, using this approach will often necessitate the project manager using strong interpersonal skills when dealing with operational managers, particularly if they are not fully behind the project.

Friction can develop as the roles of the operational manager and your role may overlap. There are various options to manage this problem. One of the favoured options is to make: 1) the project manager responsible for time and costs; 2) the operational manager responsible for scope and quality, acting as the sponsor.

When you have established the resources for the project, you may find that you have a resource shortfall. You will have to decide and then agree with the sponsor how to handle it. You could, for example decide on one of the following options, to:

- employ contract resource to fill the gap, thereby increasing costs;
- reduce the scope;
- accept a time penalty;
- accept a degradation in quality.

Project board

A project board or steering group can be established and chaired by the project sponsor, comprising the main stakeholders. The benefits that this gives you are that it:

- helps ensure that all stakeholders are in agreement with the way forward;
- shows commitment to junior members of staff by all the senior staff who are involved;
- provides a forum for debate about issues and the merits of various courses of action;
- provides help and guidance to the project manager.

MANAGEMENT OF THE PROJECT

As you now carry out your plan, the various aspects that you will have to manage are discussed below.

The people elements

As mentioned earlier, irrespective of the type of project, key to its success is the management of the people. It is vital to ensure that the people are motivated, whether you need staff to be innovative or just committed to delivering the necessary deliverables. It is also necessary to manage the expectations of the stakeholders. Don't promise that things will be delivered ahead of time. Assume the worst and allow plenty of contingency time for unforeseen circumstances.

A project will have two principal groups of stakeholders: the customers of the change, and the people who are working to make the change happen. A model showing the different strategies for dealing with the attitudes of these stakeholders is shown in Figure 12.7.

This is based on how satisfied both sets of stakeholders are with the change or project as measured by their satisfaction. The descriptions in the matrix describe an attitude strategy for the manager of the change with the people involved, as follows:

- *Crisis manager* is the strategy required where everyone is dissatisfied. This is typically the case when a change is heading for a poor result or failure. The attitude problem can be the reason for the problems or it can be the other way round where, because of inherent difficulties of the change, people become disenchanted with it. Either way, your approach should be one of crisis management. In this case, you have to get to the nub of the issues and address them as a matter of urgency. Projects that are in this state often end up being replanned as the existing plans are found to be unrealistic. You may well have to bring in fresh people to inject some energy into the project.

- *Salesperson* is the strategy required where the project team is happy but the recipient of the change is not. The strategy in this case is to use selling techniques to persuade the recipients that the project will provide them with benefits. NSS, described earlier, can help.

- *Coach* is the strategy to adopt when the internal customers are happy but the project team is not. The key skill here is the ability to be able to motivate the team by encouraging them, taking blockages out of their way etc. NSS also has a part to play here.

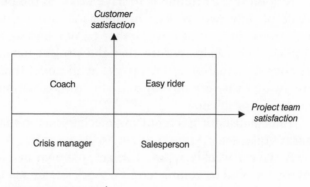

Figure 12.7 People management strategies

- *Easy rider* is where both project staff and internal customers are satisfied and happy with the project. The aim here is to have a watching brief with minimal involvement so that the staff own and develop the project themselves.

Whichever strategy you adopt, always bear in mind that it is people's self-esteem which dictates how positive they will be towards what you are trying to achieve. If you make them feel good about themselves, they will behave positively towards what you are endeavouring to do.

Managing costs and budgets

Your initial cost estimates are likely to be highly approximate. This is particularly the case when the business case is being developed. As you develop the work breakdown structure you should be able to identify the costs to a greater level of granularity.

There are several techniques for managing budgets. One of the most simple is to plot the budget on the Gantt chart. As you use funds, you plot this against the budgets, thereby giving you a simple project-based budget management system. So, if a task is completed ahead of schedule, the costs to the project can be reallocated in the project budget and variance measured.

Managing time

This is managed by having regular reports on progress of each current task. This enables progress to date to be input to the Gantt chart reflecting the reality of the current situation. Updates can be either face-to-face meetings, or formalized weekly reports.

A good rule of thumb is to have tasks on the plan which have a time-scale of only two weeks. On this basis, using a weekly reporting system, it means that a task will either be not started, nearly complete or complete. This helps ensure that the project manager knows and understands the situation of the project at all times. If dates start to slip, you are aware of it very quickly and able to take action before there is too much of a problem.

You can use formal reporting mechanisms so that you are aware of what is going on.

A typical weekly report format is shown in Figure 12.8. This type of form would be completed by a work stream manager or member of staff working on the project.

Date:	
Project:	
Completed by:	
Tasks planned for this week:	
Tasks completed this week:	
Issues:	
Opportunities:	
Tasks planned for next week:	

Figure 12.8 Example of a weekly report

You can receive these reports on a weekly basis so that you understand what is going on at all times. But please bear in mind that they are no substitute for going round and talking to the staff about how they are doing and where they might need some help for them to succeed in their tasks.

Managing quality

Quality in a project context is meeting the required specification or project vision. Achieving quality on a project principally depends on a good attitude of mind to the project from the team members and stake-holders.

In a formal sense, you should draw up a quality plan. This will mainly consist of the methods for monitoring quality to ensure a successful outcome; for example, independent acceptance testing by staff to confirm that delivered milestones are fit for purpose and meet the required specification.

You should build these tasks into the Gantt chart to ensure that they form an integral part of the project. Formal sign-off to a deliverable to confirm that it met the specification is good practice, because asking people to sign a document makes them consider the whole thing much more carefully. Likewise, if the sponsor wishes to change the scope, insist that they sign off the change within a formal framework.

Managing risk

As part of the initial work of gaining an understanding, you should have identified the high-level risks. Turner (1993) recommends identifying and managing risks at the detail task level by:

- exercising judgement;
- breaking down the plan to identify those areas where there are dependencies which will cause a knock-on effect if things go wrong, using 'what if' analysis;
- analysing the assumptions made when drawing up the project;
- decision driver analysis, which is to gain an understanding of the motivation for decisions within the project and assess whether these decisions are consistent with the project vision or to meet a hidden agenda;
- group techniques such as brainstorming, which identify risks quite effectively.

It is often more effective to use a mixture of these techniques.

From the above, a matrix can be produced showing the risks. Associated with each risk should be a method to manage the risk. This can be one of three types:

- avoidance, for example starting building projects well ahead of time to avoid the risk of bad weather;
- tasks to deflect the risk – for example taking out an insurance policy;
- contingency plans to manage the risk should it occur, such as having contract resource to be called on to work nights if a task turns out to be more complex than thought.

You should segment the risks into various categories such as technical and non-technical and examine the interrelationship of the risks. This gives a picture of the risks to the project and the risk impacts, where impact is given by multiplying likelihood by the consequence. It is normal to apply Pareto's principle (see Appendix 1) to concentrate on the top 20 per cent that tend to have the highest impact.

Also included in the risk matrix should be one owner of each risk – the person who is responsible for managing it. Often making people aware of risks helps minimize them. The risk assessment matrix is very powerful in doing this.

To manage risks, such as managers being uncooperative due to a 'hidden agenda', it is difficult to use a formal approach if the issues cannot be openly stated. If challenged, the managers would deny it. So try to predict the courses of action they might take and play a 'political game of chess' to minimize the damage they can cause. Also, if you have the power, when they do instigate things which damage the project, highlight the issue without personalizing it, so that they find it difficult to carry on with the course of action.

As you manage the project, inevitably there will be problems to overcome, such as unforeseen events, or areas of work, which only come to light later. You should have built contingency time into the plan to allow for these events, but when they do happen, don't try to fix them all yourself. Task a technician to solve the problem, get outside help, or brainstorm a solution with your project team.

GLUING THE CHANGE IN

As you manage the plan forward, eventually you will reach the point where the project team has met the plan and you have key deliverables in place. How do you make sure that the change is glued in so that you don't go back to how it was?

With a physical change such as an IT implementation, the system itself will glue in the change, particularly if it is a replacement system and the old system has been decommissioned. If you have put in place a change where it is feasible for people to go back, such as the implementation of new business processes, the main way of ensuring that they do not go back to the old ways is to have sold the change to them as you progressed the project.

Throughout the project life cycle, you should be doing this so that when the change arrives, the recipients are expecting and eagerly awaiting it. If you can get them to believe it is their change, so that they 'own' it – even better still. Coupled with this you should ensure that the managers of the staff understand the benefits of the change and ideally that their performance targets are linked to its ongoing success.

SUMMARY

In summary, the skills you will need to manage a successful outcome fall into two categories: the *task* elements and the *people* elements.

The task elements include such items as:

- good planning with the use of formal planning techniques;
- managing the tasks;
- problem solving;
- good efficient communications within the project.

The people elements include:

- gaining legitimacy to run the project;
- gaining commitment of the staff involved;
- team building;
- selling and unblocking;
- managing the politics.

You will undoubtedly have to cope with pressure. It is important to be able to handle this pressure and appear cool-headed in a crisis. Make sure you clearly identify objectives and allocate ownership of tasks to meet these objectives. Create clear, accountable plans. In doing this you will share some of the pressure and help build a team.

You must put effort into building an effective team. Make people feel significant, get them to work together and create an environment where staff are motivated and committed. Celebrate success. Understand failure and learn by it, but after that, move on to the next success. If you achieve this, you are 90 per cent of the way to a successful outcome as the people on the team will ensure you all succeed.

INCREASING PERSONAL EFFECTIVENESS

CHAPTER THIRTEEN

MANAGING YOURSELF

Clive Bonny

Managers are taught that time is one of their most precious resources, and there are many courses that managers can attend that teach them how to organize themselves more effectively.

For consultants, managing time is even more important; a consultant's stock in trade is time and – like many other professionals – consultants are usually required to keep a record of how they spend their time, for costing purposes. Consultants need to make sure that they spend no more time than is essential on any project, so effective personal organization is of the essence.

Yet time is one of the most mismanaged resources in business. This chapter focuses upon some key issues associated with time and how you spend it – ie managing yourself. Topics include goal-setting, controlling workflow, developing mind and body, managing stress and ethical dilemmas.

Use this chapter to review your day-to-day challenges and identify appropriate ways of tackling them so that your goals are more easily achieved both at work and at home. Whilst some of these points will not be new to you, as you remind yourself of them you should ask how effectively you are actually applying good practice.

GOAL SETTING

What is your mission?

The starting point is to clarify what you want to achieve. Successful people invariably talk about how setting objectives gives them a focus.

Many of them also articulate a clear sense of purpose, a mission in life, encapsulating why they exist. One of the best-known mission statements comes from the fictional Captain Kirk of Star Trek: 'to boldly go where no man has gone before'. Such a statement can not only act as a launch-pad for self-direction, it can also help others around you know your driving force and understand what makes you tick. Beware, however, of creating a statement that is long-winded or complex. Keeping it short and simple, whether written or unwritten, will avoid confusion. But it must enable you also to know what you should *not* do, as well as what you should be doing. Articulating your overall purpose is a fundamental step before setting objectives.

Setting personal objectives

Those who fail to plan, plan to fail. The next step is to set out clear goals and objectives against which you can measure achievement and success. Without these it is impossible to say if you are travelling in the right direction or when you expect to arrive at your destination. Goals should relate to a time-scale around which you wish to exercise control. Whilst in business the pace of change makes it difficult to plan more than three or five years ahead, the wider context of matters outside and beyond work should also be considered. Where do you want to be in ten years? Retirement planning is essential to start early, yet far too many, especially in smaller businesses, fail to make effective provision for themselves and their dependants. Visualize the future, and what you want it to look like. Set yourself a *lifetime* goal. Then, working backwards in time, identify key markers which will keep you on track to achieve what you want from life. By including goals that are non-work related you will avoid the trap of work becoming an end in itself rather than just a means towards a better life. On an anecdotal point, the writer comes from a family of self-employed parents and grandparents. With the same aim in mind, the writer purposefully undertook a variety of jobs at different levels in different departments and industries to become eventually a self-employed business manager. Without an eye on the long term, it would have been easy to become side-tracked into a short-term opportunity.

The components of an effective objective are described in the acronym SMART: specific, measurable, agreed, realistic and timetabled. A Specific target could be to redeem the mortgage or open a branch office, and Measurable means putting a figure on it, eg earn £75,000 pa. Agreed means obtaining the commitment of other stakeholders who may be involved in supporting your objectives. The number of objectives should be Realistically manageable and should complement and not compete with other objectives, eg the costs of opening a branch office may prevent earning £75,000 the same year. Lastly, it is essential that objectives are Timetabled – ie you have clearly stated when they are to be achieved. And beware of the trap of 'as soon as possible'; it does not mean urgent!

Change is the rule rather than an exception, and there should be an appropriate regular review of objectives so that you can respond quickly to any new circumstances that may deflect you from your aims. Your amended aims should again be shared with those stakeholders who are party to success, so that they feel shared ownership and commitment (including suppliers, customers and the local community). Business people are increasingly entering into partnerships and managing supply chains where the sharing and aligning of people's different objectives can result in more realistic expectations of yourself.

PERSONAL DEVELOPMENT

After devising personal objectives it is necessary to analyse another fundamental resource for achieving them – yourself. By looking at what you want to achieve and the tasks required, you will be able to identify the skills and knowledge needed. If you work in a primarily technical environment, then knowledge of particular products or processes may be important. If your environment is mainly people-oriented, then the skills to develop and manage others may be key. Review yourself objectively by examining the key components of your job, the ideal underpinning skills and knowledge of the jobholder and then compare yourself with this ideal. Any gaps between the ideal person specification and your own abilities will be training needs. Prioritize these and decide how these training needs should be addressed.

An effective training plan should also be 'smart' and should include both short-term training needs, and longer-term development needs. Development needs may also relate to professional education requirements, particularly if continuous professional education is mandatory. In this instance a written plan for the year and a review process are essential evidence for maintaining status within your professional body. The concept of *lifetime learning* is now accepted commercial practice, with the emphasis on your active self-development, rather than passive acknowledgement that training is merely something to do when time permits.

There are four elements to a training plan:

1.   the objectives (ie what you intend to learn or do as a result);
2.   how you will implement training (eg through projects at work, formal class-room tuition, reading or audio-visual tapes);
3.   a schedule showing the implementation plan;
4.   a review measuring what was done and its effectiveness for you.

You should also consider your preferred learning style, as selecting inappropriate methods will hinder development. Four styles are commonly referred to:

- *Activists* are often lively outgoing types who like to 'learn by doing'; these people prefer games, exercises and activities, such as role-play.
- *Reflectors* are more cautious and quieter, often observing others before getting involved; they benefit from time to analyse and review.
- *Pragmatists* like to develop new ideas and quickly link them to the job in hand.
- *Theorists* want to see the rationale for change and understand the model or system before applying it on a step-by-step basis.

Decide which of these four types is your preferred style and ensure the training method fits accordingly.

Most learning occurs naturally and informally at work, and it is worth reflecting upon the opportunities that present themselves and how you can take better advantage of them. At the simplest level, working with others allows for learning through information exchange. Beyond this, however, there may be scope for involvement in research activities. Even personal activities outside work (eg voluntary work, club secretary, school governor) provide a rich source of experience which can supplement work-based activities. If you do not take your personal development seriously you will be sending a clear message to all those who work with you or for you.

An effective way of demonstrating your intent to learn is to ask those who work with you to rate your effectiveness in your job. You will usually find this overcomes the deficiencies of your own subjective self-appraisal, particularly if you ask for their anonymous feedback and assure them of no recriminations.

CONTROLLING WORKFLOW

Any long-term or short-term plans should consider the Pareto Principle whereby 80 per cent of results are created by 20 per cent of activities. The same principle applies to managing daily workflow. There are always a few key activities which contribute to the majority of output. The most effective tactical tool for personal time management is the To Do List, which when applied effectively will significantly improve the planning of your own time, and help others to respect your own. This does not mean simply listing things to do in the day, and there are a number of rules to follow for the To Do List (whether on PC or paper) to be a workable tool.

The list should comprise a realistic number of items (maximum 20) each of which is prioritized either 'must', 'should' or 'could'. Important and urgent items take priority and must be done first, avoiding the trap of doing 'easy' tasks, which invariably divert time from difficult yet important ones. Write a start time and estimated completion time for deadlined items and bundle similar tasks together (eg telephone calls). Try to put tasks that require high quality output into the time zone when you are most alert, recognizing the natural peaks and troughs of your body clock. Decide firstly if you are an 'owl' (ie a 'pm' person) or a 'lark' (ie an 'am' person), then consider if activity sequences will help or hinder (eg a heavy lunch or a difficult meeting). Always build in contingency time to respond to external unpredicted events, and build in 'rest' or 'thinking' time before changing tasks; most people tend to generate high activity time, which can invariably be reduced by better planning. Tick or even reward yourself in other ways when completing tasks and savour achievement to maintain a desire to do more.

If you are part of a team workflow chain, then sharing To Do Lists will identify overlaps, gaps or other issues in advance. Develop your list at the same time every day so it becomes habit-forming, and try to schedule difficult tasks early on as they will otherwise hover over you like a dark cloud. Sometimes smaller chunks of larger tasks should be added and your creation of a separate 'long-term' To Do List will ensure these items are addressed before they become critical (and are rushed). It is particularly important to include personal development activities to ensure they are not continually deferred. Keep the list handy for easy reference and communication to others who may have a habit of passing tasks to you without understanding what you already have in hand.

MANAGING TIME

Organizing key tasks is a first step in managing time. If you find you are still unable to manage time, then you should perform an audit of where your time goes to diagnose and resolve the problem.

Audit how you spend your time

List the activities performed in a typical week, including making and receiving phone calls, attending meetings, travelling, lunch and rest breaks. Allow space to add unexpected activities such as interruptions from colleagues. Using this simple format, mark the number of minutes actually spent in each activity as you go through a typical week, totalling up at the end of a week. Check how these totals relate to what *should* be happening, ie under ideal circumstance where should your time have gone? You may have found that you have a persistent interrupter, in which case your interruption log may be used to help you persuade the interrupter to batch their interruptions at a time agreeable to both. Alternatively this may show you that you are 'feeding the monkey'. ('Feeding the monkey' is a phrase derived from an excellent article on time management published in *Harvard Business Review* – see References and bibliography).

Beware of monkeys

'Feeding the monkey' is an expression for doing things unnecessarily for other people. There are many time thieves, and 'monkeys' are those activities thrown to you by people who are often passing the buck. They may be suppliers, customers, people inside or outside your own business, and are often your own staff. You may even enjoy feeding the monkey because you are flattered to be asked, or it may be an interesting diversion. Unfortunately monkeys eat into your discretionary time (ie time available after fulfilling the demands of your real job) and every time you feed them, they become more dependent upon you.

Recommendations for handling monkeys are:

- feed them face to face or by phone, not by memo, at an assigned feeding time;
- keep the monkey population low;
- if you don't feed them, shoot them, and avoid saying 'leave it with me'.

The art of delegation

Monkeys are more likely to leave you alone once you have mastered the art of delegation. Decisions over routine matters can often be made elsewhere, and most people get a sense of achievement from completing entire jobs rather than doing piecework. Delegation, however, is often unsuccessful when a few key steps are omitted. Common errors include failing to explain to subordinates why the job is necessary, why you selected them to do it, what the result should look like and what other resources exist to support them. After delegating, it is useful to ask how they feel about doing it (if it is new to them) and always thank and give credit for good work.

Where appropriate, you can delegate message-taking to voice-mail, so you can choose how and when to respond at your own convenience. The best way of getting monkeys off your back, however, is to teach them how to feed themselves. There is no other way of doing this than by asking them to reflect how they could do it themselves, offering advice and encouragement, to coach them into independence. Give them a fish and you feed them for a day; give them a rod and you feed them for a lifetime.

Keep meetings brief

Communication with others is time-consuming, none more so than meetings. More than half of a manager's time is invested in conferences, either by phone or face to face, and there are some simple ways of substantially reducing time wasted. A few time-savers are as follows:

- Stick to start and end times.
- Allocate time per agenda item.
- Appoint an assertive timekeeper (separate from the chair).
- Write minutes as you go.
- Meet whilst standing up.
- Attend for only the relevant discussion points.
- Bring others back on track quickly.
- Ensure you start prepared.

Other time-saving tips

Wasted telephone calls can be equally frustrating, and for outbound calling it is useful to record the best time to reach people or let them know your own availability. A saving of only 5 per cent of your day equates to 14 days a year.

Travel time is also an area where significant savings can be made. Is the trip a necessity? Can you start early or leave late to avoid rush hour? Are there alternative routes? Do you have a dictating machine to capture important ideas en route? Could you play learning tapes in the car? There are increasing numbers of personal development books now taped for travel time.

Most busy people have difficulty finding time to read the increasing volumes of information now available and information overload is an issue we often make worse through overuse of technology's ability to copy data worldwide. Speed-reading can increase your capacity from 200 up to 1,000 words per minute, a five-fold increase. More efficient reading can also improve concentration and comprehension. For a general improvement to reading ability it is important to clear the workspace, set time limits and hold an upright posture with the material at about 45 degrees in front. Your eyes should be guided with a pointer (a pencil or finger will do) which sweeps the page with eyes following at a constant speed. Scan the first and last paragraphs for key ideas, and then focus only on nouns and verbs in the body of the text. Avoid stopping and going back, as creating a flow and momentum is important. Gently increasing speed over a period of time will ensure you develop the skill at your own pace.

The increased use of electronics has multiplied the amount of paperwork we handle; cluttered desks hinder clear or creative thinking, so the temptation to leave a number of different tasks on the desk should be resisted. Adopting the GUTS system can help: Give it away, Use it, Throw it away, or Send it. Grouping papers and putting them away quickly is essential; a waste-bin should be used frequently instead of a pending tray. When in doubt, throw it out. Removing your name from circulation lists helps, as will a daily routine of filing. At least once a year in a less busy period, review files and clear out unnecessary information. Documents should be retained only on the basis of importance and regularity of referral (about 90 per cent of filed paperwork is never referred to).

MENTAL FITNESS

The increasing volumes of information can be better managed by people with good memories, a skill which is mainly acquired rather than inherited. Your head contains three brains, not one:

- the Reptilian brain, which stems from the spinal column and controls basic instincts and functions (eg breathing and sense of territory);
- the Mammalian brain (or 'limbic system') which controls emotion, sleep and long-term memory;
- the Neocortex, the two-sided cerebrum that controls intellectual processes (eg reasoning and talking). The latter comprises the left-hand logical brain, controlling language, and the right-hand artistic brain for pictures, rhythm and creativity.

The two sides combine to assist the memory function in three stages: registration of information, retention and retrieval. Your brain has the capacity to register and retain every single piece of information encountered. The challenge lies in recalling and retrieving, and 'memory-masters' often use a few simple techniques to do this.

Linking new information to existing knowledge can be facilitated by exaggeration, humour and emotive images. The brain is stimulated by the unusual and if you have difficulty remembering people's names this technique works well. The name Clive Bonny can be transformed into Bonny and Clyde alongside the image of a gun-toting gangster into which you can insert the person's face. Music can be anchored to particular memories, so that when you learn or experience something whilst hearing a particular musical piece, its playback will recall the original context.

One of the most common memory techniques is 'mind-mapping', pioneered by Tony Buzan. Mind-maps mirror how the brain works by stimulating both left and right brain hemispheres.

The principle of mind mapping is to record information on paper (or screen) in a format that fits how your brain likes to register and retain information. Its key principles are as follows: Start with a blank sheet and a central image or word representing the theme of your subject. Draw curved lines outward from the centre with each line containing one word. Use up to four colours and vary the size of word to reflect its importance. Using the same colour for each branch of lines and images rather than words appeals to the right-hand brain; drawing arrows and patterns to connect themes appeals to the left brain. The style of the finished item may appear like a confused octopus, but your memory will prefer it to conventional alpha-numerics and you will find yourself recalling more information by scanning your mind-map than by recording in traditional methods. Its applications include speech making, project planning, problem solving, creating ideas and taking minutes. Other techniques include:

- rhyming principles, eg 'Thirty days has September, April, June and November . . .';
- acronyms, eg 'SMART' objectives;
- 'peg' systems, which hook your information to images which are more memorable, eg the number 7 can be represented by a boomerang, the letter B by a bumble-bee, the word Monday by money, or August by a gust of wind.

As with developing any new skill, such techniques will feel uncomfortable at first, but with patience and practice you will find that enhancing your memory can both astound your colleagues and improve your abilities in a wide range of activities.

Mental fitness is paramount to personal effectiveness, as it is increasingly more difficult to cope with the pressures and demands of work and home. At home there are more and more expectations related to consumer comforts and relationships. At work the pace of change in the job, new targets, technology, deadlines and flatter hierarchies combine to create an environment of pressure.

MANAGING STRESS

Everyone experiences pressure which in itself can stretch you to better performance, but too much pressure for too long leads to stress if you are unable to manage it. Stress can also occur in very short periods: making a presentation; doing a task for the first time; handling an irate person; making a mistake; being late for a meeting; or just high noise levels. Your body responds by automatically increasing heart rate and blood pressure, tensing muscles and the digestive system, and increasing breathing rate. This is your body's fight or flight response programmed by evolution for emergencies. The problem at work is that you are unable to release these physical symptoms with a physical response, thereby creating a bottleneck, which further increases pressure. This can become a downward spiral.

The first step in managing stress is to recognize the symptoms. You can identify signs by feeling impatient, depressed, frustrated or isolated. You may hear yourself slam phones or doors, drum fingers or talk quickly. Visually you may catch yourself nail-biting, blinking excessively or changing your eating and sleeping patterns. These telltale signals should be taken seriously and quickly on board. Most people suffering stress are usually diagnosed by all but themselves, and this 'loose cannon' effect only serves to further isolate the sufferer. Stressed managers are often unapproachable yet are often the first to complain that people around them are failing to communicate. The ripple effect then creates bigger problems.

Sometimes it is simply a person's perspective that generates stress – the old adage of the glass being half-full or half-empty. Those with personality 'type A' are restless high achievers and more likely than 'type B', who is more relaxed and accepting, to put pressure on themselves. You can create new perspectives by putting yourself in the shoes of others, by sharing your views, or by writing up the issues and assessing them factually. A few simple ways to put things in perspective are to think how the issue could be even more difficult to manage (making reality relatively easy) or consider how much more important other matters are (making this issue relatively unimportant). Focus on those things that you control, especially your thought pattern, which should be positive. The American habit of writing or saying out loud positive mental affirmations (PMA) is recommended.

PHYSICAL FITNESS

Mental health is governed also by physical health. Your environment must be comfortable: avoid fluorescent bulbs, have a fresh airflow, control room temperature. Your workspace should not be cramped, and your chair should assist lumbar support and a straight back. Your keyboard should allow elbows to be directly under shoulders with forearms parallel to the floor, without resting on the desktop. A two-minute break from the VDU every 20 minutes will prevent headaches, particularly standing up to stretch and changing eye focus. Closing the eyes for a minute can also help.

Using a telephone headset has been proven to reduce neck and shoulder tension, or swap a normal headset from one ear to the other. Organizations are increasingly offering lunchtime massage and short courses in self-massage are now available for office workers. The choice of colour scheme affects the thinking climate: yellow stimulates creativity, blue facilitates deeper thinking, green promotes calm, and red stimulates challenge. Some companies now have colour-coded rooms for different activities. The physical climate is also important; more than 250 different harmful chemicals have now been identified in office air, known as VOCs (volatile organic compounds). These come from photocopiers, wall insulation and floor materials and from dry-cleaned clothing. Studies by NASA have shown that plant leaves absorb many of these pollutants, purifying the air naturally, especially spider plants, chrysanthemums, azaleas, tulips and lilies.

Besides managing your environment, you should also plan your food and drink intake. Six to eight glasses of water per day is optimum, and installing a water tank in the office, instead of a coffee or cola dispenser, will also reduce the build-up of stomach acid. Vitamin supplements will overcome some of the deficiencies of fast food at lunchtime. Vitamin A (eg fish oils) improves vision and joint flexibility. B vitamins (in meat, milk and eggs) help memory (especially B5 and B6), Vitamin C is an anti-oxidant, which protects other vitamins from destruction, and Vitamin E (in grain and wheat) improves cell oxygenation. Rather than eating sweets, glucose tablets can generate 25 watts of electricity for brain functions (the brain needs 70 per cent of the body's glucose). The wrong diet equates to putting diesel into a sports car!

Your speed of thought and mental agility should be supported by a physical agility programme. Exercise is not just for the sporty types but must be seen as an essential building block to your quality of life. Fitness is an effective stress-buster and your physical fitness plan should aim for a gradual improvement in your exercise frequency and type. You should build up slowly to a half-hour workout every other day. If you have had little exercise previously, this may take several months. Select an environment in which you enjoy exercise, which could be either in a club or at home, and try to set goals which give you a sense of accomplishment. These could be stretching, from 10 to 15 lengths of a swimming pool, or be a walk to the local station rather than a drive. There are many excuses for not exercising regularly, but if you ask colleagues who do it if they would go back to inactivity they will invariably say NO. Exercise will clear your mind of worries, release physical tension, help you sleep and give you more energy to enjoy life. As one major leisure company says, 'Just Do It', but remember over-exercising is as dangerous as under-exercising.

PERSONALITY STYLES

One of the greatest causes of personal stress is to take on more than you can do. People prefer not to say NO because some are competitive (Type 'A') and want to win against all odds. Others prefer not to appear to be weak and their desire to support others results in overloading themselves. About 95 per cent of the population fall into one of these two styles – either aggressive or passive – and although most would prefer to think of themselves as assertive, only about 5 per cent of people are naturally so. The key differences between these three styles can be defined as follows:

- Assertive types express themselves at no one else's expense.
- Passive types fail to express themselves at their own expense.
- Aggressive types express themselves at someone else's expense.

The problem of aggressive types in the workplace is widely recognized and the law now protects against bullying at work. Forms of harassment, which can now lead to perpetrators becoming personally liable in the courts, include offensive jokes or gestures, purposefully excluding others from social activities and coercion and intrusion by pestering. The legal interpretation of a healthy and safe working environment now includes mental, not just physical, health and there are numerous cases of six-figure compensations being awarded against complacent employers and managers. The message to aggressives is to recognize the risks of inappropriate behaviour before it is too late, and for passive types to realize they have a final mechanism for support if all else fails. But prevention is better through assertive behaviour: by asking for what you want, directly and openly, in a way that respects others' rights.

ETHICAL DECISION MAKING

Your involvement in defending industrial tribunals will not be a threat if you make decisions and behave in an ethical manner. Ethical fitness, like physical fitness, can keep you in mental and moral shape only if you can recognize and address ethical dilemmas. The Institute for Global Ethics defines ethical practice as 'obedience to the unenforceable', and not only 'right versus wrong' but more often 'right versus right'. Effective ethical analysis is helped when the latter dilemmas are analysed according to whether they are about:

- short-term versus long-term gain;
- justice versus mercy;
- truth versus loyalty;
- self versus community.

A difficult decision can become easier when a structured process is applied to identify and balance the pros and cons of particular options, recognizing that 'lesser rights' are not necessarily 'wrongs' and that 'higher rights' are not always the only valid ethical outcomes. An example might be the decision to create redundancies when there is a small risk of business closure. The short-term gains may prejudice the long term; loyalty for individuals may be offset by loyalty for the group; a selfish desire for survival may overcome community benefits. Resolving such dilemmas will be influenced by the decision-making principles you apply.

Three common principles for resolving dilemmas are 'ends-based' thinking (ie do what is best for the greatest number of people); 'care-based' thinking (ie do what you would like others to do to you); and 'rule-based' thinking (ie acting on your highest conscience). Your choices become easier if you understand and agree with the decision-making principles of the people with whom you work. Teams discover this when they begin to discuss and agree a set of values. Consequently, finding out the values of others around you and communicating your own values can help you identify and address potentially deep-rooted conflicts before they happen.

Responding to conflict in a positive way is extremely difficult. Conflict tends to harden your attitude and stimulate the 'flight or fight' response, creating further pressure. The least stressful approach is to take a structured approach without rushing for solutions. Acknowledge a problem exists and actively listen to people's positions; identify concerns openly and search for joint solutions; finally check that everyone will commit to the agreed outcome, and ensure it is implemented to the satisfaction of all. Handling pressure in a planned way will usually result in positive outcomes.

This chapter has reviewed a number of key issues related to managing yourself: planning direction, controlling time, developing mind and body, and managing difficult situations. Much of the advice may be considered as common sense, and 'old adage'. Your greatest challenge is to review the extent you actually apply good practice. By doing so you will not only define and achieve your goals, you will also, by acting as a role model, enable others to achieve theirs.

SELF-ASSESSMENT

As reviewing your own effectiveness is a fundamental principle to managing yourself, you are invited to self-score the statements below; 0 = not at all, 1 = sometimes, 2 = usually, 3 = always.

	0	1	2	3		0	1	2	3
At **home** I have enough					At **work** I have enough				
Time with family					Management support				
Sleep					Teamwork with colleagues				
Exercise					Time to think and plan				
Financial stability					Knowledge and skills to do a good job				
Relaxation time					Time to complete tasks				
Social intercourse					Recognition when I do a good job				
Fresh food					Time for breaks				
Hobbies					Trust and respect from others				
Emotional fulfilment					Involvement in decisions affecting me				
Time to plan life goals					Reward and compensation				

Your scores will show you where strengths and areas for improvement exist. Your final step is to develop an action plan to address the gaps:

- What are your priorities and objectives?
- When could you start and complete?
- How will you implement change?
- Who will support your plan?
- How will you measure success?

And go for it!

CHAPTER FOURTEEN

DEVELOPING AND MAINTAINING EFFECTIVE RELATIONSHIPS WITH OTHER PEOPLE

Carol Harris

This chapter is designed to give you some insights into dealing with other people – whether customers, suppliers, colleagues or other stake-holders in the business. In particular it focuses on your own strengths and areas for development, and contains practical ideas for relating well to other people.

A consultant, by definition, does not have executive authority. Consultants have to work through other people. So skills in dealing with others are essential if you are to be effective as a consultant.

No one was born knowing how to make a presentation, how to elicit useful information, how to influence people to take action and how to manage difficult situations, yet effective consultants have learnt these skills, and you will already have many of them. They are the same skills needed in many other walks of life: the ability to communicate well, the ability to maintain enthusiasm, the ability to plan and orga-nize, the ability to analyse and draw conclusions. Turning these skills into ones that are relevant in consultant relationships is a small step, but a vital one if you are to be successful in managing your projects. By fol-lowing the ideas contained in this chapter, you will be able to become more aware of your present abilities, decide what you want to aim for in the future and have an idea of the steps to take to get there.

Here are a number of questions you might like to ask yourself before reading this chapter; take a few minutes to consider each of them before proceeding and, if you wish, you can make brief notes of your answers. Take each of the questions as applying to your relationships with anyone for whom you are acting in the capacity of a consultant. (At another time, you might care to answer the questions again in your capacity as, for example, a line manager, a team member or a member of your family at home, as this may be a useful process in other contexts too.) So, as a consultant:

1. Whom do you represent – yourself, a team, a function or an organization?
2. Who are the key people to whom you relate?
3. When and how do you relate to them?
4. What is your purpose in relating to your clients?
5. How good are you at relating to others generally?
6. What skills do you need to develop or enhance in this area?
7. Do you have any examples of people you know who are excellent at relating well to other people?
8. What problems have you faced in dealing with others?

Now you have thought about these questions, we will spend some time considering each of the issues they raise in turn.

WHOM DO YOU REPRESENT?

This is an important initial question. You may have been asked to contribute your personal expertise and opinions or you may have been asked to represent a wider group. For example, you may act as an internal source of specialist advice, or you might have been asked to act on behalf of your organization in an external project.

There can be significant differences in style, approach and process depending on which of the above are true, so being very clear about your role and function is an important base point at which to start.

WHO ARE THE KEY PEOPLE TO WHOM YOU RELATE?

There are various categories.

Firstly there is the obvious group: people who commission you or invite you to assist with a project. You may be dealing here with the person who needs to use your services directly, or with an intermediary or representative. Some of the people you may meet here are individual clients, management boards, other consultants, agencies and so forth.

264 / INCREASING PERSONAL EFFECTIVENESS

As well as the 'direct' client, who purchases your services, you also have other clients. One category that you may not have considered is your work colleagues. People you work with are known as 'internal clients' and they can also have claims on your time and resources. Internal clients are frequently forgotten, but building good relationships with colleagues is an important part of good project management. And, in your group of colleagues, you can include any people who work for you or to whom you report.

A further group of key people are your suppliers: people who provide you with services. Another group is contractors: anyone you take on, on a full- or part-time basis, temporary or permanent, to help with the work activities. There are also financial backers, or people interested in the progress of your business. And, finally, there are potential clients; people who are not yet in the market for your services, but who may be in the future. And it is also useful to consider that informal contacts can also be consultancy relationships: counselling a member of staff, giving advice to users of a department's services and chatting to a new contact over a business lunch can also contain consultancy elements; so awareness of the situation you are in is important, even though it may not, on the surface, seem like consultancy.

All the groups mentioned above are likely to have expectations of you and the effectiveness with which you meet these expectations (if positive), or counter them (if negative) can be a major element in the success of your entire project. It is important to consider your relationships with all relevant groups and be sure they are all dealt with effectively.

WHEN AND HOW DO YOU RELATE TO KEY PEOPLE?

Success is very dependent on how you manage relationships as well as what precisely is done; in other words, the process is as important as (and often more important than) the content of the interaction.

There are three factors that can be considered here; they are timing, format and manner.

Timing

When do you relate to other people? You might like to think of your interactions as having three phases:

- what happens before face-to-face contact;
- the contact itself;
- what happens after the contact.

Thinking about each of these stages will help you be more effective.

Format

There are various ways in which you can communicate with others. How many of these do you use?

- written communications (eg letters, briefing notes, business cards, memos, reports, progress sheets);
- electronic communications (eg phone, fax, e-mail);
- face-to-face communications (eg one-to-one interactions, meetings, presentations, negotiations).

Considering the appropriateness of various forms of communication will help you choose processes that work well.

Manner

Your own manner and style of communicating are also important. Some of the things that come into this are:

- image and appearance;
- posture, movement and gesture;
- facial expression;
- voice tonality, volume, speed, pitch and rhythm.

Paying attention to these, largely non-verbal, means of communication will help you come across as effective and professional.

It is helpful to remember that the earlier in an interaction you establish your credibility, the easier it will be for you to influence the person in some way. Your credibility is allied to the process elements we have just considered, so paying attention to them will be really useful to you. And it is worth remembering that credibility is not only developed through what you do well, but also by how you cope with difficulties. So, if you make a mistake, it may help to own up to it: you don't have to be perfect; showing you are human can work well too!

WHAT IS YOUR PURPOSE IN RELATING TO OTHERS?

You almost certainly already set objectives for a variety of work situations. For example, deadlines for projects to be completed, income generation levels, the recruitment of staff, and so forth. People often forget objectives for personal contact, however; does this apply to you?

What do we mean by objectives for personal contact? Each time you interact with others there are a variety of things going on. For example, each person has his or her own perceptions of the interaction; each person has his or her own interest in the conclusion; each person has his or her own way of valuing the process of communicating; each person has his or her own criteria for success.

By being aware of the multiplicity of factors involved in interactions, you can begin to think about what you might set objectives for. Let's consider some possibilities; you might set objectives for:

- keeping calm and relaxed;
- appearing professional to the other person;
- listening actively;
- making your point in a persuasive manner;
- encouraging the other person to feel interested in what you have to say;
- getting a commitment for future action.

Of course, there are many, many more possible outcomes than these; the important thing is to consider just how much of the process of the interaction can be subject to planning and control, while retaining necessary flexibility of response.

One simple way of thinking about objectives is to find active verbs to describe them; for example: *informing*; *challenging*; *convincing*; *agreeing* and so forth. And, still considering objectives, you might like to note the following things that are useful in setting good objectives:

- They should be stated positively (eg 'I want to come across as friendly', rather than 'I don't want to come across as unfriendly').
- They should be specific (eg 'I want to know exactly what the other person thinks about X within the first 10 minutes of the meeting' rather than 'I want to have some idea of the person's thoughts on X').

- They should be realistic (eg 'I want to create a good impression' rather than 'I want to come across as the most effective person s/he has ever met').
- They should be measurable (eg 'I will know I have been successful if the person telephones me to agree the proposal' rather than 'I want the person to be positive about my ideas').
- They should have a time-scale associated with them (eg 'I need to arrange a meeting with this person by the end of the week' rather than 'I need to arrange a meeting soon').
- You should have considered the pros and cons of achieving the objective (eg 'If I am really friendly with this person I may gain a useful ally; however, s/he may take up a good deal of my time over the next few weeks, so I may have to give up some of my independence'); by doing this you can better assess whether the objective is really one you wish to pursue.

When considering objectives or purposes it helps if you are able to shift your perspective so that you can have some concept of the other person's point of view. So many people simply go into a meeting thinking about what they want to get out of it, or speak on the telephone without any thought as to whether the person at the other end has the time, or inclination, to listen and respond. By thinking more clearly about the other person, you will be better able to deal with him or her effectively and in a mutually beneficial manner. (And do avoid 'mind reading'; it certainly helps to understand the other person, but do so in an informed way, not by making assumptions, which could be incorrect.)

So, although your own objectives are the only ones you can really control, it can help to think about the other person's objectives too (a technique which is also the foundation of effective negotiating).

HOW GOOD ARE YOU AT RELATING TO OTHERS GENERALLY?

If you believe you are excellent at relating to others, you will not have too much to do in this section! If, however, you feel you could do with some help in enhancing your relationships, you might like to think about the difference between situations in which your interactions work well and situations in which they work less well.

Take two or three occasions when you felt things were going really well, and two or three when you were rather disappointed with the process. Take a little time to explore and analyse these situations and see if you can work out what made the difference.

For example:

- Were you feeling energetic and enthusiastic, or tired and bored?
- Was the other person someone you liked or someone you were indifferent towards, or disliked?
- Did you feel knowledgeable about the subject or were you rather at sea with it?
- Did you possess the required skills, or lack some particular expertise?
- Did you think, in advance, that things would go well, or did you anticipate them going badly?
- Did you believe the interaction would be a success, or did you believe it would be a failure?

Once you have identified the factors that distinguish high from low performance, you are better placed to work towards generating the more positive factors whenever you need them.

WHAT SKILLS DO YOU NEED TO DEVELOP OR ENHANCE IN THIS AREA?

There is a wide range of skills involved in interpersonal relations and you may already have thought of several. Some skills that are particularly important are the following.

Self-awareness

Being able to monitor what you do, as you do it, is important in allowing you to assess the effectiveness of your behaviour. Some people are remarkably self-aware and usually very much in touch with how they come across; others are frequently unaware of their impact on others and, if you asked them, would find it hard to describe exactly what they did in a particular interaction.

One consultant I know tries very hard to give the impression that she is always inundated with work and has to juggle her diary around to fit in even the shortest of meetings with clients. She doesn't realize that it is transparently obvious to anyone with a shred of sensitivity that this is a front and she really isn't as much in demand as she likes to make out.

If you would like to develop your own self-awareness, have a go at these short activities; they are designed to be carried out in neutral situations, not when you are in an important meeting with a client:

- Next time you walk into a newsagent to buy a paper, notice how quickly or slowly you are walking, where you are looking and what expression you have on your face as you look at the shop assistant.
- Next time you make a telephone call to a friend, or member of your family, notice how quickly or slowly you are speaking, what tone of voice you are using and how loud or soft your voice is; also notice if you pause often or little as you speak.
- Next time you go to a cinema, theatre or concert, notice how you are sitting in your chair, whether you are keeping still or fidgeting, where you have placed your hands, what position your feet are in and how deeply you are breathing.

There are many more such self-observation exercises and paying definite attention to what you are doing is an excellent precursor to effectiveness in interpersonal skills.

Awareness of others

The other side of self-awareness is awareness of the people with whom you are dealing. Being able to pick up signals that indicate how others are thinking and feeling is an essential element in business communications.

You may have come across the term 'body language', but this is a very gross representation of the significance of people's behaviour. For example, the fact that someone has folded arms may, as the body language texts indicate, mean they are defensive or aggressive, or may simply mean they are feeling cold or are comfortable with their arms crossed.

So, to be really sensitive to others, it is important to notice the 'micro' signals they give off, which really tell you about that person's actions and reactions as an individual. Have a go at the following exercises, which will help you become more sensitive to other people's behaviour and feelings:

- Watch a quiz programme on television. As each contestant answers questions, notice his or her facial expression. Notice the differences between how the person's face looks when they get an answer right and when they get it wrong. This development of your acuity will help you become more aware of people's appearance when they are feeling positive and negative (and, because each individual will have his or her own pattern of positive and negative, these patterns will differ between individuals). With practice you will become more sensitive to the slight differences in appearance which relate to internal thoughts and feelings.

- When you are with someone you know very well, listen out for the differences in voice tone when they are pleased, when they are annoyed and when they are upset. As you get better at this, do the same exercise with people you know less well, so you can enhance your skills in noticing tonality differences that differentiate between different emotional states. This exercise will help you become more sensitive to voice tone as an indicator or response (and it works excellently on the telephone too).

Understanding others

Being able to shift perspective, and put yourself in another person's shoes, is vital to creating good relationships. If you stay where you are, you are likely to miss factors which are important to the other person.

There are a variety of ways in which you can begin to understand other people. You may find the following useful.

Absorbing information

If you are to understand other people, it is important to really concentrate on the process of absorbing information. The process can be thought of as having five stages:

1. *hearing* (this is simply taking in the person's words as they speak);
2. *listening* (this is making sense of the words you hear);
3. *understanding* (this is checking with the other person to make sure what you thought you understood was actually what they meant);
4. *acknowledging* (this is letting the person know you have understood, and appreciated, their views);
5. *acting* (if you need to take action, it is important that you go through the first four stages first, otherwise your action may be based on false premises).

Following this process through, and especially the understanding and acknowledgement parts of the process, will ensure that you really understand and that the other person feels that his or her thoughts and views are appreciated.

Three-level questioning

This is a technique whereby you start by questioning at 'level one', which is to ask questions of fact, for example: 'How many staff work for you?'; 'What is your budget?' and so forth. At the second level you question about feelings; for example: 'How do you feel about the changes that are proposed?'; 'What do you feel about having to spend time on this activity?' At the third level you question about values; what is important to the other person. The simple question here is: 'What's important to you about . . .?' (eg 'What's most important to you about getting this project in on time?'). This question will get to the root of the issues that concern the other person and will help you work out what to do to respond effectively.

Surveys/audits

The design and conduct of surveys is covered elsewhere in this book. Suffice it here to note that they can be used to collect data about attitudes and feelings as well as more 'hard' data.

Self-management

We have discussed the importance of self-awareness; it is also important to be able to manage yourself if you are to do well in social interactions. Some of the things that come into self-management include being able to generate self-confidence and motivation, being able to control negative emotional states, being able to use assertive behaviour and maintaining high levels of self-esteem.

One thing which many consultants tell me is that they often find that the way they feel is governed by their expectations of a situation. For example, if they have to give a presentation to very senior executives, or if they have to give 'bad' news to people, or if they have to 'sell' a project to someone, they can feel disempowered, apprehensive and demotivated. If you would like to avoid such feelings, have a go at the following exercise.

Find a quiet place, sit in a comfortable position and then think back to a time when you felt very confident about something. Remember where you were at that time and picture how the place looked; the colours and shapes you could see, what objects or people were around and so on. Then recall any sounds you heard at the time; how loud or soft they were and where they came from. Now allow yourself to re-experience the physical sensations you had at the time; how warm or cool you were, how your clothes felt on you and so forth. Finally, remember the feeling of confidence and notice where it is located in your body: is it in your head, your stomach or chest, or all over? Now notice your breathing and your posture. Now stand up and keep the feeling of confidence with you and notice your posture and your breathing as you stand. Now walk around, maintaining the feeling of confidence and, again, notice your breathing and also the speed at which you are walking, how you are moving your arms or legs, where you are looking and what expression you have on your face. In future, when you want to feel more confident, all you have to do is remember these postures, movements, breathing patterns and expressions and you will be able to create a feeling of confidence at will.

Creating and maintaining rapport

One mark of a good consultant is the ability to develop, quickly and easily, effective relationships with a variety of people. There is a simple key to this process of developing rapport and that is to do what we call 'matching' the other person.

Matching involves making yourself a little like the other person, because most people tend to get on well with someone who is similar to themselves. Matching simply means copying small elements of another person's behaviour or thinking; it is definitely not mimicking, which can really irritate or embarrass people, and it is not 'mirroring', which is copying exactly everything the other person does, as this is too exaggerated.

When you learn to match people you will find they naturally gravitate towards you and the ensuing rapport is the first stage in being able to influence and persuade them. The following are some things you might do in order to match someone:

- Wear similar clothes to them.
- Speak at a similar speed to a person on the telephone.
- Sit in a similar (not identical) position to the person you are with.
- Talk about detail if the person you are with is talking about detail; talk in broader terms if the person tends to generalize and talk in terms of bigger concepts.
- Get the person to assess something for themselves if they seem self

opinionated, but give them evidence of how others have benefited from the kind of thing you are proposing if they seem to be easily influenced by others or need constant feedback from others.

- Use processes which fit in with the ways in which the person absorbs information and learns (there isn't space here to go into detail on this topic, but reading a book on Accelerated Learning will help you with this process, as will reading about Honey and Mumford/Kolb's learning styles – see References and bibliography for references for these).

Flexibility

A key to successful interactions is the ability to act and respond in appropriate ways, whatever the circumstances. This means selecting what you do in accordance with the context and not necessarily just using the same behaviour, ideas or solutions you have used before.

The greater your flexibility, the more likely it is that you will be able to alight on a good approach for the situation you are in as different people require different approaches. For example, some of the things you might wish to be flexible about are:

- arrangements you make for meetings;
- the degree of humour you use;
- how you respond to feedback.

Ongoing interest

Finally, it is important to remember to make managing relations an ongoing process. Even when a project has ended, it is good to maintain contact with your client. It is nice to remember the client's personal interests and activities. It is rewarding to make your client feel valued.

Doing this, even when there is no obvious benefit to yourself, can pay real dividends in terms of client satisfaction and recommendations to others.

DO YOU HAVE ANY EXAMPLES OF PEOPLE YOU KNOW WHO ARE EXCELLENT AT RELATING WELL TO OTHER PEOPLE?

If you really want to enhance your people skills, it helps to find one or more role models you can emulate. You probably know some people who are good at getting on with others and getting results from personal contact. Some of these might be people you know personally and others might be people you know indirectly (for example, politicians) or even fictitious characters (for example, characters in plays or films). If you take time to watch and listen to others in similar situations to yourself, and find out what they do that works, you will get invaluable guidance for your own interactions.

Some of the things you might do to pursue the role-modelling concept are:

- watch and listen to shop assistants as they sell you items, and notice what they are doing that either interests you or puts you off;
- notice the techniques used by television interviewers either to put people at their ease or make them feel challenged; notice which techniques you feel you could use and which you feel would not fit with who you are;
- notice how your own colleagues, team members or bosses relate to you; notice what they do that makes you feel good and what they do that makes you feel bad;
- ask other people what they appreciate or dislike in contact with others; see if you can work out any patterns here about things that are useful to do or to avoid doing.

Developing your people skills on a continuing basis is essential to good relations. Even if you are good now, see how much better you can become with further development.

WHAT PROBLEMS HAVE YOU FACED IN DEALING WITH OTHERS?

We have all, at some time, had difficult moments. The following scenarios relate to predicaments that are commonly experienced by consultants. See if any of them sound familiar; there are suggestions about how to handle each.

What to do if the senior manager with whom you are dealing is causing poor morale or conflict within the client organization

This is one of the most common difficulties. Very often, managers rise to the positions they are in because of their ability to disregard people's feelings and needs. Being able to do this means that they can concentrate all their efforts on making decisions, and managing 'non-human resources' without being distracted by considerations of how they impinge on others, especially the people who report to them. However, this kind of management can, and does, lead to problems with staff morale, resentment, antagonism, stress-related problems and consequent apathy or hostility.

In some cases the consultant may be seen as allied with the manager and the negative feelings towards the manager can rub off on the consultant. But it can be more common for staff to treat the consultant as a confidante and sounding board, and attempt to get the consultant to side with them against the manager. This can be a no-win situation for the consultant and needs great sensitivity in dealing with the situation appropriately.

Two real organizations come to mind in this context. In the first, the manager was a quiet, unobtrusive individual, who found it difficult to relate well to people. Because of these difficulties with relationships, decisions were often made which either antagonized, or appeased, staff – rather than keeping them informed or taking them along – and morale dropped rapidly because management was seen as weak, problem avoiding and engendering favouritism.

In the second organization, the manager was a very tough individual, who was frequently aggressive towards staff and insensitive to their problems and concerns. Again, morale was low as people felt they were not valued and believed there was nothing they could do to influence workplace issues.

In both cases, these managers lacked self-awareness and had little idea of how they came across to staff. They were out of touch with staff concerns and spent most of their time fire fighting and avoiding staff contact. In both cases consultants had been called in to help, ostensibly with organizational issues but, in practice, to help and support the managers in carrying out their own roles within the organization.

So, what can you do if you are running a consultancy project and find that your client is, for one reason or another, ineffective or actually causing the problems?

There are a number of options here; they tend to diverge between assisting the manager and assisting the other staff within the organization.

If you wish to assist the manager, you can have a go at coaching, helping the manager learn and develop skills that will equip him or her to carry out the role better. An extension of coaching is mentoring, where you can offer personal support and guidance in a way that goes beyond simple skills development. Mentoring is becoming a popular approach within organizations and is a skill that the experienced consultant can utilize in a wide range of situations.

If you wish to assist the staff to cope with the situation, and perform effectively in it, you can help them to be more confident and assertive, and develop skills in influencing and feedback, so they can feel more capable of telling the manager how they feel and what effect he or she is having on them, and can be more influential in helping the manager to act differently.

To do these things it helps if you have strong interpersonal skills, as well as experience in coaching or training. If you do not, you might wish to bring in another specialist who can provide assistance to staff in developing their own resourcefulness and communication skills. In either case, it is useful to develop coaching and support skills as part of your longer-term portfolio.

If you do believe the manager is the problem, however, be sure that he or she is not acting deliberately in antagonizing staff. If the manager's behaviour is part of a strategy to rid the organization of (in his or her opinion) unproductive or uncooperative staff, or an attempt to demonstrate his or her power, or an attempt to adopt a low profile so that increasing demands are not made of him or her, your efforts at change management may well fail and you may be forced to ask yourself if you can ethically work within such a situation.

What to do if your client is unable or unwilling to devote sufficient time to the project or to contact with you as consultant

Your job as a consultant is made considerably easier when you have an internal contact able to spend time liaising with you, briefing you, dealing with internal problems that arise and generally discussing progress. If this facility is missing, it can be much harder for you to work effectively.

There are a number of possible reasons for this lack of contact: the person might believe he or she is simply too busy to make the project a priority or might not want to devote time to the project. This latter situation may come about for a range of reasons:

- not thinking the project is important;
- not wanting to be seen to be associated with it;
- wanting to make sure it fails (and, yes, this can happen!);

or a myriad of other reasons.

One thing you might do if the person really does not make time available is to develop your assertiveness skills, so you are able to face the person with the reality of the situation and explain, clearly and confidently, what the consequences of the unavailability are for the project's success. (And, when considering assertiveness, it is useful to do a mental rehearsal of what you are planning to say and how you are planning to say it. Doing this as if you were really there lets your mind know that you really are capable of doing it, and makes it so much easier when it really happens.) It is also helpful to make sure that you do not take up unnecessary time, so the person knows that, if you do want time with them, it is used to good effect. It may help, too, to put things in writing, so you do not have to keep asking for face-to-face time in a busy day. You can also see if there is another person in the organization you could work through instead; this will at least ensure the project continues, even if it does not necessarily get the top-level support you feel it requires.

Finally, you could suggest running a time management course for people in the organization (not, of course, targeted at the manager who always fails to make time for you!); if this succeeds, you may find that everyone gets better, including the person with whom you were having the difficulty.

What to do if your client lacks the ability to manage a consultancy project effectively or to establish effective administrative procedures in relation to it

If you embark on a consultancy project, it is vital that it is managed effectively. Your client within the organization therefore needs skills in project management and administration.

Very often, however, the person who is responsible for commissioning a project either has too many other commitments to give priority to yours or, alternatively, lacks the skills needed for effective project management.

If either of these is true, you could try to persuade the person to delegate the management of the project to another staff member. You will need good influencing skills to carry this off and, to develop these skills, you might like to consider the following:

- *Showing how the person could benefit from someone else managing the project* (benefits might include saving his or her time and being seen as helping the other person develop their project management skills).
- *Pointing out the effects of not delegating.* A good way of doing this is to utilize cause–effect chains where you show what the immediate consequences would be, then the consequences of the consequences and so forth; at some stage in this process the real issues become very apparent.
- *Using influencing language.* People may be influenced through language in various ways, some of which are as follows:
  - The use of *matching* (see 'Creating and maintaining rapport' above). When you match someone's language patterns they tend to be more open to persuasion as you are, literally, 'speaking their language'. For example, if you are with someone who is continually talking of the future, and doesn't seem to be able to concentrate on what is happening here and now, you could start off by speaking of future events too, rather than trying to get the person back to the present. Once you have their attention, you can then have a go at bringing them more into a present-day reality. (For more on this process, see *Words that Change Minds* (Charvet)).
  - The use of *metaphor.* Using metaphors is a powerful aid to change. An example would be if you said: 'We had a small dinner party yesterday. We were given one of those hostess trolleys some time ago, which we thought would be more trouble than it was worth, but it turned out that it just seemed to keep everything under control. There were hotplates at just the right temperature, it had places to keep all the cutlery and plates and it was very flexible and could go from place to place very easily. It took all the trouble out of having to organize these things ourselves; it was just like another pair of hands to make sure the meal went well.' This may sound an odd metaphor, but it could just back up the idea of delegating in a work situation.
  - Using *pre-suppositions.* With this, you simply speak as if certain things were bound to happen. So, you might say: 'When you hand this project over to James you will feel much better, knowing you can get on with other things which you need to do; he will do a really good job of it and can still keep you in touch with everything that is going on.' That sentence

contained many indirect 'instructions' or 'assumptions'. The next few lines have the words you could emphasize high-lighted, so you can see the ones which are likely to be most influential: **When** you hand over (not if); **you will** feel much better; you can **get on with other things**; he **will** do **a really good job**; and can still **keep you in touch with everything** that is going on. The highlighted words go straight to the person's unconscious mind and have a major impact.

What to do if you have difficulty in gaining sufficient access to your client while the project is under way

This is another common problem, which can happen for different reasons. It may be that the person is constantly in meetings, or travel-ling, and access is simply difficult for logistical reasons. It may be that there are other people in the organization acting as barriers to you meeting the person, either because they are trying to protect the person's time or because they do not agree with the need for the project. Or it may be that you are constantly fobbed off with another member of staff because nobody understands that the person you really need to see is the actual client.

So, what can be done? Firstly, it is important to identify which of the above factors is the real problem; until you know that, it will be hard to tackle. If the problem is someone else acting as a block, you can use some of the techniques covered above to influence that person. If the 'real' client is simply not available, you have a number of choices. One is to just get on with what you think is most appropriate, and put a few things in writing so there is evidence that you have provided the opportunity for your actions to be considered in advance of you carry-ing them out. Another choice is to write and outline some options and ask for feedback by a particular date; otherwise you will take no action. And a further option is simply to refuse to continue with the project unless you do get access to the person concerned. If you cannot get access to the person who needs to agree with you what needs to be done, there is a very real chance that there will be a later dispute about action you have taken or recommendations you have made. So, the choice is up to you, as it generally is with consultancy. That's just what makes it so challenging and (if you are the kind of person who thrives on autonomy and goal achievement) rewarding!

HELPING OTHERS DEVELOP TOO

So far, we have mainly discussed your own development, but another facet you might like to consider is your role in developing those with whom you work, so they can also enhance their skills in these areas. We talked a little above about the possible need for you to assist others to become more confident and assertive; in addition, you may have staff who report to you, or people you mentor (either formally or informally), who would also really benefit from your coaching and feedback.

Even if you don't see yourself as a trainer, it can be very worthwhile to take the opportunity to develop others (and it is often in the process of developing others that we learn the most ourselves). So take a little time to think how you might go about this; it may be by doing a presentation, running a workshop, suggesting books for people to read or simply being there to act as a sounding board.

And remember that, these days, CPD (continuing professional development) is a requirement of most professional bodies, so the more opportunities you can take to develop both your own skills and those of others, the more your own standing and expertise will be enhanced.

FINAL OBSERVATIONS

Good personal relationships are an ongoing process. They require responsiveness, flexibility and enthusiasm, and the more you develop your skills in these areas, the better you become.

If you would like a simple framework by which to assess your performance or development, you might consider Figure 14.1, based on work by Miller, Gallanter and Pribram, which shows how feedback can inform and enhance an action or interaction.

The diagram shows an input (this may be a behaviour, such as speaking to someone on the phone, or a thought, such as thinking someone is being aggressive, or a feeling, such as feeling apprehensive, and so on). The 'Test' element is about checking whether what you want to achieve, or what you expect to happen, is in fact what results. So, a test might be 'Does the person sound helpful on the phone, or is the person shouting?', or 'Am I apprehensive because I am late for the meeting?' The 'Operate' element only applies if the test is negative. In other words, if you do not get a result that fits with your expectations, you need to do something else. So, if you checked whether someone was being aggressive by asking them a simple question and noting their tone of voice as they answer, if you get a voice tone that is consistent

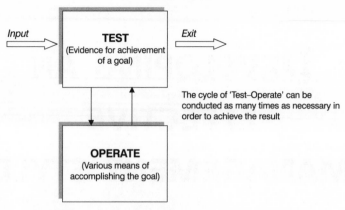

Figure 14.1 A framework for assessing performance and development

with aggression it confirms your judgement. If you get a voice tone that is inconsistent with aggression you could change your original opinion.

You can use this process to test assumptions or to help others develop. For example, in coaching, you could ask a person how they currently deal with their boss and, if the results they get are not positive, they can work through the test–operate loop until they come up with a more effective behaviour.

So, this chapter has covered some of the important skills that you may wish to develop and enhance. What you do with this information is now up to you; it is certainly well worth the small commitment in time and effort to know that you are able to work effectively and enjoyably with people across a wide range of client situations.

CHAPTER FIFTEEN

DEVELOPING AN EFFECTIVE MANAGEMENT STYLE

Bill Peace

The performance of a business depends not only on the quality of people in it, but also on how well they are managed. Consultants often have to engage in a management role, for example if leading a project team. They also need to be acute observers of managers and management within a client organization, if they are to engage effectively with them. So this final chapter deals with the world of managers and management. In this chapter we start by looking at the specific tasks a manager has to perform, and then move on to the subject of self-knowledge, or what you believe about yourself. Management style is a function of what you believe about others – the next topic – which can then be manifest in different approaches. Finally, management style both influences and is influenced by organizational culture – a topic that emerges in every discussion of people and organizations.

WHAT MANAGERS DO

Doing the thing right is not the same as doing the right thing. This is now a management cliché, but the truth remains! Effective management starts with a clear vision of what the things are that the manager has to do. The issue is who or what is in control: the manager or his or her environment. Many managers fall into the trap of fire fighting. Their staff, colleagues and boss feed them a steady diet of urgent problems. Able managers become very able fire fighters. They build a reputation for being able to handle tough, urgent problems, and it's addictive, because there's rapid feedback of success. Before long, these managers lose interest in fire prevention: compared to fire fighting, it's boring, mundane stuff. With next to no fire prevention in place, fire fighting becomes the norm. In this situation, the company begins to suffer, because every time a fire breaks out, something is at risk: a relationship with a customer or supplier, a lawsuit, a financial loss, etc. Moreover, fire fighters (in business at least) aren't really in control, and they aren't doing what managers are paid to do: to manage.

The 'rewards' for the firefighter may not just be personal; there may be a climate of praise for such people within the organization. So be sensitive to what is praised in any organization – it will influence what managers do and their style.

What is needed is a climate of fire prevention rather than fire fighting. Figure 15.1 gives a checklist of tasks for the fire prevention manager.

DEVELOPING SELF-KNOWLEDGE

We engage with the world through our own eyes; we interpret the world through our experience and knowledge. Both of these are personal to each one of us and – as everybody knows – this often leads to different interpretations of the same situation by different people.

Self-knowledge is helpful in engaging with the world. To take a simple analogy, I may find it incredible that my friend can see that road sign so clearly when I can't. Perhaps he's making up the information on it? But if I know I'm short-sighted, I will value my friend's clear-sightedness, and even get some spectacles to improve my vision.

Self-knowledge can help us build on strengths and address weaknesses. Indeed, one of the main purposes of performance review is based on this assumption.

A consultant may wish to use a psychometric profile to acquire an insight into some aspect of an individual or group of individuals with whom the consultant is working. There are some 'health warnings' about using these profiles:

- The profile should be fit for purpose. There are many profiles, so choose the one that measures the feature you are particularly interested in examining.
- Use only those profiles that you are qualified to use. There are many, of course, for which no qualification is required, but there will still be directions for their use.

Key tasks	Task aspects
Setting the agenda for your company or unit	• Defining/redefining goals and objectives • Clarifying scope: what business the company/unit does/doesn't do
Strategy: clarifying how we will reach our objectives Process: the way we will organize the vital systems (see Chapter 2)	
Priority setting (we can't do everything)	• What tasks we will do (or not do) and why?
Resource allocation (resources are limited)	• Who will get what resources and why?
Problem management	• Surfacing problems (while there is time to take action on them) • Gathering information • Defining and evaluating alternatives
Decision making	• At the right management level (the lowest level which has a clear perspective, and can be held accountable for the outcome) • On a timely basis
Communication	• More than 'need to know': want to know and should know • Complete, non-selective with information • Up, down and laterally
Measurement and control	• Relevant metrics in place • How are we doing? • Corrective actions agreed, implemented, checked
Delegation and accessibility (with employees)	• The boss is accountable, subordinates are responsible • The boss delegates, provides trust and confidence • The boss is available for coaching and advice, as needed
Developing people resources	• Coaching, advising, mentoring, teaching

Figure 15.1 Tasks for the fire prevention manager

- Remember that profiles illuminate rather than define, so the interpretation of a profile should be discussed with the person who completed it.
- Profiles should, of course, be used ethically. This means that people who complete them should know why they are being asked to do so, and what they are meant to do with the results.

Two important conclusions can be drawn from 'psychological instruments'. First, it is important for each of us, as managers, to understand our own particular strengths and vulnerabilities. None of us is completely 'well rounded'. Second, each of us can benefit from having colleagues at work who have different styles than we do. We can call upon their strengths, especially if their particular strength happens to be one of our weaknesses.

MANAGEMENT STYLE

There are, of course, as many different management styles as there are managers. Each of us has a style, which is as unique as our fingerprints. But can't one generalize about some characteristics that are more desirable than others?

Unfortunately, it's not quite that easy. Individual managers may use a particular set of personal skills (style) in a way that makes their business successful. In another time, place and business, the same skill set could be a disaster.

General George Patton (also known as 'Old Blood and Guts') won great respect from his men: he was a strong, charismatic leader, with a powerful sense of destiny, and he was an expert in the use of armoured forces. He was very successful in throwing back the German armies in World War II. Would he have been as successful in the Gulf War as was General Norman Schwarzkopf? Schwarzkopf was a great strategist, planner and leader, who, once the ground war started in early 1991, overran the Iraqi armies in a matter of days. Would Schwarzkopf have been a better Patton? It seems to us that each of these men was singularly equipped to succeed in his own situation in his own time.

Most observers of management like to distinguish between *leadership* skills and *management* skills. By *leadership* skills one typically means the ability to *motivate people*, and show them the way toward the successful achievement of a common goal. By *management* skill one tends to mean the *organization and direction of work* in order to achieve a business success: profitability, growth, etc.

Theory X vs. Theory Y

The style of management any individual adopts will depend on their own 'theory of human behaviour'. So, if you believe someone is untrustworthy or lazy, then you will manage them as if that were the case, whether it is true or not.

Douglas MacGregor, in a seminal book, *The Human Side of Enterprise*, characterized two extreme theories of human behaviour, which he labelled Theory X and Theory Y. These embodied assumptions about people's behaviour at work.

One fundamental difference between the two styles is that 'Theory X managers' believe that trust has to be earned. 'I will extend trust to this employee *after* she *demonstrates* her trustworthiness.' The 'Theory Y manager' takes a different view: 'Because this person is my employee, I will trust her *from the outset*; as she sees that I trust her, she will be more confident and will perform better.' Theory X and Theory Y represent two different views of human nature. It has to be said that neither approach is universally right or wrong. Sometimes it is better not to be too trusting (because the company might be taking too great a risk).

Having said that, however, theories can be self-fulfilling: if we treat people as untrustworthy, then they will respond as such. MacGregor's theme was that Theory Y was more widely applicable than is usually assumed to be the case.

A useful way in which these ideas can be applied in practice is in a decision-making model developed by Victor Vroom. This is described in some detail in Appendix 2.

In his model, Professor Vroom makes clear that there can be a rational basis for withholding trust. For example, his 'Goal Congruence Rule' requires that when employees may not share the organization's goals, the manager must decide. In such cases it is almost certainly best for the manager to make clear that he or she has decided on a particular course of action because the action will best support the company's goals. While employees may have felt that trust was being withheld in reaching a decision that wasn't *their* choice, they will understand that the company's needs must take priority.

Trust

Trust is a precious commodity in organizations: it holds us together, enhances relationships, strengthens values, builds respect, mutual confidence and patience. There is a useful formula for understanding trust:

$$T = (I \times C)/R$$

Trust is proportional to Intimacy and Credibility and inversely proportional to the Risk we are asked to take in the relationship. Intimacy is openness, transparency: how well do we feel we really *know* the other person, their *true* values and beliefs. Credibility is the extent to which this person's actions match his words. Does he deliver what he says he'll deliver (or perhaps a little more)? Or does he always come up 'a little short' (or a lot short), with or without an excuse? The risk is the *perceived* risk I will be taking in the relationship with this person. As we think about our relationship with another person, it is important to be conscious of how the other person will see the risks. If, for example, a new salesman is asking a new buyer to try a new product, the relationship is more likely to continue successfully if the new product is provided as a trial sample, rather than a run of 100,000 pieces which will go straight into the buyer's product!

Approaches used by CEOs

While we are on the subject of management style, it may be useful to mention the five different approaches to leadership, which have been identified by two consultants from Bain and Company. In their research, Charles Farkas and Philippe De Backer interviewed 160 chief executives around the world. They expected to find nearly 160 different approaches to leadership. Instead, they found five. (See Figure 15.2.) They also found that the approach used by a given CEO was more likely to reflect the CEO's perception of the needs of the business, than it was likely to reflect his or her personality style.

The *Strategy Approach* is used by CEOs who believe their most important job is to create, verify and implement long-term strategy. Less than 20 per cent of the 160 CEOs used this approach. The complexity of the industry (or the company) – particularly in terms of geography or technology, and the breadth and rate of change – was one of the key determinants for CEOs choosing the Strategy Approach. If the business is complicated and changing rapidly, these CEOs see the need for navigational leadership from the top.

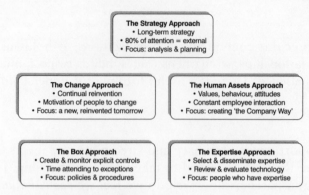

Figure 15.2 The five leadership strategies

The *Human Assets Approach* is used by CEOs who believe it is essential for them to influence values, behaviours and attitudes in the organization. They take considerable interest in the growth and development of individuals. This approach was used by 22 per cent of CEOs surveyed. Those who used this approach tended to take the view that strategy belonged at a lower level in the organization, and that in their particular companies, success depends on superior execution. Their key focus, therefore, is to make sure that the company hires and develops the right kind of people. They pay considerable attention, also, to the development of a 'company way' set of values and behaviours, by establishing clear procedures, systems and policies.

The *Expertise Approach* seeks to strengthen the knowledge or technology of the company as a means to achieve competitive advantage. These CEOs devote much of their personal time to understanding their technology, studying research and talking with the experts. They make a particular effort to bring the expertise into the company by hiring, training or research. If the expertise is a process, they will build the skills of the company in using the process. By whatever means, these CEOs (less than 15 per cent of the total) believe that building the expertise of their company is the most effective way to create and sustain competitive advantage.

The *Box Approach* is used by CEOs who believe that the success of their companies depends on the ability to satisfy customers in a consistent way. They achieve this consistency through an explicit set of controls (financial and cultural), as well as systems and procedures. A considerable proportion of these executives' time is spent finding and correcting exceptions to the desired values and behaviours. They tend to promote from within to reinforce the focus on consistent performance to standards. The Box Approach is frequently used in regulated industries, such as banking or utilities, or in industries, such as airlines, where safety is essential. About 30 per cent of CEOs use the Box Approach.

Finally, we have the *Change Approach*. The CEOs using this approach are not so much concerned about the specific destination of the company as they are about the process of getting there. They are willing to accept anxiety, confusion, some strategic errors and disappointments in financial performance. Change, it is felt, is the best way to consistently deliver extraordinary results. These CEOs value aggressive, independent people, the innovators and risk-takers, who are open to a new, reinvented tomorrow. While most CEOs recognize the value of change (to their customers and shareholders, for example), only about 15 per cent of CEOs are truly change agents who focus their energies almost entirely on the process of change in their companies.

In the case of your company, what is the right approach? The answer depends on the position of your company in the marketplace, its resources and its culture. In fact, you may well conclude that a combination of approaches, *Strategy* and *Change*, for example, may be best for your company. An interesting exercise for the top management team of any company would be to review the article from the *Harvard Business Review*, 'The ways chief executive officers lead' (Farkas and Wetlaufer, 1996), and discuss the advantages and disadvantages of each of the approaches for that team's business. A consensus may be reached on what is the best approach, or combination of approaches, for your particular company.

LEARNED SKILL SETS

An executive we know, the chairman and chief executive of a marketing services company, has an extraordinary ability to develop new concepts and sell them to clients. He personally built the company from nothing to over £35 million turnover, and profitably. He has great vision, imagination and conceptual skills. Without him the business would suffer. But he is not good at (or particularly interested in) the practical details. How his people are to plan and implement the programmes he sells isn't really 'his thing'. If he personally *had* to do it, he wouldn't enjoy it, and it probably wouldn't get done very well. But David's a clever fellow. He has a chief operating officer who is an excellent detail man and implementer. David has also provided his people with the software and the training they need to be good programme managers. The company runs very well. It has both the imagination, creativity and vision to attract clients, and the detailed, practical programme management skills to 'deliver the goods' and keep the clients happy. The separate skills reside in different people. The only real problem in this situation (and it's one to which we, as consultants, pay particular attention) is the hand-off between the creators and the implementers. These groups tend not to speak the same language, and to have entirely different concepts of work. Careful, complete communication at the interface is required.

Let's consider now four pairs of *skills* (see Figure 15.3), all of which are essential for successful managers and all of which can be learned and enhanced. Each pair is mutually exclusive: it is not possible to behave at both ends of the spectrum at the same time. Also, most managers have a preference for where they like to behave on the spectrum. But, depending on the situation, it may be more effective to behave at one extreme, rather than at the other. These are skills that all managers need – at both ends of the spectrum. Unfortunately, many of us find it difficult to move out of our comfort zone, even when the situation calls for it.

Self-confidence vs. vulnerability

Many top managers pride themselves on their charisma – their ability to influence others. They are, in many cases, supremely self-confident. This behaviour is appropriate, even necessary, if one is, for example, a management consultant presenting to a new client. The consultant's confidence inspires confidence in the client: 'This fellow certainly sounds as if he can help me solve my problem!' Charisma and confidence are also appropriate when managers are presenting their strategic

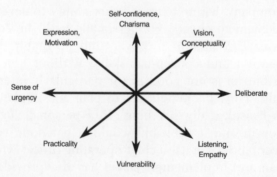

Figure 15.3 Essential management skills

plan to a large group of employees. The employees, too, will have confidence in the managers and their plan!

But what if managers are 'managing by walking around' (MBWA, to use the popular acronym)? Here, managers want to relate *personally* to employees, to see and be seen. They don't want to be distant 'ivory tower' figures who are perpetually sheltered in their offices. They want to be real, human, flesh and blood, even fallible. They want to be vulnerable! If they are not vulnerable, there will always be that shield of rank and position which will insulate them from their employees. That insulating shield will keep managers from succeeding at one of the objectives of MBWA: finding out what's really going on. Employees are much less likely to open up to authority figures than to a friendly visitor.

So, while managers are MBWA, they'll use employee first names and insist that employees reciprocate. They'll want to talk about employees' work, taking an interest in problems and congratulating successes. If the opportunity presents itself, they'll want to express an interest in the employees' personal concerns; see Figure 15.4 for an illustration.

Being vulnerable is absolutely essential when people are being made redundant. It sends a very uncaring, unfeeling signal to the employees who will stay with the company when the boss takes a decision to make a dozen people redundant, then hides in his or her office until the unhappy employees are gone.

From personal experience we can tell you that it makes a great difference in employee attitude and morale if the manager *personally* meets with the redundant employees, explaining the necessity for the step and allowing them to ask questions and express their anger and disappointment. The employees who stay feel: 'Well, it's a tough step, but we understand the reasons for it, and at least they were honest and caring about it.'

Being vulnerable doesn't mean being 'soft'. In fact, being vulnerable can mean being very tough. It means being open, empathetic and patient. But at the end of the day, there's a business to be run, and we're here to make a profit.

Vision vs. practicality

For you as a manager, it's important that sometimes you be the imaginative visionary, and at other times the practical 'doer'. It's not easy for most people to do both, but your company almost certainly needs both.

'Are those your kids in the picture there, Alan?'

'Yes, that's Martin and Jenny.'

'Very nice looking kids! Are they enjoying school?'

'Well, Jenny's very keen on her studies, but I'm afraid Martin would rather play football.'

(Now comes the chance for the boss to demonstrate that he's not from another planet.)

'I know what you mean, Alan. My younger boy, Tommy, was always very rebellious and couldn't be bothered with his studies. Margaret and I had quite a time with him, I can tell you. Now, he's a maintenance technician in the RAF. I have to admit I was pretty disappointed he didn't go to university, but he seems to be doing what's right for him.'

There's some further conversation about the work Alan is doing, and the boss makes a mental note to check on a computer system problem which Alan mentions.

Don't underestimate what a tremendous difference this kind of interchange makes to employees! Those of Alan's colleagues who didn't observe the discussion will certainly hear about it before the day is over. Imagine the conversation between Alan and his wife, when he gets home that evening.

Alan: 'I had a chat with Michael, the new boss.'

'Why? Did he call you into his office?'

'No, nothing like that. He was just walking around the department, talking to people.'

Wife: 'Why was that, then?'

'Well, he says he wants to get to know all the people and understand what we do.'

'So he knows your name is Alan and you do electrical design work.'

'And we also talked about kids.'

'What? Does he have kids?'

'Yeah, a couple, I guess. He has one like our Martin who didn't want to study, but now he's in the RAF – not as an officer, mind you. Michael said he was disappointed the kid didn't go to university, but now he thinks the kid made the right choice and he's doing OK.'

'So did you tell this Michael fellow about that stupid buyer who always orders the wrong control boards?'

'No, but I did tell him about how you have to enter part numbers three times on the system, and he said he'd look into it.'

Figure 15.4 MBWA

If you can't do both, be sure the complementary skills are available and that there is an effective deliberate process for bridging between the skill sets.

Sense of urgency vs. deliberate

We all know people who are in a hurry, who have a tremendous sense of urgency: 'Time is money, let's get on with it!' We also know others who are deliberate, careful and want to think things through.

The receivers who come into a business that is unable to pay the banks and its creditors invariably have great sense of urgency. 'This company is bleeding to death! Action is needed now!'

The same behaviour which is appropriate in a receivership would be entirely counter-productive in an accounting firm of five partners which is trying to decide how to grow. Personal feelings, skills, many alternatives, pros and cons need to be surfaced, discussed and digested.

But the concept of time is not just a reflection of the kind of business we're in. It's also a reflection of the kind of problem we face. It may be entirely appropriate for the five accountants to take a year to sort out their growth strategy; it would be inexcusable for them to take more than a week to sort out a problem with debtors, where the average debtor days has climbed to 64.

While it may be easier for most of us to vary our concept of time, depending on the situation (even receivers have demonstrated patience, sometimes), most of us have an internal clock which sets the pace at which we like to work. But, with a conscious effort, we can speed up, or slow down, when we see the particular need. To a large extent, the importance of time as a variable is related to the kind of problem we face.

Expression vs. listening

Finally, we have these opposite skills of listening and demonstrating empathy on the one hand vs. expressing oneself, motivating and persuading on the other hand. A bereaved employee or an angry customer needs listening and empathy as an immediate response. An under-performing employee or supplier may need some motivation and persuasion. It is impossible to be both empathetic and persuasive at the same time. If you're not sure which is called for, start with listening, and then try persuasion. (Your credibility will suffer if you decide to persuade and then find you need to listen.)

It is correct to say that as a matter of personality or style, some of us are better empathizers and some are better persuaders. Most management jobs require both, at one time or another. Certainly it is possible to train yourself and enhance the weaker skill. The other alternative is to call on others to help you when the required skill is needed. For example, you might call in the HR manager to help you console a bereaved employee. The employee is left with the impression that *both* of you were concerned, while the HR manager *actually* did most of the consoling.

Six thinking hats

The value of diversity is illustrated by an approach to handling matters in meetings of groups devised by Dr Edward de Bono, which he called 'Six thinking hats'. He suggested that if teams are to be effective, several conflicting perspectives need to be employed by the team in order to fully understand a problem and to optimize the solution to it.

He calls these perspectives 'hats', because it is possible for any of us to put on a 'hat' (each with a distinctive colour – see Figure 15.5) and play that particular role.

The *White Hat* focuses on *facts and figures*: what we *know* about this situation.

The *Black Hat* takes a *logical, but pessimistic view*, reminding the team of what could go wrong.

The *Yellow Hat* takes a *logical, but optimistic view*, emphasizing the positives in the situation

White Hat
• Facts & figures
• Neutral
• 'The facts are...'

Red Hat
• Emotions & feelings
• Hunches, intuitions
• 'I feel that...'

Black Hat
• Logical – negative
• Pessimistic view
• ' It's wrong, incorrect...'

Yellow Hat
• Speculative – positive
• Optimistic view
• 'The glass is half full...'

Green Hat
• Creative, lateral thinking
• New ideas, change
• 'Another possibility...'

Blue Hat
• Control of thinking
• Problem-solving process
• 'The way ahead...'

Figure 15.5 Edward de Bono's 'Six thinking hats'

The *Red Hat* focuses on *feelings and intuition*.

The *Green Hat* is the *creative, innovative idea generator*.

And the *Blue Hat* is concerned with *process*: how are we going to address and solve the problem?

De Bono's suggestion is that all six hats need to be represented on a team so that the team can most effectively process and resolve the issues it faces. While any of us is actually capable of putting on each of the hats (and acting out that role), we tend to have two or three pre-ferred hats. Similarly, most teams will have heavy weightings of several hats, and other hats will be under-represented. For example, if a team tends to take an optimistic view of the world (Yellow Hat), it's impor-tant for someone on the team, preferably with the understanding of the other team members, to put on a Black Hat, and raise the possible risks, so that a sound decision is made.

Therefore, it's not unusual in experienced and successful teams for someone to say something like: 'Well, if I put the Red Hat on for a moment, I would say that our employees may be feeling that . . ..'

Speaking generally, teams need to be especially aware of the experience, perspective and skills that each person brings, to respect that unique contribution, and to encourage that it be brought into play when it is needed. Similarly, individual team members need to remind the team to consider the issue from another perspective, even though that perspective may be somewhat uncomfortable.

CULTURE

The culture of an organization isn't just something that 'happens' or is simply the result of 'the people we've hired'. Culture is primarily the result of management behaviour, and the perceived values that underlie that behaviour.

Culture can make a company enormously successful: the cus-tomer focus, market aggressiveness and technical pride of Microsoft have made it the world's largest software company. We have also observed companies, in regulated industries, for example, where employees are entirely focused on pay, benefits and getting the job done 'quick and easy', and where customer dissatisfaction was rampant. Culture can, in fact, destroy such a company. When competition is introduced, customers desert the 'quick and easy' company in droves and never come back.

Fortunately, culture is changeable, but it is not easy to change. The problem is primarily getting managers *throughout* the organization

to understand the need for change, to feel top management commitment to change, and to behave with credible *new* actions, not just
words.

The simple message here is that actions speak louder than
words!

A working definition of culture is 'the way we do things around
here'. Management style is clearly an important component, and it is
useful to deduce the culture of an organization by eliciting what the
unwritten rules are. We have found that employees at middle management levels and below, in a workshop where comments are not
attributed to individuals, are able to develop very accurate pictures of
the culture of their organization. These pictures may be quite different
from the organization's public statement of values, and might include
such items as:

- Please the boss.
- It doesn't matter whether necessary or not, you need to show com-
  mitment by working long hours.
- Sales are more important than customers.
- Time spent on training is a poor investment.
- New ideas rock the boat.

Figure 15.6 shows a list of the cultural values an organization might
have.

1. 110% commitment/loyalty expected	8. Majority rule not rule of logic
2. Individualism discouraged	9. Money is not an obstacle (except headcount)
3. Low tolerance for bad news	10. Employees are kept informed
4. Hardware/production oriented	11. People are friendly
5. Bullying based on perceived lack of performance	12. We strive for excellence
6. Time is the most important variable (more than £, people, quality)	13. We're measurement conscious
	14. Management is approachable
7. Team is more important than the individual	15. Crucial issues: informal settings vs.
	16. Ordinary issues: meetings

Figure 15.6 Example of a list of cultural values

Once you have your 'as is' list of values in hand, you should plot them on a strength vs. positive/negative impact chart – see Figure 15.7.

The next step is to identify the values and behaviours that you *want to have*. These values should reflect your strategy and the competitive differentiators that you have selected for your business. For example, if your strategy is to respond quickly to customer requests and inquiries, you will want to have values such as: a sense of urgency re our customers; commitment to please our customers.

If a major differentiator vs. competition is the unique technology that your company uses, your culture values might include: understanding of and pride in our technology; commitment to developing our technology further.

Now begins the difficult part! With the 'as is' and 'to be' charts in front of you, how and what are you going to change? In particular, what are: 1) the 'as is', strongly held values that have a negative influence and which we want to abolish? and 2) the 'to be' strongly held values, which will have a positive influence on the business, and which we must put in place?

The reason that this step is difficult is not so much identifying what values we want to instil or which we want to abolish, but *how* we're going to do that. For many companies, the temptation is to 'tell the people that these are our new values, and we believe in them'. This

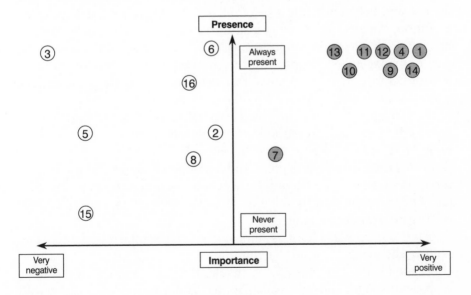

Figure 15.7 The presence and importance of the key aspects of culture

approach is almost completely ineffective, because it is *behaviours,* not words, that drive the culture.

The culture change plan *must* include:

- actions (and behaviours)
- of the top management team
- which are unambiguous (so that there can be no confusion in the message)
- and which are different/unique/innovative (because employees will tend to see new actions as some sort of extension of the status quo, unless the new action is truly different)
- with results measured continually, and
- relentless follow-up.

This is a prescription for hard work! We haven't mentioned above the obvious need to communicate clearly to the organization why the change is needed. This is a very necessary step to lay the foundations for the actions that we have mentioned above. Employees will want to understand the rationale for the changes that are planned. But communication is the relatively easy warm-up which precedes a long, vigorous exercise (after which we are more fit, perhaps a little weary, but certainly proud).

The importance of the *unique* and *unambiguous* nature of the actions and behaviours must be emphasized. This is what gets people's attention. We were involved in a culture change process nearly 20 years ago in which one of the values we wished to adopt was openness on the part of management. (Previously, the culture had been very hierarchical and autocratic.) The consultants who were involved with us stressed the need to make clear, innovative public demonstrations of openness. One of the managers, a man in his late 40s, understood this. For years he had worn a toupee (and everyone knew it), but one day he came to work without it, and he never wore it again. It was, he said, his way of demonstrating that he was going to be an open manager. The effect on the organization, even though he was not a senior manager, was electric. Other managers scrambled to show *their* openness, and, of course, the organization did change.

And, conversely, it is almost always essential to identify and remove the managers (and the employees) who – for whatever reason – reject the change. In some cases, this 'removing the dinosaurs' is done with dignity. The manager is confronted about his or her lack of willingness to change, and after some reasoned discussion, the manager and the company agree to part on a sensible basis. In too many cases, the manager is 'booted out', often without really understanding what happened. In these unfortunate cases, while other managers get the message that top management is serious about 'this new stuff', the aggressive, insensitive behaviour demonstrated by top management may run directly counter to the values being espoused.

Culture change can happen, and surprisingly quickly, but it takes hard work, innovation and real commitment.

CONCLUSIONS

There is no one 'right' management style. In fact, the styles we use are, to an extent, a reflection of our unique personalities. It is true that managers must apply different skills and different approaches in different business situations. To some extent we are able to broaden our skills as managers so that we can have a better portfolio of capabilities. But we can also use the complementary skills of colleagues to assist us in situations where we would not be at our best, on our own. In fact, management teams need to have a broad range of skills, styles and experience in order to provide a total management capability that is far better than the best of its parts.

Managers must be conscious of their proactive roles, refusing to be relegated to a reactive role. Senior managers are accountable for the culture of their organizations. Changing culture is sometimes necessary for the survival of an organization. It is hard work to change culture because it takes real commitment and persistent action, but the results can be well worth the efforts.

APPENDICES

MISCELLANEOUS ANALYTICAL TOOLS AND TECHNIQUES

PEST REVIEW

When formulating a strategy, a marketing plan or any matter looking ahead, you need to consider what is happening in the world outside the organization.

You can assess the environmental forces at work by conducting a PEST review. This is a disciplined way of examining your business environment for issues and forces which will affect your future operation but over which you have no control. PEST is an acronym for the main headings involved. First look at the Political environment (municipal, regional, national, global issues). Here you will find regulatory matters, export markets, grants and subsidies. Next look at your Economic environment (interest rates, cost of labour, inflation, etc). In PEST the S is for Sociological and the T for Technological issues. Sociological issues have to do with the society from which you draw your labour or perhaps where you sell your product. In the final category you build up your picture of the IT environment, and other technological matters relating to your product under this heading as well.

Sometimes the initials L (for legal and regulatory) and E (for environmental, meaning ecological considerations) are added to the list.

SWOT ANALYSIS

Whereas a PEST analysis looks only outside the organization, a SWOT analysis considers the enterprise itself – its Strengths, Weaknesses, Opportunities and Threats.

First look at the Strengths of your organization. What are you really good at? Next look at your Weaknesses. Are there some problem areas? Some companies have used a weakness analysis as a starting point for discovering possible weaknesses of a competitor. Might this lead to a discovery of a location where you could gain a major competitive advantage?

Whereas the examination of strengths and weaknesses looks at your business, the consideration of opportunities and threats looks outside.

Under the heading of Opportunities there will always be a healthy set of issues related to the business you are already in. Take care to look broadly at this area for it is often here that the competitive advantage ideas are born. Success stories from the past include new systems of order taking and customer care, direct access to stocks, pricing and availability on computers in the customers' buying departments. The e-commerce business possibilities will also produce new kinds of opportunities.

Finally, look at Threats – where might you be vulnerable, either to competition or to other external factors? (A PEST analysis could help with this last point.)

The table below summarizes how SWOT might be considered in a marketing context.

Strengths (S)	What are the real strengths (USPs) of the business and its products?
Weaknesses (W)	Shortfalls, inadequacies identified within the business and its products/marketing
Opportunities (O)	As yet un- or under-tapped avenues for business benefit or improvement
Threats (T)	Usually external and substantive (ie technological, environmental, legislation, financial)

A well-executed SWOT critique with a marketing focus undertaken by management, or by independent consultants on its behalf, will provide an invaluable understanding of likely forward needs.

PARETO'S PRINCIPLE

Pareto became famous for his study of the distribution of wealth, where he found (perhaps not surprisingly!) that most of the wealth is owned by only a small percentage of the people. If a government wished to levy a wealth tax, it would be more economical therefore to apply its efforts to only that small percentage rather than the population as a whole.

Pareto's rule therefore states that in many situations, a small number of causes account for the bulk of effects. This is sometimes known as the 80/20 rule (80 per cent of the effects are caused by 20 per cent of the causes) or the law of diminishing returns.

Thus 80 per cent of output is usually produced by about 20 per cent of the products. Eighty per cent of the complaints come from 20 per cent of the customers. In general it means that by making a few critical changes it is possible to have a large effect.

Pareto's rule is therefore helpful to consultants, who need to make an impact in a short time. Things it might be useful for are, for example:

- Risk analysis – what are the major sources of risk, and how might these be contained?
- People – which people are crucial to get on side in respect of a change?
- Technology – what elements are crucial to the success of this operation?

FORCE FIELD ANALYSIS

Force field analysis is a useful technique for determining how you might change a situation. It assumes that in a stable situation, the forces resisting change are balanced equally and oppositely by those opposing it. Any change in the forces will result in a change in the equilibrium, and shift the balance (see Figure A1.1).

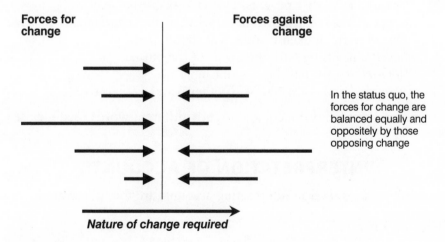

Figure A1.1 Force field analysis

The method of conducting force field analysis is as follows:

1. Determine the nature of the change required; if possible, quantify it.
2. Brainstorm a list of forces that assist or oppose the change.
3. From the list, identify which are the Pareto forces.
4. Make an action plan based on this analysis.

You can use this technique in a workshop, where you would get the people to identify the forces for and against the change. If you wish, you can assign weightings to the forces. So those forces which are major drivers would have a larger arrow than less important forces. In this way, you draw up a picture of what helps and hinders you. To be effective, you should endeavour to include both covert and overt objectives.

The use of force field analysis with a group of people in a workshop environment is a useful way of enlisting help and commitment in joint problem solving.

DESCRIBING OBJECTIVES

Objectives must be clear, tangible and understood in advance by the parties involved. Employees must know what they are committing themselves to; the manager needs to be clear in his or her expectations.

A useful process in defining objectives is to ensure that they meet the definition of being SMARTI objectives. That means:

S   *Specific* so that no one can misunderstand what has been agreed
M   *Measurable* so that progress and success can be seen
A   *Achievable* so that individuals feel that they can actually achieve their objectives, even if some will stretch them
R   *Realistic* in fitting with the needs of the business
T   *Time-related* so that there is finishing line
I   *Integrated* and consistent with other people's objectives

(Sometimes the I is dropped, and slightly different words used – eg see Chapter 13.)

INTERPRETATION OF ACCOUNTS

Important ratios used in interpreting accounts are the following.

Liquidity ratios

Current Ratio = Current Assets/Current Liabilities

Even when this shows that Current Assets exceed Current Liabilities it is necessary to examine the accounts to see that Assets can be realized in the timeframe available to cover liabilities. This ratio is important during any expansion phase to track whether the business is overtrading.

The Acid Test = (Current Assets − Stocks)/Current Liabilities

The Acid Test removes stocks, which generally can be difficult to liquidate and can be overvalued in the accounts. It is therefore a much more cautious test of liquidity.

Profitability ratios

Return on Capital Employed = Profit before Interest and Tax/Capital Employed (percentage)

This can be expressed in different ways (eg before tax or after tax) so care needs to be taken in benchmarking to ensure that like is compared with like. It is a valuable ratio for comparing different divisions of a business.

Return on Shareholders' Funds = Net Profit after Tax/Shareholders' Funds (percentage)

Any company wishing to raise further funds on the stock market needs to be aware of the return being given to the shareholder. The after-tax figure is more important than the pre-tax one, which is sometimes quoted. Sometimes profits are massaged in the final accounts to provide for a steady increase in this ratio.

Profit Ratios = Profit/Turnover (percentage)

Gross Profit, Operating Profit and Net Profit before Tax can be useful measures of 'profit' to use for this ratio. It is a valuable benchmark ratio to measure how competitors are performing and to compare different divisions of a company or home sales and exports, to make pricing decisions or drive down costs.

Efficiency ratios

Stock Turnover = (Stock/Cost of Sales) × 365

This is a vital ratio for any retail or wholesale business and is important too for manufacturers. Reducing the number of days' stock that is held can release capital tied up in stock for expansion. A sharp increase in days held indicates problems with turnover and warehousing and can mean production should be cut.

Debtor Turnover = (Trade Debtors/Turnover) × 365

This is the measure of effectiveness of credit control and collection of debts.

Creditor Turnover = (Total Creditors/Total Credit Purchases) × 365

The ratio shows how effectively the business is using other businesses' money to finance itself. The ratio should be similar to the average terms of business with suppliers. Where it is considerably higher, creditors could exert pressure that could ultimately damage the business.

Fixed Asset Turnover Ratio = Turnover/Fixed Assets

This ratio varies considerably with the type of business and the method of financing. A contracting firm can work on a very low profit on turnover because they can have very few fixed assets and so still achieve a good return to their shareholders. On the other hand, a farm is likely to have a high value of fixed assets and will require a large margin to get a good return. In looking at this ratio it is important to be aware of how the business is financed. A farm can own all the land and have high capital assets or it can rent land and lease machinery to keep the fixed asset value down. The turnover will not have altered.

Stock market ratios

Earnings per Share = Profit after Tax/Number of Shares in Issue

The Russian stock market has suffered from share dilution where additional shares have been issued without the approval of the current shareholders, resulting in the profit being spread over many more shares. From a shareholder's point of view, a steady increase in earnings per share is a good measure of a successful company.

Price Earnings Ratio = Market Price of the Share/Earnings per Share

Many businesses are not concerned about the market price for their shares in the belief that, providing profits continue to rise, the market will look after itself. Yet more and more businesses are offering share options to their Board with the objective of maintaining their interest in increasing the market price. This ratio varies considerably for different sectors of the stock market and comparisons should be drawn within sectors when benchmarking.

Dividend Yield = Dividend per Share/Market Price per Share

When raising money for a business, this will be a critical ratio. It will influence strongly the price of the money that can be raised.

VROOM AND YETTON'S DECISION-MAKING MODEL

Professor Victor Vroom (then at the Yale University School of Organization and Management) developed a model for decision making which he recommended to managers. The model is shown in Figure A3.1. Starting from the left, Professor Vroom asks seven questions (A through G) about the problem which is to be resolved. The 'yes' or 'no' answers to these questions lead us through a decision tree to 13 distinct types of problems. For example, a type 6 problem is one that has the following characteristics:

- A quality requirement (the decision is an important one whose outcome can make a significant difference).
- The manager does not have sufficient information to make a quality decision on his or her own.
- The problem is structured (alternatives are known and the parameters for evaluating the alternatives are also known).
- It is important for effective implementation of a decision that the employees will accept the solution.
- It is not certain if the manager makes the decision alone that employees will accept it.
- Employees do not necessarily share the organization's goals in solving the problem.
- Finally, there is likely to be conflict amongst the subordinates over the preferred solution.

Notice the designation 'CII' after problem type 6, under 'feasible set'.

A. Does the problem possess a quality requirement?
B. Do I have sufficient information to make a high quality decision?
C. Is the problem structured?
D. Is acceptance of the decision by subordinates important for effective implementation?
E. If I make the decision myself, will it be accepted by my subordinates?
F. Do subordinates share the organizational goals to be attained in solving the problem?
G. Is conflict among subordinates over preferred solutions likely?

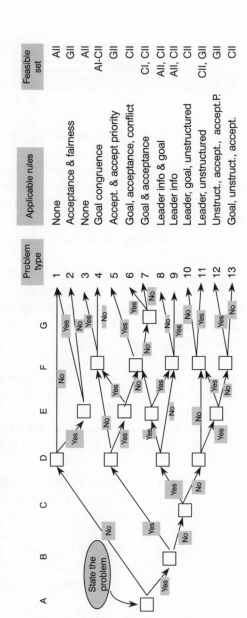

Figure A2.1 The Vroom decision tree

Professor Vroom identified five styles of management decisions, each with its own short label, from AI, completely autocratic, to GII, completely participative as follows:

- AI: The manager makes the decision alone, using only the information immediately available.
- AII: The manager obtains information from subordinates and then makes the decision. Subordinates may be made aware of the purpose of the information requested, but they play no role in defining the problem or in generating or evaluating alternative solutions.
- CI: The manager shares the problem with subordinates individually, getting their ideas or suggestions, but without bringing them together as a group. Then the manager makes the decision.
- CII: The manager shares the problem with the subordinates in a group meeting, obtaining ideas and suggestions. Then the manager makes the decision.
- GII: The manager shares the problem with subordinates as a group. The manager acts as chairman, keeping the discussion focused, raising issues, contributing ideas, but does not 'press' for any particular solution. The manager accepts the decision that is supported by the group.

As regards problem type 6, for example, Professor Vroom's decision tree (and the rules that underlie it) allows only a CII style decision for this type of problem.

Fortunately, it is *not* necessary for you to memorize the decision tree. Instead, there are just seven rules that underlie the tree:

- *Leader Information Rule*: If there is a quality requirement, and the manager doesn't have sufficient information, don't use style AI. (There is a need to obtain information that the manager does not possess.)
- *Goal Congruence Rule*: If there is a quality requirement and subordinates are not likely to share organizational goals, don't use style GII. (The manager must maintain control so that the organization's goals are satisfied.)
- *Unstructured Problem Rule*: If there is a quality requirement, and the leader doesn't have sufficient information, and the problem is unstructured, don't use styles AII or CI. (To effectively deal with unstructured problems, group interaction is required.)

- *Acceptance Rule*: If acceptance of the decision by subordinates is important for effective implementation, and it's not sure the manager's decision will be accepted, don't use styles AI or AII. (Because in AI and AII, the manager is completely in control.)
- *Conflict Rule*: If acceptance of the decision by subordinates is important for effective implementation, if it's not sure the manager's decision will be accepted, and if conflict amongst subordinates over the preferred solution is likely, don't use style CI. (Because, when there is conflict amongst subordinates, it is best to resolve it through a group process.)
- *Fairness Rule*: If there is no quality requirement and acceptance of the decision by subordinates is important for effective implementation, and it is not sure that the manager's decision will be accepted, don't use styles CI or CII. (Because styles CI and CII involve decisions by the manager.)
- *Acceptance Priority Rule*: If acceptance of the decision by subordinates is important for effective implementation, it's not sure the manager's decision will be accepted, and subordinates share the organizational goals, don't use styles CI or CII. (Because a group decision will give priority to acceptance of the decision by the subordinates.)

Figure A2.2 is a diagram of the seven rules. If we refer back to Figure A2.1, we can see which of the rules apply to each of the problem types. The decision styles which remain after application of the rules are what Professor Vroom calls the 'feasible set'. This means that any decision

Rules:	Quality requirement	Enough information	Structure	Acceptance by subordinates	Management decision accepted	Shared goals	Conflict amongst subordinates	Decision types excluded
•Leader information	Yes	No						AI
•Goal congruence	Yes					No		GII
•Unstructured problem	Yes	No	No					AII, CI
•Acceptance				Yes	No			AI, AII
•Conflict				Yes	No		Yes	CI
•Fairness	No			Yes	No			CI, CII
•Acceptance priority				Yes	No	Yes		CI, CII

Problem Attributes →

Figure A2.2 Vroom model rules

style contained in the feasible set is an appropriate response by management to that type of problem. For many problems, therefore, a range of responses, from autocratic to participative, is appropriate.

There is one other interesting point about the feasible set. Professor Vroom calls the decision style at the left-hand limit of the feasible set (the most autocratic decision style permitted) the 'time efficient' model. This is because the least amount of time is invested in these decisions: the minimum time is spent interacting with subordinates. The right-hand limit of the feasible set (most participative choice) is called the 'time investment' model. Extra time is required to make decisions in this way, but it represents an investment in the understanding (and commitment) by employees.

For those who wish to pursue the Vroom decision-making model further, there is a series of 'situations' which Professor Vroom developed. Each situation is modelled around one of the 13 problem types. Having read the situation (without trying to relate it to a problem type) a manager is asked which of the five decision styles he or she would use in that situation. There are, as we now know, some right and wrong answers. As a result of analysing his or her answers, the manager can learn:

- how his or her decision-making style compares to others on an autocratic to participative scale;
- rule violations;
- the effect of problem attributes (the seven questions shown in Figure A2.1) on management behaviours.

REFERENCES AND BIBLIOGRAPHY

CHAPTER 1: CONSULTANCY AS A JOURNEY

Hanzhang, General T (1995) *The Art of War-Sun Tzu*: Forward by Norman Stone, Wordsworth Editions Ltd, ISBN 1 85326 305 2. The various items of ancient wisdom have become highly regarded as valid metaphors for many kinds of strategic, competitive and business conflicts.

Markham, C (1997) *Practical Management Consultancy*, Accountancy Books. An introduction to the basis skills of consultancy.

Markham, C (2001) *The Top Consultant*, Kogan Page, London. Covers operating, selling and managing in a consultancy practice.

Porter, ME (1985) *Competitive Advantage*, Collier Macmillan, ISBN 0 02 925090 0. Very good models for understanding the value-adding proposition of any business, and good value as a basis for strategic planning.

CHAPTER 2: DIAGNOSING THE HEALTH OF YOUR BUSINESS

Crainer, S (ed) (1995) *The Financial Times Handbook of Management*, Pitman Publishing, ISBN 0 273 60694. This is an excellent reference book, which should be on every manager's bookshelf.

Hall, G, Rosenthall, J and Wade, J (1993) How to make re-engineering really work, *Harvard Business Review, November-December 1993*. This and the *HBR* article below deal with the practicalities of making change programmes work.

Hammer, M and Champy, J (1993) *Reengineering the Corporation: A Manifesto for Business Revolution*, Nicholas Brealey Publishing, ISBN 1 85788 029 3. This is the 'original manifesto' of business process re-engineering. It still contains an abundance of wisdom on the subject.

Johansson, H, McHugh, P, Pendlebury, J and Wheeler, W (1993) *Business Process Re-engineering: Break Point Strategies for Market Dominance*, John Wiley & Sons; ISBN 0 471 93883 1. A more practical, 'how to' book, written by four PricewaterhouseCoopers consultants.

Kotter, JP (1995) Leading Change: Why Transformation Efforts Fail, *Harvard Business Review*, March-April

CHAPTER 3: MARKETING

Janelle, DG (1969) Spatial reorganization: a model and concept, *Annals of the Association of American Geographers*, 59, pp 348–64

CHAPTER 4: WINNING AND MANAGING SALES

Bonny, C *et al* (1998) *The Corporate Communications Handbook*, Kogan Page, London, ISBN 7494 2233 5. Expert advice and case studies on best practice.

Bonny, C (1999) *The Salesperson's pocketbook*, Management Pocketbooks, ISBN 1 870471 09 1. A summary of tips and techniques in direct selling.

ICSA (1999) *In Business: The Essential Factfile*, ICSA. A practical sourcebook on business management.

CHAPTER 5: USING CUSTOMER FOCUS TO GENERATE REPEAT BUSINESS

Armistead and Clark (1992) *Customer Service and Support*, ISBN 0 273 03273 9. Systematic guide to implementing a service and support strategy by two Cranfield School of Management lecturers. Useful checklists in each chapter.

Hand and Plowman (eds) (1992) *Quality Management Handbook*, ISBN 0 7506 0143 4. Contains 13 chapters covering most of the principles and foundations of total quality management and related topics of customer satisfaction. A useful work of reference.

Peters, T (1987) *Thriving On Chaos*, ISBN 0 333 45427 8. America's most financially successful writer-consultant who rose to fame with *In Search of Excellence* may not be to everyone's taste, but his books contain many ideas and case studies within an anarchic structure. This book is about challenging conventional ways of managing. Wide in its scope, one of the book's many themes is to exploit the chaos of fast-changing markets to introduce new services that will attract new customers and keep the ones you already have.

Seddon, J (1992) *I Want You To Cheat*, Vanguard Press, ISBN 0 951 19731 0. An unconventional, easy to read book which encourages 'unreasonable' thinking to challenge the way in which organizations have a habit of putting up with things that are clearly wrong and do not serve the interest of the customer. Written by a UK occupational psychologist and consultant.

Whiteley, RC (1991) *The Customer Driven Company*, ISBN 0 7126 5235 3. Written by a director of a US consultancy, this book contains practical tools assessing how customer-focused your business is and could be. Chapters give many examples of the exceptional efforts to provide good service from US and European companies. Tools provide techniques for detailed analysis of causes (of customer dissatisfaction) and for effecting change.

CHAPTER 6: IMPROVING OPERATING PERFORMANCE

Johnson, B (1997) *Managing Operations*, Institute of Management/Butterworth Heineman. Alternative general approach to operations management – brief, concentrating on important elements.

Slack, N, Chambers, S, Harland, C, Harrison, A and Johnstone, R (1998) *Operations Management*, 2nd edn, Pitman, ISBN 0 273 62688 4. Up-to-date general approach to operations management with examples of effective operating performance.

CHAPTER 7: IMPROVING BUSINESS INFORMATION

Business Accounting

Horngren, Foster, Datar (1997) *Cost Accounting*, Prentice-Hall
Drury, C (1997) *Management and Cost Accounting*, 3rd edn, Chapman and Hall

Broadbent, M and Cullen, J (1997) *Managing Financial Resources*, Institute of Management. Alternative general approach to business accounting – brief, concentrating on important elements.
Two general works on management accounting that cover all aspects.

Business Information

Norton, B (1995) *Managing information in a week*, The Institute of Management Foundation, Headway, Sevenoaks. Brief approach to managing business information with many good ideas.

Wilson, DA (1993) *Managing Information*, Institute of Management/ Butterworth Heineman, ISBN 0 750 60667 3. Fuller consideration of the subject.

General

Management Checklists (1998) The Institute of Management Foundation, Corby. Provides pithy comments and ideas for managers and consultants.

Management Today – The Best Factory Awards (1998) Excellent examples of ideas that work.

CHAPTER 8: CONSULTING APPROACHES TO INFORMATION TECHNOLOGY

Earl, MJ (1989) *Management Strategies for Information Technology*, Prentice-Hall International, ISBN 0 13 551664 1. Standing at the beginning of a new era in IT (the early 1990s) this work contains important observations that the management of IT is not like that of the other traditional business functions. In the next era (the early 21st century) the technology will move on, but many of the management issues will remain unchanged.

Parsons, J (1999) *Enterprise.Com*, Nicholas Brealey, ISBN 1 85788 207 5. Everyone needs to be on the Web. It is no longer 'optional'. There are many views on what this means in practice and this book from IBM/Lotus is a good place to start your thinking on the matter.

Ward, J and Griffiths, P (1998) *Strategic Planning for Information Systems*, John Wiley and Sons, ISBN 0 471 96183 3. This is an up-to-date and comprehensive treatment of the subject. It is a valuable overview for any size of business, but if you are running a small company, remember there are some things that are not meant for you.

CHAPTER 9: MANAGING PEOPLE EFFECTIVELY

Belbin, M (1987) *Management Teams: why they succeed or fail*, Heinemann, ISBN 0 434 90127 X. Belbin's book describes the different interpersonal and teamwork skills and attributes that people bring to working with others. He emphasizes that we can choose to adapt our style rather than feel that we have but one style to choose from.

Covey, SR (1994) *First Things First*, Simon & Schuster, 0 671 71283 7. This American book describes a leadership approach and personal discipline that managers can choose to adopt at work and generally. He emphasizes the important of self-awareness and the kind of model of appropriate behaviours or habits that managers should present to their staff.

Goldratt and Cox (1995) *The Goal*, Gower, ISBN 0 566 07418 4. An unusual management textbook written as a novel that argues that managers must look really hard to find the fundamental causes of problems and bottlenecks in their work and personally. The book makes it clear that there are no easy answers and problems need to be addressed with hard thinking.

Handy, C (1986) *The Future of Work*, Blackwell, ISBN 0 631 14278 9. One of Handy's older books but addressing important issues about how work will be done and organized; and some of the issues remain to be addressed even though the book was written in 1985.

Plant, R (1987) *Managing Change and Making it Stick*, Fontana/Collins. The title well describes the book. Sets out some tools and techniques for managers to use that can help them make change actually happen rather than just being something they would like to happen.

Sadler, P (1991) *Designing Organizations*, Mercury, ISBN 1 85251 088 9. Lots of good advice and examples of what can make organizations work well and effectively.

Schutz, W (1988) *Profound Simplicity*, WSA, ISBN 0 89384 066 1. A US New Age book that will help managers think hard about their beliefs and ways of doing things. As Schutz says 'there is no such thing as an accident' – and if we suspend our immediate disbelief, we might actually end up agreeing with him.

Senge, P (1994) *The Fifth Discipline Fieldbook*, Nicholas Brealey, ISBN 1 85788 060 9. Lots of different organizational examples, case studies and questionnaires to help managers involve others in planning and implementing change. The examples are there to be copied or amended as needed by the reader.

Stewart, V (1990) *The David Solution*, Gower, ISBN 0 566 02843 3. An optimistic book about people's potential to grow and contribute much more to their organization. Worth reading to check out if your business has too many of the bureaucratic/cover your back characteristics than you would like.

CHAPTER 10: FINANCING THE BUSINESS

There are many books in accounting and finance. See also references for Chapter 7.

CHAPTER 11: INFLUENCING OTHERS

Bandler, R and Grinder, J (1982) *Frogs into Princes*, Eden Grove, California. There are countless other books from the world of NLP – see Dilts, Andreas, O'Connor and Seymour, Charvet etc.

Cannon,W (1932) *Wisdom of the Body*, Norton & Co, New York

Lewin, K (1952) *Field theory in social science*, Tavistock, London.

LIFO *(Life orientation)* (1976). A programme for better utilization of strengths and personal styles, Allen Katcher International Inc. This personality approach provides complete workbooks for handling a vast range of situations and other personality types as a manager, salesperson, team leader etc.

Maslow, AH (1970) *Motivation and Personality*, Harper & Row, New York. Maslow's famous hierarchy is known to most people but is far more complex than many realize.

Ottaway, RN (1980) *A taxonomy of change agents*, UMIST, Manchester

Schein, EH (1969) *Process Consultation*, Addison-Wesley, Reading, MA. Schein's work has become something of a bible to some consultancies although he was working in specific markets in the US and at the highest level while his primary role was as an academic.

Shepard, HA (1970) Personal growth laboratories, *Journal of Applied Behavioural Science*, 6 (3)

Smith, M and Beck, J (1986) *Introductory organizational behaviour*, Macmillan, London

CHAPTER 12: CHANGE AND PROJECT MANAGEMENT

Handy, CB (1985) *Understanding Organizations*, Penguin

Kaplan, RS and Norton, DP (1992) The Balanced Scorecard – Measures That Drive Performance, *Harvard Business Review*

Schein, EH (1987) *Process Consultation Volume II*, Addison-Wesley

Turner, JR (1993) *The Handbook of Project Based Management*

CHAPTER 13: MANAGING YOURSELF

Economy, P (1997) *Consulting for Dummies*, IDG Books

Fleming, I (1998) *The Time Management Pocketbook*, Management Pocketbooks

Oncken Jr, W and Wass, DL (1974) Management time: Who's got the monkey, *Harvard Business Review*, November-December

Richards, M (1998) *The Stress Pocketbook*, Management Pocketbooks

CHAPTER 14: DEVELOPING AND MAINTAINING EFFECTIVE RELATIONSHIPS WITH YOUR CUSTOMERS

Armstrong, T (1993) *7 Kinds of Smart*, Plume Publishing. An excellent book on accelerated learning techniques. Useful if you want to know more about identifying people's learning styles in more depth.

Charvet, SR (1997) *Words that Change Minds*, Kendall Hunt Publishing Co. A book about influencing people through using language which relates to their own motivational patterns. Straightforward, entertaining and practical.

Harris, C (1998) *NLP: New Perspectives*, Element Books. A simple introduction to NLP (Neuro-Linguistic Programming). Many of the ideas in this chapter have been based on NLP principles, and this book gives you both an overview of the subject and many practical exercises that will take your personal and interpersonal skills to greater heights.

Harris, C (2001) *Consult Yourself: the NLP guide to being a Management Consultant*, Crown House Publishing. Practical techniques for new and established consultants.

Harrison (1988) *Training and Development*, Institute of Personnel Management. There is a reference to the Honey/Mumford-Kolb learning styles in this book.

Hay, J (1995) *Transformational Mentoring*, McGraw-Hill. A very useful book, which discusses 'developmental alliances'. A wealth of information about many processes which underlie consultancy, but not for the absolute beginner, as it assumes some prior knowledge of people management processes.

Jensen (1995) *Super Teaching*, Turning Point Publishing. An excellent book on Accelerated Learning techniques. Useful if you want to know more about identifying people's learning styles in more depth.

Scholes (ed) (1997) *The Handbook of Internal Communications*, Gower. An excellent book for those involved in communicating with others in organizations. Provides an overview of corporate communications media, their pros and cons and advice for enhancing effectiveness.

Training Extras series: Institute of Personnel and Development. Various dates. A very good, basic series of booklets on various skills which are essential to good management and consultancy. Some that you might find especially helpful are those on Customer Care, Feedback, Questioning and Listening, Time Management and Negotiating. A good series of small booklets on various business skills topics.

CHAPTER 15: DEVELOPING AN EFFECTIVE MANAGEMENT STYLE

De Bono, E (1986) *Six Thinking Hats,* Little Brown & Co., ISBN 0 316 17791 1. The master of thinking explains what it takes to make good team decisions.

Farkas, CM and De Backer, P (1998) *Maximum Leadership: the World's Leading CEOs Share Their Strategies for Success*, ASIN, 0 80504 151 6. This book, now out of print, describes the research and the results leading to the Five Leadership Styles.

Farkas, CM and Wetlaufer, S (1996) The ways chief executive officers lead, *Harvard Business Review*, May-June. This is a summary of the Five Leadership Styles work done by Farkas and De Backer.

Keirsay, D and Bates, M (1984) *Please Understand Me: Character and Temperament Types*, Prometheus Nemesis Book Co., ISBN 0 960 69540 0. This book contains an abbreviated version of the Myers-Briggs questionnaire.

McGregor, D and Bennis, WG (1985) *The Human Side of Enterprise*, McGraw-Hill, ISBN 0 070 45098 6

Myers-Briggs, I and Myers, PB (1995) *Gifts Differing-Understanding Personality Type*, Consulting Psychologists Press, ISBN 089106074X. This is the original explanation of the Myers-Briggs Type Indicator, and while it covers the history of the work and the type indicators in detail, it does not include the questionnaire.

Pearce, W (1991) The Hard Work of Being a Soft Manager, *Harvard Business Review*, November-December. A personal treatise on why vulnerability helps make better leaders/managers.

Vroom, VH and Yetton, PW (1976) *Leadership and Decision-Making*, ASIN, 0 822 95265 3. This book, originally published in 1976 and now, unfortunately, out of print, contains the Vroom decision-making tree.

OTHER SOURCES OF INFORMATION

The environment within which businesses now operate is increasingly controlled by legislation from Europe. Relevant laws and regulations proliferate and management needs to be aware of these, and assess their impact on their products, channels, and customers. The following are worth consideration:

- The Trade Descriptions Act 1968
- The Consumer Protection Act 1987
- The Consumer Safety Act 1978
- The Consumer Credit Act 1974
- The Misrepresentation Act 1917
- The Sale of Goods Act 1979

- The Supply of Goods & Services Act 1982
- The Unfair Contract Terms Act 1977
- The Consumer Protection Approval Order 1988
- The Data Protection Act 1984

There are a number of industry bodies that businesses can turn to for advice in these areas, plus knowledge of prevailing self-regulatory codes of practice, including:

- The Advertising Standards Authority (ASA)
- The Advertising Association (AA)
- The Direct Marketing Association (DMA)
- The Incorporated Society of British Advertisers (ISBA)
- The Institute of Sales Promotion (ISP)
- The Market Research Society (MRS)
- British Printing Industries Federation (BPIF)

All of these have offices in central London, and their contact telephone numbers found in the London Telephone Directories.

External Statistics

There are copious volumes of marketing information and data in the public domain. Some of it is free, some by payment of a fee or by sub-scribing to a service. Using Internet search engines it is readily possible, using keyword (company, sector, specialism) searches, to locate many of these sources (some online and downloadable).

THE INSTITUTE OF MANAGEMENT CONSULTANCY

The aim of the Institute of Management Consultancy (IMC) is 'to be recognised as the UK's professional institute promoting excellence in management consultancy'. It is the custodian of the internationally rec-ognized Certified Management Consultant qualification in the UK. But it is also an inclusive institute; there is scope for other individuals and organizations to become involved.

The Institute has a Client Support Service for organizations wanting advice on the use of Consultants. It may be contacted via its Web site at www.imc.co.uk.

INDEX